LISBON & BEYOND

CARRIE-MARIE BRATLEY

CONTENTS

1	Sintra's Moorish Castle wall
2	*azulejo* tile
3	Rua Augusta in Lisbon
4	tram 28 in Lisbon
5	grilled sardines
6	Monument to the Discoveries

DISCOVER
LISBON & BEYOND

Stretched languidly along the banks of the Tagus River, almost midway up Portugal's west coast, Lisbon is magnetic.

Consistently ranked among Europe's top destinations for tourism and quality of life, Lisbon is a thriving city packed with contemporary attractions that sit comfortably among its time-honored facets, a city that effortlessly manages to blend tradition with trendy. Add exciting cuisine, welcoming hospitality, and first-class accommodations, and you get a hugely appealing destination. Another major bonus is that it is a gateway to a vast array of distinct day-trip destinations.

The wonderfully scenic Marginal Road to the Portuguese Riviera offers regal towns and some of the finest beaches in the region. Just north is Sintra, a town whose whimsical buildings could be straight out of a children's storybook. Slightly farther north still is majestic Mafra, with its extravagant Baroque national palace and beautiful gardens, easily paired with the surfy town of Ericeira or the wonderfully preserved medieval town Óbidos.

Just across from Lisbon, on the south bank of the Tagus River, is the sea-salt-kissed Setúbal Peninsula, where wines and fresh fish are as abundant as vast golden beaches. From the sunny Costa da Caparica and its endless stretch of amber sand, south to quaint seaside town Sesimbra, and east to the vibrant port town of Setúbal, this outcrop of land cradles the lush Sado Estuary, where a pod of wild bottlenose dolphins can be admired in their natural habitat. Finally, to the east in the deep Alentejo region is Évora, a fantastically preserved historic town with strong Roman ties.

A trip to Lisbon should be a priority for any European escapade—not only for the quintessentially Portuguese experience it provides, but for the opportunity it offers to explore a wealth of other incredible destinations, all within easy reach of the capital.

MY FAVORITE
EXPERIENCES

1 Touring the out-of-this-world **Pena Palace** in Sintra, whose colorful turrets and towers are the stuff of magic (page 116).

2 Walking the alluring **Estoril-Cascais boardwalk,** a perfect way to take in the sights, sounds, and smells of Lisbon's most famous coastal retreats (page 98).

3 Visiting the ancient **Almendres Cromlech** outside Évora, a mysterious set of standing stones thought to be older than Stonehenge (page 203).

4 Immersing yourself in Templar history at Tomar's massive **Convent of Christ** (page 189).

5 Seeing wild dolphins, along with more than 200 bird species, in the glistening **Sado Estuary** (page 150).

>>>

6 Taking in a soulful **fado** show in the historic Lisbon neighborhoods of Alfama (page 77) or Bairro Alto (page 81).

<<<

7 Indulging in one of Portugal's many **regional delicacies;** any trip to Lisbon is incomplete without a mouthful of delicious *pastel de Belém* (page 16).

>>>

8 Hopping on the convenient **Transpraia tourist train** along Costa da Caparica's beaches, a 30-kilometer (19-mile) stretch of pristine sand (page 143).

9 Catching a ride up one of Portugal's many hills, whether it's via the **riverfront cable cars** in Lisbon's Park of Nations (page 53) or on the historic **Nazaré funicular** up to the dramatic Sítio headland (page 177).

<<<

EXPLORE
LISBON & BEYOND

BEST OF LISBON

Lisbon can get very busy and hot in summer, so a **hat, sunscreen, water,** and a healthy dose of patience are useful in warmer months. If you plan to visit in June, make sure you book well ahead, as this is the month in which the **Santo António Festival** causes the city to explode into party mode.

The Portuguese capital is also rather hilly, which can mean steep climbs. That said, **public transport** is pretty reliable, and all those hills mean amazing views from the many *miradouros* (viewpoints) dotting the city. If your feet get tired, the historic and famed **No. 28 tram** is one of the quirkiest ways to explore the city, trundling through authentic neighborhoods on the time-honored tracks.

After spending three days in the city, experience a few great day trips within a quick drive or train ride, from Lisbon's favorite **beach resorts** to the world-famous castles and palaces of **Sintra.**

>DAY 1

- Spend the morning discovering downtown Lisbon, beginning at the main **Avenida de Liberdade,** exploring **Comercio Square's museums** and **landmarks.**

- After lunch, take the tram to **Belém,** where you can visit the **Belém Tower** and **Jerónimos Monastery** before indulging in a famous *pastel de Belém* custard tart.

- Head back Lisbon's **Chiado Square** for a sunset cocktail before walking up to **Bairro Alto** for dinner and a show at a typical **fado restaurant.** After dinner, let loose in one of the many nearby bars.

>DAY 2

- Today, explore the **Baixa, Alfama,** and **São Vicente** neighborhoods by Lisbon's famous **trams,** visiting sights such as the **National Pantheon,** the **Fado Museum, Lisbon Cathedral,** and the **Graça viewpoint.**

- After all that walking, hop on the train toward **Park of Nations** and some much-needed retail therapy at **Vasco da Gama shopping center.** Here you can visit **riverfront gardens,** explore the **Oceanarium,** and rest your feet on a scenic **cable car ride.**

- End your day at one of the many **restaurants** and **bars** along the Park of Nations waterfront.

MAAT—Museum of Art, Architecture and Technology

>DAY 3

- Enjoy some of Lisbon's quirkier sights today, starting by browsing the many stalls of the **LX Factory** in Alcântara.

- From here, walk across the road to the futuristic-looking **MAAT— Museum of Art, Architecture and Technology**; be sure to take in the views from the rooftop.

- Head toward the **25 de Abril Bridge,** where you can take the **Pillar 7 Experience,** a unique tour in, around, and up one of the pillars of this iconic bridge.

- Finish your night with a sundowner at one of the many bars and lounges on the **Santo Amaro docks.**

>DAY 4: THE PORTUGUESE RIVIERA

- Do as the locals do escape from the city for a few days: just a 40-minute drive from Lisbon is the Portuguese Riviera, one of Lisbon's most popular beach resorts. You can get there either along the **A5 motorway** or the amazingly scenic coastal **Marginal Road.**

- Stop first in **Estoril.** Spend the day on the **beach,** popping into the

famous **Pastelaria Garrett** for a coffee and sweet treat.

- Stroll along the 3-km (2-mi) promenade to **Cascais,** enjoying the chic **boutiques** and dinner at one of the many **restaurants** on the marina.

- Taxi back to Estoril to spend the night at the legendary **Hotel Palacio Estoril.**

If You Want ...	Destination	Why Go	Getting There from Lisbon	How Long to Stay
Beaches	Costa da Caparica (page 134)	spacious beaches; fun seaside feel; close to Lisbon	bus or car (25 minutes)	1 day
	The Portuguese Riviera (page 92)	beautiful beaches; cool bars; glamorous hotels	car or train (40 minutes)	overnight
	Nazaré (page 173)	surfing; soaring cliffs; a historic funicular; fascinating folklore	car (1.5 hours) or bus (2 hours)	1 day
Palaces	Sintra (page 112)	magical palaces and castles; shady woodland	car (30 minutes) or train (1 hour)	1 day
	Mafra and Ericeira (page 122)	an extravagant royal palace within 15 minutes' drive of a beach; laid-back vibes	car (50 minutes)	1 day
Historic villages	Óbidos (page 160)	a well-preserved medieval town; *ginjinha*	bus or car (1 hour)	1 day
	Tomar (page 185)	the remnants of a Knights Templar stronghold; river-town charm	car (1.5 hours), train (2 hours), or bus (1 hour 45 minutes)	overnight
Nature	Setúbal Peninsula (page 144)	wild dolphins; unspoiled coastline; fresh fish	car (45 minutes) or bus/train (1 hour)	overnight
Rural Portugal	Évora (page 197)	excellent wines; the thrilling Bone Church; a glimpse into rural life	car (1.5 hours) or bus/train (2 hours)	1 day

>DAY 5: BOCA DO INFERNO, CABO DA ROCA, AND SINTRA

- Wake up early to continue your drive west, stopping at the dramatic **Boca do Inferno** coastal rock formation and **Cabo da Roca,** Europe's westernmost point, before swinging inland toward Sintra.

- Park on the outskirts of Sintra, as the city center can become quite congested. Purchase a day ticket on the local **434 tourist hop-on hop-off bus** (€6.90) so you can save on the leg work and time between monuments, and start by visiting the iconic **Sintra National Palace.**

- Be sure to visit the fairytale **Pena Palace,** the **Moorish Castle,** spooky

Regaleira Estate, and the historic Monserrate Park and Palace.

- After all that sightseeing, order as many small plates as you can eat at Nau Palatina tapas restaurant, followed by a good night's sleep at Aguamel Sintra Boutique Guest House before heading back to Lisbon in the morning.

BEACHES AND CASTLES: NORTH OF LISBON

Within a quick drive of Lisbon, you can find atmospheric medieval towns and world-renowned surfing. A few places on this itinerary, especially Óbidos, can feel somewhat overrun by tourists. It helps to spend the night to see the towns before and after the tour buses have left, and to park in the outskirts if you're driving.

Be sure to pack a swimsuit for a beach day, and, as always in Portugal, a comfortable pair of shoes for walking hilly, cobblestoned streets is also advisable.

The towns on this itinerary are beach towns and therefore summertime destinations; however, they all have something to offer year-round. For example, although Nazaré is a beach town, November is a top time to visit, as this is when the town's famous waves are at their most formidable.

the Medieval Fair in Óbidos

>DAY 1: MAFRA AND ERICEIRA

- From Lisbon, head straight to Mafra, just less than an hour's drive north, to visit the monumental **Mafra National Palace.** Afterward, enjoy an al fresco lunch on the patio of one of the local restaurants, such as **Sete Sois.**

Mafra National Palace

- After lunch make the short drive to the edge of Mafra to the **Royal Tapada hunting grounds,** where you can hike, take an archery class, or maybe even spot some majestic animals.

- From here, head to Ericeira to take in the laid-back barefoot vibes of the popular surfing resort. Enjoy a couple of hours on the **beach** before a fresh seafood dinner at **Marisqueira Furnas,** and take advantage of Ericeira's **cool bar scene** before heading back to your hotel for the night.

>DAY 2: NAZARÉ

- The next morning, time and sea conditions allowing, book an invigorating **surf lesson** before heading out for the hour's drive north to Nazaré.

- On the way into Nazaré, stop at the impressive nearby **Alcobaça Monastery.**

REGIONAL DELICACIES

ginjinha poured into chocolate cups

- *Pastel de Belém:* Delicious eggy tartlets made from freshly baked, crisp, buttery pastry filled with rich custard, usually enjoyed with a sprinkling of cinnamon, found only in Belém, a short train ride north of central Lisbon (page 75).

- *Queijadas:* Despite being made from cheese, there is nothing cheesy about these sweet, stodgy, sticky delicacies. Many towns are renowned for their own versions of *queijadas,* but Sintra's are especially famous (page 118).

- *Ginjinha:* This sweet cherry liqueur, a specialty in the town of Óbidos, is sometimes served in a chocolate cup, with or without a cherry (page 169).

- *Canja de Carapau:* A fishy broth made from mackerel, *canja de carapau* is the trademark dish of Costa da Caparica (page 141).

- *Peixe-Espada Preto:* Sesimbra is renowned for its freshly caught black-scabbard fish—a fluffy, meaty piece of fish served simply, just charcoal-grilled (page 156).

- *Polvo á lagareiro:* Reflecting the town's fishing roots, *polvo á lagareiro* (octopus cooked in a pressure cooker covered in hot olive oil) is synonymous with Nazaré (page 182).

Santa Maria Church in Óbidos

- Park on the streets set back from the beachfront or in one of the various car parks. Spend the morning strolling along the **beachfront** and enjoy lunch in one of the town's many offbeat little eateries, such as **Rosa dos Ventos.**

- In the afternoon make a beeline for the vertiginous **funicular**

up to **Sítio old town.** Up at the top, the Nazaré promontory, the oldest part of town, is high above the beach and packed with folklore-infused sights, such as the **Memorial Hermitage** and the landmark **lighthouse** and **fort.**

- Have dinner at **Tosca Gastrobar** and spend the night at **Hotel Mar Bravo.**

>DAY 3: ÓBIDOS

- Stop at **Quinta do Gradil** winery on the way into Óbidos for a winery tour and delicious lunch.

- Set aside a couple of hours to wander around the **medieval walled town,** ambling its mazelike cobbled backstreets and following its high walls.

- For a small town there's plenty to fill a morning or an afternoon, not

least sampling the local *ginjinha* and visiting the main **Santa Maria church** and the **Municipal Museum.**

- Have dinner away from the main tourist drag at **A Nova Casa de Ramiro,** followed by a night at the **Pousada Castelo Óbidos,** your chance to sleep in a real castle.

DOLPHINS AND THE BONE CHURCH: SOUTH OF LISBON

For this three-day itinerary, pack your **swimsuit** and **beach towel** for a jaunt to Portugal's largest uninterrupted stretch of beach. As with most places in Portugal, **comfortable walking shoes** are a must, and you may want **hiking shoes** to experience the Setúbal Peninsula, a land of seaside cliffs and the spectacular Arrábida Natural Park.

Though the beaches of Costa da Caparica are popular, they are so extensive that they rarely feel crowded, and many parts of the Setúbal Peninsula feel almost deserted. One attraction worth booking in advance is the popular **Sado Estuary dolphin excursions.**

>DAY 1: COSTA DA CAPARICA

- From Lisbon, drive just over a half an hour via the **25 de Abril Bridge** over the **Tagus River** to Costa da Caparica.

- Take the tiny **Transpraia tourist train** to spend the day on one of the Costa's various **beaches**— with 30 kilometers (19 miles) of sand making up Europe's longest beach, there are dozens of spots to choose from.

- When the weather is cooler at the end of the day, walk the **promenade** along Costa da Caparica town south to the authentic **Fisherman's Quarters,** stopping at a bar for a sundown drink.

- Have dinner at **Borda d'Agua** and spend the night at **Tryp Lisboa Caparica Mar Hotel.**

Costa da Caparica

CAPES, CLIFFS, AND VIEWPOINTS

Dramatically situated along Europe's most beautiful coastline, with many cities and towns famously set into picturesque hills, Portugal is a great place to get some altitude and take in awe-inspiring views of the sea. The following are some of the most jaw-dropping viewpoints, or *miradouros*, covered in this book.

- **Lisbon's Best Views:** Gorgeous *miradouros* abound in Lisbon, from the famous Graça viewpoint to the romantic Miradouro da Nossa Senhora do Monte (page 48).

- **Cabo da Roca:** Be amazed by the vastness of the Atlantic Ocean as you stand on the high cliffs of mainland Europe's westernmost point (page 111).

- **Cabo Espichel:** Walk paths where dinosaurs once roamed on the eerily remote and rugged Espichel Cape (page 158).

- **Sítio Headland:** Take the vertiginous funicular up to Sítio headland, where the bird's-eye views over Nazaré give as big an adrenalin rush as watching the monster-wave surfers (page 177).

>DAY 2: SETÚBAL PENINSULA

- Set off early toward Setúbal, stopping at the **Costa da Caparica Fossil Cliff Protected Landscape** en route.

- Drive 40 minutes south to the **Cabo Espichel promontory,** where you can see a **lighthouse** and **dinosaur footprints.**

- Head east to **Sesimbra,** where you can enjoy an hour on the **beach** before lunch in one of the excellent quay-side fresh fish restaurants.

- After lunch set off for Setúbal city via the **Arrábida Natural Park,** stopping at the postcard-perfect **Portinho de Arrábida** for refreshments.

- In Setúbal, walk the town and enjoy its unpolished attitude. Join a late afternoon **dolphin excursion** to the Sado Estuary, before spending the night in one of Setubal's dockside hotels.

>DAY 3: ÉVORA

- Head straight east into the Alentejo region, to its largest city, Évora, a city of **intriguing monuments** and **offbeat sights.** Park in one of the various car parks on the outskirts of town.

- Spend the morning visiting the chilling **Chapel of Bones,** the **Roman Temple of Diana,** and the nearby **Convent.**

- Enjoy lunch in the bustling **Giraldo Square** or sample authentic local fare at the **Cartuxa Wine Cellar,** near the Roman Temple.

- After lunch and exploring Évora city, leave time for a couple of compelling sights on the city's outskirts: the **Cartuxa Estate winery** and the fascinating **Almendres Cromlech neolithic stone site.**

BEFORE YOU GO

WHEN TO GO

HIGH SEASON

May–September offers the **best beach weather;** average temperatures for this time of year will range from the mid-20s to the mid-30s Celsius (mid-70s to mid-90s Fahrenheit). **June–August** constitutes the peak of high season, when Portugal is at its busiest—and priciest. Most of the country's major events, such as the traditional **Popular Saints** festivities and **local festivals,** are held in summer. But don't feel obliged to visit Portugal when it's at its hottest; peak summer season can mean extremely busy monuments and beaches, packed hotels, and parking at a premium. **Inland areas** such as the **Évora** in **Central Portugal** can be sweltering (more than 40°C/104°F) in summer and are much more enjoyable in **spring** or **autumn.** Just outside peak season—June and September, even October—are also beautiful times to visit, when the weather is milder and the pace is more relaxed.

LOW SEASON

Spring, autumn, and winter are mild and mostly sunny, with temperatures that can range from the mid-teens to low 20s Celsius (mid-50s to low 70s Fahrenheit), although Portugal does have **rainy months, December** being the wettest; January is the coldest, when

traditional *Manjerico* plants are given as gifts during Popular Saints festivities

WHAT YOU NEED TO KNOW

- **Currency:** Euro (€)

- **Conversion rate:** €1 = £0.87 GBP; $1.11 USD (at time of publication)

- **Entry requirements:** No visa needed for travelers from the US, Canada, UK, Europe, Australia, or New Zealand. South African nationals need to apply for a Portugal-Schengen visa.

- **Emergency number:** The common European emergency number is 112.

- **Time zone:** Western European time zone (WET)

- **Electrical system:** 230-volt, 50-hertz electricity and type C or F sockets (the standard European round, two-prong plugs)

- **Opening hours:** Vary; most businesses open between 9am and 10am and close between 6pm and 7pm. Shops may close 1pm-3pm for lunch, but this is increasingly rare.

thermometers can sometimes dip to single digits (30s Fahrenheit), particularly at night. **Sintra, Tomar,** and **Évora,** are **year-round** destinations. Hotels will again be close to full over Christmas and New Year, but outside that, low season in most of Portugal will mean fewer tourists and a more tranquil, relaxed pace of life.

GETTING THERE

FROM EUROPE

Traveling to Lisbon Airport from anywhere within Europe is quick and easy—and even better, it's less expensive, thanks to the growing number of low-cost airlines. Gatwick, Stansted, Heathrow, and Luton in **London** usually have two or three daily flights to Lisbon on low-cost carriers such as **Ryanair** and **easyJet.** Flag carriers **TAP** and **British Airways** also fly direct to Lisbon from London.

Bus and **train** services connect Portugal with Spain, France, Belgium, the Netherlands, and the United Kingdom. **Driving** to Lisbon from within Europe is also possible thanks to a good international road network and the EU open-borders policy.

FROM OUTSIDE EUROPE

There are **direct flights** from the **United States** to Lisbon from cities including New York, San Francisco, Miami, Boston, Washington D.C., and Chicago, and from Toronto in **Canada.**

There are no direct flights between **South Africa** or **Australia** and Lisbon, but travel is possible on flights with main European carriers via other major European cities such as Madrid, London, Paris, Frankfurt, and Amsterdam, or via Dubai, Doha, and Luanda. There are directs flight between Lisbon and Dubai with Emirates and Doha with Qatar Airways.

GETTING AROUND

Thanks to its compact size and a good road network, Portugal is easily traveled by **car.** Hiring a car also provides greater flexibility for exploring off the beaten track. But an efficient bus and train network also connects most major towns and cities. **Train travel** can often be more **scenic** and **cheaper** than the bus, but train stations can sometimes be located far outside the town centers. **Bus travel** is almost always **quicker** than the train.

CAR

Portugal's road system is decent and major routes are kept in good condition, although the same cannot be said about smaller regional or municipal roads. Some are in urgent need of repair, particularly in rural areas, and on certain stretches signage could use updating.

Motorways are generally in good condition, although major motorways (autoestradas) have **tolls,** signaled with a large, white V on a green background. Cars drive on the **right-hand** side of the road—the same as the rest of mainland Europe and the United States.

TRAIN

Portugal's train service **Comboios de Portugal (CP)** (www.cp.pt/passageiros/en) is efficient and inexpensive but complex. Despite being comprehensive, the national rail network isn't as direct as bus services, and, oddly, some major cities have no train station, while many cities and towns have their train stations on the outskirts, requiring a taxi ride to the center. On

the plus side, Portugal's trains tend to be spacious and clean on the inside, and offer cheaper second-class tickets and more privacy and comfort in first class, sometimes in private compartments.

Lisboa Oriente train station

BUS

There are many different bus companies in Portugal, including three major intercity long-distance bus companies; most of the regions in this book are serviced by national **Rede Expressos** (www.

rede-expressos.pt). Local and regional buses link towns, villages, and parishes within municipalities. In Lisbon, the local public transport company is **Carris,** which operates buses, trams, and funiculars. Lisbon also has a safe and efficient subway, the **Lisbon Metro,** whose four lines total 44.2 km (27.5 mi) of route and serve 56 stations. Bus travel in Portugal is inexpensive but not always the most comfortable, although long-distance express buses are mostly equipped with air-conditioning, TVs, toilets, and even onboard drinks and snacks.

TRAVEL DOCUMENTS

All travelers entering Portugal are required to have a **valid ID.**

European Union nationals traveling within EU or Schengen states do not require a visa for entering Portugal for any length of stay. They do require a valid passport or official ID card. European citizens traveling between **Schengen Area** countries are not required to present an identity document or passport at border crossings, as an open-borders policy is in effect. However, it is recommended that travelers have ID documents with them, as they may be requested at any time by the authorities.

Citizens of the **United Kingdom** and **Ireland** must produce a passport to enter Portugal, valid for the duration of the proposed stay, and can stay for up to three months. Further documentation might be required post-Brexit.

People from **non-EU countries** always require a passport, valid for at least six months; some may require a visa. **Australian, Canadian,** and **U.S.** travelers require a valid passport but do not need a visa for stays of up to 90 days in any six-month period. While it is not obligatory to have an onward or return ticket, it is advisable.

South African nationals need to apply for a Portugal-Schengen visa. This should be done three months before travel. Applicants must have a South African passport valid for six months beyond date of return with at least three blank pages.

WHAT TO PACK

Key items to pack include **mosquito repellent** and **sunblock** (sunblock is expensive in Portugal) plus a **hat** for May-October, a **windbreaker** for all seasons (Portugal can be breezy year-round), and **warm sweaters,** a **jacket,** and a light **raincoat** for winter.

Comfortable shoes for walking are advised if your trip is more than a beach holiday, and don't forget a **plug adapter** for chargers. Pack a **concealable pouch** to carry documents and cash while out and about exploring, and **never carry cash and documents together.**

LISBON

Portugal's magnificent capital is currently one of Europe's most up-and-coming cities—vibrant and culturally rich, where the historic blends seamlessly with the cool and contemporary. At the mouth of the Tagus River (Rio Tejo), the "City of Seven Hills" is buzzing and cosmopolitan, home to melodic fado music and a vivid nightlife scene. Traditional tile-clad facades and redbrick roofs conceal a tangle of charming cobbled streets and elegant avenues that beckon to be explored.

Lisbon's impressive monuments, historic

HIGHLIGHTS

✪ **SÃO JORGE CASTLE:** On a hilltop in the heart of Lisbon, this imposing Moorish monument commands spectacular views of the historic city center and the Tagus River (page 37).

✪ **NATIONAL TILE MUSEUM:** Where else can you see a collection of traditional hand-painted tiles housed in a 16th-century convent (page 40)?

✪ **CALOUSTE GULBENKIAN MUSEUM:** One of Lisbon's less-celebrated treasures, the collection ranges from Greco-Roman antiquity to contemporary pieces (page 42).

✪ **CARMO CONVENT:** Once the largest church in Lisbon, these ruins starkly show the devastation of the 1755 earthquake (page 43).

✪ *CHRIST THE KING:* Arms outstretched high above the Tagus River, this iconic statue affords dazzling views over the city (page 49).

✪ **BELÉM TOWER:** At the mouth of the Tagus River, this fortified tower was the last and first sight the country's intrepid sailors had of their homeland when setting off and returning from their voyages (page 50).

✪ **JERÓNIMOS MONASTERY:** Home to the national archaeological and naval museums, Belém's stunning centerpiece is a marvel of ornate Manueline architecture and took the entire 16th century to construct (page 51).

✪ **AVENIDA DA LIBERDADE:** An appealing mix of historic and contemporary buildings, high-end boutiques, and tree-shaded cafés lines the country's most famous avenue (page 61).

✪ **BAIRRO ALTO NIGHTLIFE:** Historic Bairro Alto has reinvented itself as the city's liveliest and coolest nocturnal hangout, with chic wine bars, historic fado houses, and renowned jazz clubs (page 79).

neighborhoods, and edgy vibe welcome visitors to drink in stunning bird's-eye views from many panoramic *miradouro* viewpoints or hip hotel rooftop bars. Stroll the chic boulevards with their many boutiques, admire striking riverfront monuments, explore the many museums, or for the classic Lisbon experience, take the famous tram 28 around the city's historic nooks and crannies before enjoying mesmerizing fado in one of the many original haunts in Alfama or Bairro Alto.

Less than an hour from the heart of the city are the upscale towns of Estoril and Cascais as well as magical Sintra, which famously has a microclimate all its own.

ORIENTATION

Hilly Lisbon is divided into many neighborhoods and parishes, or *bairros*. The heart of Lisbon's historic area is the **Baixa Pombalina,** often simply referred to as the Baixa; it's the main downtown commercial and banking area along the river. Baixa

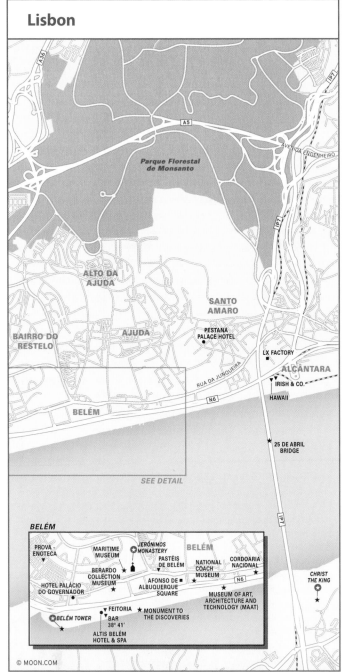

Lisbon

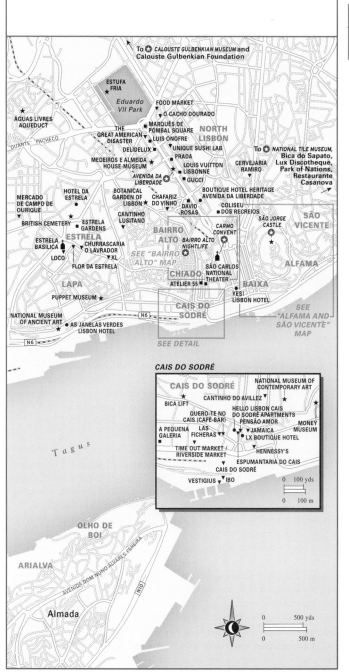

To CALOUSTE GULBENKIAN MUSEUM and
Calouste Gulbenkian Foundation

ESTUFA
FRIA

Eduardo
VII Park

FOOD MARKET

ÁGUAS LIVRES
AQUEDUCT

O CACHO DOURADO

MARQUÊS DE
POMBAL SQUARE

NORTH
LISBON

THE
GREAT AMERICAN
DISASTER

LUIS ONOFRE

DUARTE PACHECO

DELIDELUX

UNIQUE SUSHI LAB

To NATIONAL TILE MUSEUM,
Bica do Sapato,
Lux Discotheque,
Park of Nations,
Restaurante
Casanova

PRADA

MEDEIROS E ALMEIDA
HOUSE-MUSEUM

LOUIS VUITTON
LISBONNE

CERVEJARIA
RAMIRO

AVENIDA DA
LIBERDADE

GUCCI

MERCADO
DE CAMPO DE
OURIQUE

HOTEL DA
ESTRELA

BOTANICAL
GARDEN OF
LISBON

CHAFARIZ
DO VINHO

BOUTIQUE HOTEL HERITAGE
AVENIDA DA LIBERDADE

DAVID
ROSAS

COLISEU
DOS RECREIOS

SÃO
VICENTE

BRITISH CEMETERY

ESTRELA
GARDENS

CANTINHO
LUSITANO

ESTRELA

BAIRRO
ALTO

SÃO JORGE
CASTLE

ESTRELA
BASILICA

CHURRASCARIA
O LAVRADOR

CARMO
CONVENT

BAIRRO ALTO
NIGHTLIFE

LOCO

XL

SEE "BAIRRO
ALTO" MAP

ALFAMA

FLOR DA ESTRELA

LAPA

SÃO CARLOS
NATIONAL
THEATER

CHIADO

PUPPET MUSEUM

ATELIER 55

BAIXA

CAIS DO
SODRÉ

YES!
LISBON HOTEL

NATIONAL MUSEUM
OF ANCIENT ART

N6

SEE
"ALFAMA AND
SÃO VICENTE"
MAP

AS JANELAS VERDES
LISBON HOTEL

N6

SEE DETAIL

Tagus

CAIS DO SODRÉ

CAIS DO SODRÉ

NATIONAL MUSEUM OF
CONTEMPORARY ART

CANTINHO DO AVILLEZ

BICA LIFT

HELLO LISBON CAIS
DO SODRÉ APARTMENTS

QUERO-TE NO
CAIS (CAFÉ-BAR)

PENSÃO AMOR

MONEY
MUSEUM

A PEQUENA
GALERIA

LAS
FICHERAS

JAMAICA

LX BOUTIQUE HOTEL

TIME OUT MARKET /
RIVERSIDE MARKET

HENNESSY'S

ESPUMANTARIA DO CAIS

CAIS DO SODRÉ

VESTIGIUS

IBO

0   100 yds

0   100 m

OLHO DE
BOI

ARIALVA

AVENIDA DOM NUNO ÁLVARES PEREIRA

N10

Almada

0   500 yds

0   500 m

27

is immediately fringed by several of the city's other most famous neighborhoods: labyrinth-like **Alfama** and hilltop **São Vicente,** cultural and hip nighttime hangout **Chiado** and **Bairro Alto,** cool and arty **Cais do Sodré,** and chic **Estrela** and **Lapa. Alcântara,** a former docks area currently enjoying a hipster revival, is west of the downtown area.

Heading north from downtown is the **Avenida da Liberdade,** one of the city's most famous avenues, surrounded by some excellent museums and historic monuments. On the western extremity of the heart of Lisbon is the culturally rich area of **Belém,** while at the opposite side, on the northeast, is the modern area of **Park of Nations (Parque das Nações),** dramatically developed for the 1998 World Exposition. And if you want visit a palace without venturing to Sintra just yet, just a 20-minute drive north is the commuter suburb of **Queluz,** home to the beautiful **Queluz National Palace and Gardens.**

BAIXA

Fronted by the Tagus River, the Baixa Pombalina (BYE-shah pom-bah-LEE-nah) or just Baixa, or "downtown Lisbon," is the city's central shopping and banking district—and its tourist hub. The name derives from the distinctive Portuguese Pombaline architectural style employed to rebuild the city after the 1755 earthquake, under the guidance of Sebastião José de Carvalho e Melo, the 1st Marquis of Pombal. Elegant neoclassical facades and patterned cobbled streets give the neighborhood an air of graceful uniformity. Two main streets, **Rua Augusta** and **Rua da Prata,** are laden with buzzing shops and restaurants. The main Metro stops in the Baixa

area are Avenida, Restauradores, Rossio, Baixa-Chiado, and Terreiro do Paço, on the Green and Blue Lines.

ALFAMA

Alfama (al-FAH-mah), just east of Baixa, is Lisbon's oldest and most soulful neighborhood and claims to be the birthplace of fado, although Bairro Alto also makes this claim. Inhabited from the 5th century by the Visigoths, the narrow cobbled streets of this unpolished neighborhood create a stepped labyrinth of historic houses and quirky shops. It was once rough and home to dockworkers and seafarers. As the city's port prospered, so did Alfama, although its rugged charisma remains. Alfama boasts monuments, traditional **fado houses,** and many fabulous **viewpoints** along its slopes.

In the northern part of Alfama, the stately and traditional area around **São Jorge Castle,** is known as Lisbon's birthplace and often called **Castelo.** One of the city's finest neighborhoods, it has fabulous views from almost every street corner.

SÃO VICENTE

Two major monuments, the **National Pantheon** and the **São Vicente de Fora Church,** are in São Vicente (sown vee-SENT), among a cascade of historic homes on the hillside toward the Tagus just east of Alfama. Peaceful and poised most of the week, São Vicente comes alive every Saturday morning for the famous **Feira da Ladra** flea market, next to the National Pantheon.

AVENIDA DA LIBERDADE

This broad, leafy avenue is home to some of Lisbon's most upscale shops and priciest real estate. The Avenida terminates in **Marquês de Pombal Square,** with the towering statue of the Marquis de Pombal guarding the entrance to **Eduardo VII Park,** and is surrounded by some of the city's best museums, such as the **Calouste Gulbenkian Museum.**

CHIADO AND BAIRRO ALTO

Just northwest of Baixa, centered on the **Chiado Square,** Chiado (SHEE-aah-doo) neighborhood is the core of Lisbon's cultural scene—a district packed with theaters, museums, and galleries. Sandwiched between the Baixa and Bairro Alto, the emblematic square is lined with traditional commerce, fashionable boutiques, and cultural venues galore.

A bit further northwest, Bairro Alto (BYE-rroo AL-too) has long been Lisbon's bohemian hangout, a favorite haunt for artists and writers. In the evenings, its grid of steep streets echoes with melancholic fado. Visit after 11pm, when the innumerable **small bars** and **colorful nightspots** really start to hit their stride. The neighborhood's historical significance dates to its expansion in the 16th century to accommodate the city's booming economic and social transformation.

CAIS DO SODRÉ

Fronting Lisbon's downtown to the west is Cais do Sodré—or the Sodré Docks—a trendy, underrated part of Lisbon on the riverside. Historically important and one of the city's busiest areas for nightlife, Cais do Sodré is also the location of one of the main **ferry terminals** for crossing the Tagus as well as the train terminus for the **Lisbon-Cascais train line.** Because of this, the area sees heavy traffic of students and commuters passing through daily.

ESTRELA AND LAPA

Northwest of Cais do Sodré, with **grand properties** and **elegant streets,** peaceful Estrela (eesh-TREH-lah) was settled by the well-heeled during the city's expansion in the 1700s and remains one of Lisbon's most affluent areas. The adjoining Lapa (LAH-pah) neighborhood is home to many **foreign embassies.**

ALCÂNTARA

Wedged halfway between downtown Lisbon (Baixa) and Belém, directly beneath the **25 de Abril Bridge,** is Alcântara (al-KHAAN-ta-ra), a riverside area of significant urban revival, popular among locals. Said to take its name from the Arabic word for "bridge," the former port and industrial area is today one of the city's busiest **nightlife** spots, its old warehouses having given way to hip bars and restaurants. With a growing art scene, it is one of Lisbon's liveliest areas.

Across the 25 de Abril Bridge, technically in the town of Almada, is the the **Christ the King** statue, whose outstretched arms dominate the skyline of the Tagus' west bank.

BELÉM

Just west of downtown in bright and breezy Belém (beh-LAYN), iconic landmarks such as the **Jerónimos Monastery** and **Belém Tower** pay tribute to key chapters in Portugal's history, sharing a riverside location with modern museums, cafés, and gardens. During the Age of Discoveries, this is where ships set off to explore the globe. Belém, home of the famous *pastel de Belém* tart, can be uncomfortably busy, particularly in the heat of summer; expect long queues.

To get to Belém from downtown Lisbon, take tram 15 or 127 from the main Comércio Square, or the Cascais train from Cais do Sodré to Cascais. Jump off when you see the Jerónimos Monastery, and walk to the sights. A taxi from downtown Lisbon costs around €14 one-way.

PARK OF NATIONS

Northeast of Lisbon, Park of Nations, or Parque das Nações (park dazh nah-SSOYNS), is an über-modern neighborhood developed for the 1998 World Exposition, with mirrored high-rise apartment blocks and twin sail-shaped skyscrapers. It is linked to the south side of the Tagus River by the sinewy, 17-kilometer-long (10.6-mile-long) Vasco da Gama Bridge, Europe's longest. Family attractions such as the Altice concert arena and the Lisbon Oceanarium are here, along with cosmopolitan restaurants and bars.

SAFETY

As with many tourist destinations, Lisbon is afflicted by petty and opportunistic crime. Take basic precautions such as not walking along dark streets alone at night, not leaving valuables in rental vehicles, and not carrying large amounts of cash. Pickpockets are an issue, so make sure backpacks are worn in front in crowded areas and on public transport. Better still, use concealed pouches and never keep cash and documents in the same pouch. Call the PSP tourist police (tel. 213 421 623) or visit the nearest police station. In an emergency, call 112.

PLANNING YOUR TIME

Much of Lisbon's city center can be covered in a day, but it's worth spending at least two or three days. A great way to cover the must-sees is either a hop-on hop-off bus that stops at all main attractions and landmarks, or tram 28, which circumnavigates Lisbon's main neighborhoods. Other good options to explore include a neatly organized subway, nifty tuk-tuk carts, and a hop-on hop-off ferryboat. Set aside more days to explore the many day trips within a few hours' drive of the city. While in Lisbon, an absolute must is dinner at a fado restaurant in Bairro Alto. Make reservations well in advance, as these are popular attractions.

In mid-June, the traditional Santo António festivities, dedicated to the city's patron saint, explode into party mode. In December, Christmas trimmings and roasted chestnuts bring warmth to the city. July and August can get very hot, and even though many of the city's residents head south for summer vacation, it is still packed with tourists. Summer and New Year are tourism high seasons, when hotel prices soar and the city is full of visitors. Good times to visit are March-May and September-October, when the weather is pleasant and the hotels less expensive.

Itinerary Ideas

DAY 1: BAIXA AND BAIRRO ALTO

1 Spend the morning discovering downtown Lisbon. Begin by walking the main **Avenida da Liberdade,** heading south toward the Tagus River. Peruse the glamorous window displays and stop for a mid-morning coffee at one of the picturesque cafés.

2 In the main downtown area, explore famous **Comércio Square** and its museums and landmarks—they're all within walking distance. Make sure you climb to the top of the Triumphal Arch on Rua Augusta.

3 A few streets back from the main square is the **Santa Justa Elevator,** also called the Carmo Lift. This historical contraption transports passengers from downtown up to the famous Bairro Alto neighborhood. Hop onto the elevator and admire how the old-fashioned machinery comes to life, taking you to the viewing platform at the top.

4 Once up in Bairro Alto, visit the **Carmo Convent.**

5 For lunch, hop on the Metro (from Baixa-Chiado to Cais do Sodré) or take a 20-minute walk west to the bustling **Time Out Market Lisboa,** set back from the Cais do Sodré quay. This eclectic food hall showcases the finest Portuguese products.

6 Head back to downtown Lisbon via tram, bus, or taxi, stopping at Chiado Square to enjoy a late afternoon cocktail on a panoramic terrace. The **Hotel Mundial Rooftop Bar & Lounge,** just off Chiado Square, is a good choice.

7 From here, it's a 20-minute stroll west to Bairro Alto for dinner at the typical fado restaurant **O Faia.** After dinner, let loose in one of the many nearby bars.

DAY 2: ALFAMA AND PARK OF NATIONS

1 From Lisbon's Baixa, head to the historic Alfama and São Vicente neighborhoods on one of the city's emblematic trams (no. 12 or 28). Spend a few hours ambling Alfama's maze of ancient cobbled streets, visiting sights including the **Lisbon Cathedral.**

2 Don't miss the **Graça viewpoint,** a short 15-minute walk north from the Cathedral.

Itinerary Ideas

DAY ONE	DAY TWO	LISBON LIKE A LOCAL
1 Avenida da Liberdade	1 Lisbon Cathedral	1 LX Factory
2 Comércio Square	2 Graça Viewpoint	2 MAAT— Museum of Art
3 Santa Justa Elevator	3 São Jorge Castle	3 Jerónimos Monastery
4 Carmo Convent	4 Vasco da Gama Shopping Centre	4 Pastéis de Belém
5 Time Out Market Lisboa + Riverside Market	5 Lisbon Oceanarium	5 25 de Abril Bridge
6 Hotel Mundial Rooftop Bar & Lounge	6 Riverside Cable Car	6 Feitoria
7 O Faia	7 Restaurante D'Bacalhau	

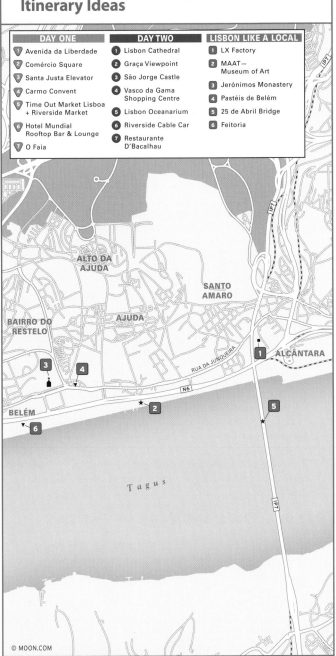

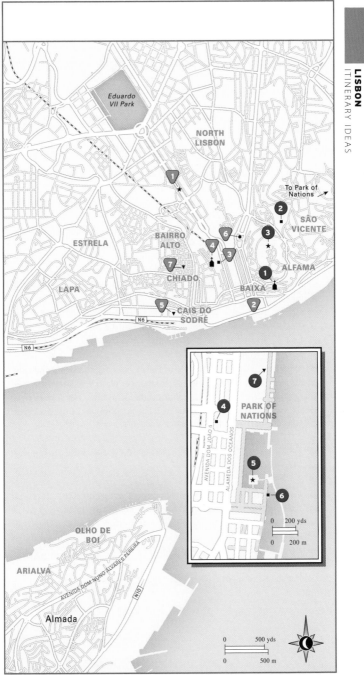

3 Make your way toward São Jorge Castle for a spot of lunch with a view.

4 After lunch walk northeast toward the river to the Santa Apolónia train station. Jump on a train for a 10-minute journey north toward Park of Nations (Azambuja line; trains run every 15 minutes). Exit at modernist Oriente station. Here you can spend the afternoon browsing the huge Vasco da Gama Shopping Centre and walking the riverfront gardens.

5 Kids of all ages will enjoy exploring the Lisbon Oceanarium.

6 Follow this up with a fun ride on the scenic riverside cable car.

7 End the day with a meal at Restaurante D'Bacalhau, along the Park of Nations waterfront, maybe followed by a boogie in one of the many bars nearby, before heading back to your hotel in a cab or an Uber.

LISBON LIKE A LOCAL

1 For a slower-paced day in the city, start by heading to the LX Factory in Alcântara (halfway between Baixa and Belém) for a leisurely browse of the stalls, enjoying a spot of brunch.

2 From here, walk across the road to the futuristic-looking MAAT museum; take in the views from the rooftop.

3 Walk west along the riverside to Belém, enjoying the sights and cafés on the way, or rent one of the many bicycles or electric scooters scattered along the stretch. Find a shady spot near the Jerónimos Monastery to sit and relax for a while, before enjoying a late lunch in one of the many restaurants located just behind it.

4 Now it's time to visit the famous Pastéis de Belém bakery to sample a *pastel de Belém* custard tart.

5 Catch a train back into downtown Lisbon, getting off at the Alcântara-Mar stop, to enjoy a sundowner at one of the many bars and lounges on the Santo Amaro docks underneath the 25 de Abril Bridge. Don't miss the Pillar 7 Bridge Experience while you're here—a unique tour in, around, and up one of the pillars of the iconic bridge.

6 Finish your day with a delicious meal at Feitoria.

Sights

BAIXA
COMÉRCIO SQUARE
(Praça do Comércio)

This vast square, with views of the Tagus River, bustles with visitors and has the statue of King José I on his horse. The impressive colonnades that frame it on three sides house several ministries, museums, shops, and restaurants. It's one of the city's main transport hubs, with many trams and buses running from here; it's also directly across from the Cais do Sodré ferry terminal. Two museums on the square are worth a visit—the Beer Museum and the Lisbon Story Centre.

Beer Museum
(Museu da Cerveja)

Terreiro do Paço, Ala Nascente 62-65, tel. 210 987 656, www.museudacerveja.pt, daily 11am-midnight, €5, Metro Terreiro do Paço, Blue Line

The Beer Museum (Museu da Cerveja) boasts a plethora of different beers and ales from around the world.

The Lisbon Story Centre

Praça do Comércio 78, tel. 211 941 099, www.lisboastorycentre.pt, daily 10am-8pm, €7, Metro Terreiro do Paço, Blue Line

The Lisbon Story Centre recounts the key chapters of Lisbon's history through state-of-the-art interactive multimedia.

AUGUSTA TRIUMPHAL ARCH
(Arco da Rua Augusta)

Praça do Comércio, tel. 210 999 599, www.visitlisboa.com, daily 9am-8pm, viewing terrace €2.50, Metro Terreiro do Paço, Blue Line

The formal entrance to the Baixa neighborhood, the decorative Augusta Triumphal Arch was built to mark the city's resilience and glorious rebirth following the 1755 earthquake. Historical Portuguese figures such as explorer Vasco da Gama and the Marquis of Pombal adorn the gateway's six columns, gazing over Comércio Square and out to the river. Inside the arch a narrow, spiral staircase made from solid stone climbs to a viewing terrace that offers sweeping views of the plaza.

ARCHAEOLOGICAL CENTER OF RUA CORREEIROS
(Núcleo Arqueológico da Rua Correeiros)

Rua dos Correeiros 15-23, tel. 211 131 004, Mon.-Sat. 10am-6pm, free, Metro Baixa-Chiado, Green/Blue Lines

Overlooked by many tourists, the Archaeological Center of Rua Correeiros showcases a wealth of Roman artifacts uncovered during the construction of the bank next door. Free guided tours of Roman ruins beneath the streets of Lisbon must be booked in advance and are available in English.

MONEY MUSEUM
(Museu do Dinheiro)

Largo de São Julião, tel. 213 213 240, www.museudodinheiro.pt, Weds.-Sun. 10am-6pm, free, Metro Baixa-Chiado or Terreiro do Paço, Blue Line

Part of the Bank of Portugal's premises in the heart of downtown Lisbon, this fascinating, interactive multimedia museum is probably one of Lisbon's more underrated sights. It

LISBON'S BEST RESTAURANTS

✪ **CAFÉ NICOLA:** Frequented by poet Manuel du Bocage, this art deco landmark epitomizes European coffee culture (page 65).

✪ **SOLAR DO BACALHAU:** This is one of the best spots to enjoy the Portuguese specialty *bacalhau* (page 66).

✪ **CERVEJARIA RAMIRO:** Expect long queues at this famed institution where a steak sandwich replaces dessert (page 66).

✪ **CHAPITÔ À MESA:** This restaurant is part of a famous circus arts school, so expect a fun and fanciful meal (page 67).

✪ **CASA DO LEÃO:** Dine inside the São Jorge Castle, where the dishes are culinary masterpieces and the views are remarkable (page 67).

✪ **CERVEJARIA TRINDADE:** This beautiful brewery and banquet hall dates from the mid-1800s, when it was the place of choice for writers, poets, and politicians (page 72).

✪ **TIME OUT MARKET LISBOA:** Hundreds of gastronomic goodies are under one roof (page 73).

✪ **PASTÉIS DE BELÉM:** No visit to Lisbon is complete without a stop at this birthplace of Portugal's famous *pastel de Belém* tart (page 75).

takes visitors on a trip covering the entire history of global currency, from pre-currency civilization to payments in the modern world. In a lofty, converted 17th-century church, you can handle a real bar of gold, visit old Roman ruins in the basement, see currency from all over the world, and learn about how money is made, before popping into the on-site café.

SANTA JUSTA ELEVATOR
(Elevador de Santa Justa)

www.carris.pt, daily 7:30am-11pm May-Oct., daily 7:30am-9pm Nov.-Apr., round-trip €5.15, Metro Baixa-Chiado, Green/Blue Lines

Also called the Carmo Lift, the 19th-century neo-Gothic, wrought-iron Santa Justa Elevator is the only vertical lift in Lisbon, connecting the Baixa area to the Bairro Alto neighborhood, saving a steep climb. Inaugurated in 1902, it is classified as a national monument. Standing at 45 meters (148 feet) tall, it was designed by engineer Raoul

Mesnier de Ponsard in a style similar to that of the Eiffel Tower. The lift is stunning at night when lit up and has a fabulous viewing platform at the top. Intriguingly, it can transport more people going up than coming down. It is accessed via Rua do Ouro at the bottom or Carmo Square at the top. The viewing platform (€1.50) is also accessible directly from Carmo Square, up the hill behind the lift.

ROSSIO SQUARE
(Praça Dom Pedro IV)

Metro Rossio, Green Line

The beating heart of Lisbon, located downtown, Rossio Square has long been one of the city's main meeting places, a lively, genteel square of Pombaline architecture lined with cafés, trees, and two grand Baroque fountains at either end. Housed in the impressive buildings framing the square are the stately **Dona Maria II National Theater (Teatro Nacional**

✪ **YES! LISBON HOSTEL:** This hostel has it all: excellent location, fantastic service, and budget-friendly prices (page 83).

✪ **HOTEL MUNDIAL:** The rooftop bar at this four-star hotel has one of the best views in Lisbon (page 83).

✪ **SOLAR DO CASTELO:** Sleep in medieval-contemporary style at this eco-retreat within the walls of the São Jorge Castle (page 83).

✪ **MEMMO ALFAMA DESIGN HOTEL:** This chic urban retreat blends in with the historic Alfama neighborhood (page 84).

✪ **BAIRRO ALTO HOTEL:** This grand 18th-century hotel enjoys a dominant position on the main square, within walking distance of shops and restaurants (page 84).

✪ **HELLO LISBON CAIS DO SODRÉ APARTMENTS:** These self-catering apartments reflect the youth and energy of frenetic Pink Street (page 85).

✪ **HOTEL PALÁCIO DO GOVERNADOR:** Located in the 16th-century Governor's Palace is an oasis of tranquility in one of Lisbon's prettiest neighborhoods (page 85).

✪ **VIP EXECUTIVE ARTS:** This streamlined four-star hotel is close to convenient transportation, shopping, and nightlife (page 85).

de Dona Maria II) and the historic **Café Nicola,** which dates to the 18th century and was one of the first cafés to emerge in Lisbon. Also nearby is the ornate **Rossio train station,** which is typically Manueline in its architecture. One of the square's distinguishing features is the wavy black-and-white cobblestone paving.

GLÓRIA FUNICULAR
(Elevador da Glória)

www.carris.pt, Mon.-Thurs. 7:15am-11:55pm, Fri. 7:15am-12:25am, Sat. 8:45am-12:25pm, Sun. and holidays 9:15am-11:55pm, round-trip €3.60

The quirky Glória Funicular puts the "fun" in funicular. It has become an emblem of Lisbon, its graffiti scrawl only adding to its charm, mirroring its urban surroundings. Inaugurated in 1885, it connects the Baixa (Restauradores Square) to the São Pedro de Alcântara viewpoint in Bairro Alto via a steep track that cuts straight through a dense residential area packed with 19th-century buildings. Practical for locals, it's a treat for visitors.

ALFAMA
✪ SÃO JORGE CASTLE
(Castelo de São Jorge)

Rua de Santa Cruz do Castelo, tel. 218 800 620, www.castelodesaojorge.pt, daily 9am-9pm Mar.-Oct., daily 9am-6pm Nov.-Feb., €8.50

The São Jorge Castle sits on a summit high above historic Baixa. The original fortress was built by the Visigoths in the 5th century and expanded by the Moors in the mid-11th century due to its prime defensive location. It contains the medieval castle, ruins of the former royal palace, stunning gardens, and part of an 11th-century citadel.

A permanent exhibition of relics

uncovered here includes objects from the 7th century BC to the 18th century. The Black Chamber, a camera obscura, provides 360-degree views of the city through an optical system of mirrors and lenses, while an open-air viewpoint looks over the city center and the Tagus River. Renowned restaurant Casa do Leão and a casual café are also within the castle walls. To get there from downtown Lisbon, take tram 28 or the Castelo Bus, line 737.

PORTAS DO SOL VIEWPOINT
(Miradouro Portas do Sol)

Largo Portas do Sol, tram 28, open 24/7, free

Midway between São Jorge Castle and the Sé cathedral, this is one of Lisbon's most iconic viewpoints, a vast terrace looking over rooftops down to the Tagus River. It's also an obligatory stop for weary walkers. At the viewpoint is the cool, contemporary **Portas do Sol** (Portas do Sol Drinks & Food,

Largo das Portas do Sol, Beco de Santa Helena, tel. 218 851 299, https://portasdosol.pt, daily 10am-midnight), a café, restaurant, and cocktail bar all rolled into one—it's a great place to drink in the views, enhanced by a lively soundtrack of street entertainers mixed with the bustle of the city.

LISBON CATHEDRAL
(Sé de Lisboa)

Largo da Sé, tel. 218 866 752, www. patriarcado-lisboa.pt, daily 9am-7pm, main cathedral free, tram 28 or 12

Between the Alfama neighborhood and Castelo, Lisbon Cathedral is the oldest and most famous church in the city. Its official name is the Church of Santa Maria Maior, but it is often simply called the Sé. Construction began in 1147, and successive modifications and renovations span the centuries. Its exterior is austere, with two robust towers. Inside, a wealth of decorative

São Jorge Castle

Alfama and São Vicente

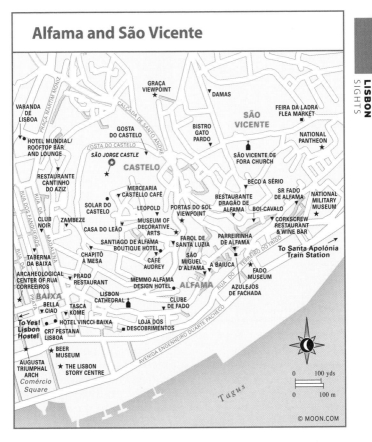

GRAÇA VIEWPOINT

DAMAS

CALÇADA DE SANTO ANDRÉ

PRAÇA MARTIM MONIZ

VARANDA DE LISBOA

SÃO VICENTE

FEIRA DA LADRA FLEA MARKET

GOSTA DO CASTELO

BISTRO GATO PARDO

NATIONAL PANTHEON

HOTEL MUNDIAL/ ROOFTOP BAR AND LOUNGE

COSTA DO CASTELO

SÃO JORGE CASTLE

SÃO VICENTE DE FORA CHURCH

CASTELO

RESTAURANTE CANTINHO DO AZIZ

MERCEARIA CASTELLO CAFÉ

BECO A SÉRIO

RESTAURANTE DRAGÃO DE ALFAMA

SR FADO DE ALFAMA

NATIONAL MILITARY MUSEUM

RUA DOS FANQUEIROS

RUA DA MADALENA

SOLAR DO CASTELO

LEOPOLD

PORTAS DO SOL VIEWPOINT

BOI-CAVALO

CLUB NOIR

ZAMBEZE

CASA DO LEÃO

MUSEUM OF DECORATIVE ARTS

CORKSCREW RESTAURANT & WINE BAR

SANTIAGO DE ALFAMA BOUTIQUE HOTEL

FAROL DE SANTA LUZIA

PARREIRINHA DE ALFAMA

To Santa Apolónia Train Station

TABERNA DA BAIXA

CHAPITÔ À MESA

CAFÉ AUDREY

SÃO MIGUEL D'ALFAMA

A BAIUCA

RUA DO TERREIRO DO TRIGO

ARCHAEOLOGICAL CENTER OF RUA CORREEIROS

PRADO RESTAURANT

MEMMO ALFAMA DESIGN HOTEL

ALFAMA

FADO MUSEUM

BAIXA

LISBON CATHEDRAL

CLUBE DE FADO

RUA DO

AZULEJOS DE FACHADA

RUA DA PRATA

BELLA CIAO

TASCA KOME

To Yes! Lisbon Hostel

HOTEL VINCCI BAIXA

CR7 PESTANA LISBOA

LOJA DOS DESCOBRIMENTOS

AVENIDA ENGENHEIRO DUARTE PACHECO

BEER MUSEUM

AUGUSTA TRIUMPHAL ARCH

THE LISBON STORY CENTRE

Comércio Square

Tagus

0   100 yds
0   100 m

© MOON.COM

features reflect different eras. The neoclassical and rococo main chapel contains the tombs of King Afonso IV and his family. You'll also see lofty Gothic vaults, sculptured Romanesque motifs, stained-glass rose windows, and a Baroque sacristy. The **Cloister** (Mon.-Sat. 10am-5pm, Sun. 2pm-5pm, extended hours until 7pm May-Sept., €2.50) houses Roman, Arab, and medieval relics excavated during archaeological digs. The **Treasury** (Mon.-Sat. 10am-5pm, €2.50) on the second floor contains jewels from various periods. Tram 28 stops right outside the cathedral's door.

FADO MUSEUM
(Museu do Fado)

Largo Chafariz de Dentro 1, tel. 218 823 470, www.museudofado.pt, Tues.-Sun. 10am-6pm, €5, Metro Santa Apolónia, Blue Line

The Fado Museum showcases traditional fado, a soulful and often mournful musical genre that is to Portugal what the blues are to Memphis. Fado's origins are debated, but the consensus is that it was born in Alfama in the 1820s. This interactive museum hosts a permanent exhibition with photographs, records, and instruments. There are also sometimes live performances.

NATIONAL MILITARY MUSEUM
(Museu Militar)

Largo Museu da Artilharia, tel. 218 842 300, www.exercito.pt, Tues.-Fri. 10am-5pm, Sat.-Sun. and holidays 10am-12:30pm and 1:30pm-5pm, €3, Metro Santa Apolónia, Blue Line

Across the square from the Santa Apolónia train station, the National Military Museum is Portugal's largest and oldest military museum. Beautiful, lofty, tile-clad rooms contain 26,000 pieces of military paraphernalia spanning centuries, including the former Royal Arsenal. The building is a striking monument, built on the site of a 16th-century foundry.

✪ NATIONAL TILE MUSEUM
(Museu Nacional do Azulejo)

Rua da Madre de Deus 4, tel. 218 100 340, www.museudoazulejo.gov.pt, Tues.-Sun. 10am-6pm, €5, Metro Santa Apolónia, Blue Line

Located in a 16th-century convent, the National Tile Museum contains a collection of traditional hand-painted *azulejo* ceramic tile plaques, some dating from the 15th century. It explores the history and tradition behind the

tile from the National Tile Museum

art and craft of tilework, and the building is a splendid example of the magnificence of Portuguese Baroque, with carved and gilded wood features, old paintings, and historical *azulejo* panels.

MUSEUM OF DECORATIVE ARTS
(Museu De Artes Decorativas Portuguesas)

Largo Portas do Sol 2, tel. 218 881 991, www.fress.pt, Weds.-Mon. 10am-5pm, €4, bus 737, tram 12 or 28

Located near the Portas do Sol viewpoint, the 17th-century Azura Palace is home to the Museum of Decorative Arts. Part of the Ricardo do Espirito Santo Silva Foundation, this wonderful museum offers a glimpse into how 18th- and 19th-century Portuguese aristocracy lived. While the palace itself retains many of its original features, it also showcases furniture and fixtures of the era. Among them are a priceless silver collection, Chinese porcelain, and ancient Flemish tapestries.

GRAÇA VIEWPOINT
(Miradouro da Graça)

Calçada da Graça, open 24/7, free, tram 28

Also called the Sophia de Mello Breyner Andresen viewpoint after Portugal's most famous poetess, this bird's-eye terrace was built in 1271 and offers dramatic sweeping vistas over Lisbon. Particularly magical at sunrise and sunset, the view of São Jorge Castle is striking. A little on-site **café** (Esplanada da Graça, tel. 218 865 341, daily 10am-2am) is a great spot for refreshments while drinking in the views. Located in front of the Graça church, this is often the starting point for exploring Bairro Alto.

Graça Viewpoint

SÃO VICENTE

NATIONAL PANTHEON
(Panteão Nacional)

Campo de Santa Clara, tel. 218 854 820, Tues.-Sat. 10am-6pm Apr.-Sept., Tues.-Sat. 10am-5pm Oct.-Mar., €4, Metro Santa Apolónia, Blue Line

The National Pantheon—otherwise known as the Church of Santa Engrácia—has Baroque architecture and a distinctive domed roof that can be seen from most of central Lisbon. It is on the site of the original Santa Engrácia church, which began renovations in 1681 and took more than 300 years to complete. Construction dragged on for so long that the Portuguese call any lengthy project "work of Santa Engrácia." In 1916, the church was converted into a pantheon, a process that took another 50 years. Today, the building boasts a majestic nave with a polychrome marble decoration typical of Portuguese Baroque architecture. It is home to tombs of historic personalities such as writer Almeida Garrett, fado singer Amália Rodrigues, legendary soccer star Eusébio, and Portuguese presidents. The views from the front steps and the terrace around the dome are breathtaking.

SÃO VICENTE DE FORA CHURCH
(Igreja de São Vicente de Fora)

Largo de São Vicente, tel. 218 824 400, www.patriarcado-lisboa.pt, Tues.-Sun. 10am-6pm, €5, Metro Santa Apolónia, Blue Line

In its present guise, the São Vicente de Fora Church, or Monastery of São Vicente de Fora, is considered one of the finest examples of mannerist architecture in the country. Rebuilt from a 12th-century church, it dates to the 16th century and houses one of the biggest collections of Baroque glazed tiles in the world, used to clad the cloisters, stairways, and aisles. There are also two mausoleums, one belonging to the Royal House of Braganza and the other to the city's archbishops, known as the Patriarchs of Lisbon. The must-see Patriarchate's Museum showcases beautiful historic works of religious art. Enjoy fabulous views from the roof terrace.

AVENIDA DA LIBERDADE

MARQUÊS DE POMBAL SQUARE
(Praça Marquês de Pombal)

The massive statue of the Marquis of Pombal towering in the middle of this busy roundabout is one of Lisbon's most recognizable landmarks. Sebastião José de Carvalho e Melo, the 1st Marquis of Pombal, was prime minister in the 18th century. His soaring statue faces the Tagus River, strategically between Eduardo VII Park and the cosmopolitan Avenida da Liberdade, the start of several main thoroughfares. Get here by taking the Metro to Marquês de Pombal station (Blue/Yellow Lines).

EDUARDO VII PARK
(Parque Eduardo VII)

Just behind the Marquês de Pombal Square is a sprawling, manicured garden of lush lawns and box hedges that give it a regal feel, consistent with the historic buildings surrounding it. Stand at the top of the park and enjoy magnificent views down to the Baixa and the Tagus River. Covering 26 hectares (64 acres), the park was renamed in 1902 for Britain's Edward VII, who visited Portugal that year. It is also home to the Estufa Fria (Cold Greenhouse, www.estufafria. cm-lisboa.pt, €3.10), one of the most important gardens in the city center, comprising lakes, waterfalls, brooks, statues, and hundreds of different plant specimens from all over the world. It's a great place to take refuge on a hot day.

☉ CALOUSTE GULBENKIAN MUSEUM
(Museu Calouste Gulbenkian)

Av. de Berna 45A, tel. 217 823 461, www.gulbenkian.pt/museu, Weds.-Mon. 10am-6pm, €14, Metro São Sebastião, Blue/ Red Lines

A major hub of the arts, the Calouste Gulbenkian Museum is one of Lisbon's less-celebrated treasures. Its collection ranges from Greco-Roman antiquity to contemporary pieces, with 18th-century French art well represented. The stunning works of French glass and jewelry designer René Lalique (1860-1945) are a highlight. The museum is housed in two separate buildings, connected by a lovely garden.

Calouste Gulbenkian Museum

ÁGUAS LIVRES AQUEDUCT
(Aqueduto das Águas Livres)

main entrance at the EPAL Municipal Water Museum ticket office, Calçada da Quintinha 6, Campolide neighborhood, tel. 218 100 215, www.epal.pt, Tues.-Sun. 10am-5:30pm, €3

Climb above the city to explore the formidable Águas Livres Aqueduct, whose name translates as "Aqueduct of the Free Waters." Built between 1731 and 1799 to supply the city with water from Sintra, it is considered a remarkable example of 18th-century engineering, snaking over 58 kilometers (36 miles) along the trajectory of an old Roman aqueduct. Despite its size, it blends into its surroundings. Visitors can walk the main portion of the platform, crossing the 1-kilometer (0.6-mile) stretch over the Alcântara Valley, the aqueduct's highest point at 68 meters (223 feet), with views of Lisbon. Guided tours (first Saturday every month, 11am) require advance booking.

Take the Portas da Benfica bus 758 (every 15 minutes, €2) from the Glória Funicular to Campolide, then walk west for 5 minutes to the aqueduct. A taxi from central Lisbon to the aqueduct costs around €8.

MEDEIROS E ALMEIDA HOUSE-MUSEUM
(Casa Museu Medeiros e Almeida)

Rua Rosa Araújo 41, tel. 213 547 892, www. casa-museumedeirosealmeida.pt, Mon.-Sat. 10am-5pm, €5, Metro Marquês de Pombal, Blue/Yellow Lines

Once a private residence, this house museum is another of Lisbon's lesser-known attractions but definitely worth a visit. It houses a massive collection of 17th- to 20th-century artifacts in more than two dozen rooms, including furniture, clocks, Chinese porcelain, and, word has it, Napoleon Bonaparte's tea service, European paintings, and silverware. The house itself is a handsome, stately mansion that was the home of one of the most successful Portuguese businessmen of the 20th century, António de Medeiros e Almeida.

CHIADO AND BAIRRO ALTO
GARRETT STREET
(Rua Garrett)

Named after acclaimed Portuguese poet Almeida Garrett, Garrett Street (Rua Garrett) is the main vein traversing Chiado, a pulsing shopping street flanked by handsome cultural venues, such as the **São Carlos National Theatre, Livraria Bertrand,** believed to be one of the oldest bookstores in the world, and the century-old **A Brasileira Café,** once the meeting point of Lisbon's intellectuals and luminaries.

Carmo Convent

✪ CARMO CONVENT
(Convento do Carmo)

Largo do Carmo, tel. 213 478 629, www. museuarqueologicodocarmo.pt, Mon.-Sat. 10am-6pm May-Sept., Mon.-Sat. 10am-5pm Oct.-Apr., €4, Metro Baixa-Chiado or Rossio, Green/Blue Lines

Once Lisbon's largest church, the Carmo Convent is a stark reminder of the vast devastation caused by the 1755 earthquake, which razed the city and large swaths of Portugal. Originally built in 1389 by order of Nuno Álvares Pereira, an influential knight who led the Portuguese army, the church and convent sit on a hill directly opposite the São Jorge Castle. Today only its naked Gothic ruins still stand. The site is also

43

Bairro Alto

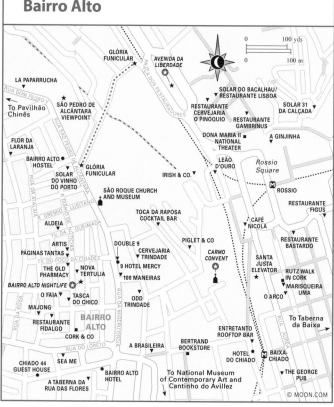

Map labels:
GLÓRIA FUNICULAR
AVENIDA DA LIBERDADE
PRAÇA DOS RESTAURADORES
LA PAPARRUCHA
RUA DOM PEDRO V
SOLAR DO BACALHAU/ RESTAURANTE LISBOA
SOLAR 31 DA CALÇADA
SÃO PEDRO DE ALCÂNTARA VIEWPOINT
To Pavilhão Chinês
RESTAURANTE CERVEJARIA O PINÓQUIO
RESTAURANTE GAMBRINUS
A GINJINHA
FLOR DA LARANJA
RUA SÃO PEDRO DE ALCÂNTARA
DONA MARIA II NATIONAL THEATER
BAIRRO ALTO HOSTEL
GLÓRIA FUNICULAR
SOLAR DO VINHO DO PORTO
RUA DA ATALAIA
LEÃO D'OURO
Rossio Square
IRISH & CO.
RUA DO GRÉMIO LUSITANO
SÃO ROQUE CHURCH AND MUSEUM
ROSSIO
R. GREMIO LUSITANO
RUA DA QUEIMADA
ALDEIA
TOCA DA RAPOSA COCKTAIL BAR
RESTAURANTE FIGUS
CAFÉ NICOLA
ARTIS
PÁGINAS TANTAS
TV. DA CARA
DOUBLE 9
PIGLET & CO
RESTAURANTE BASTARDO
CERVEJARIA TRINDADE
CARMO CONVENT
SANTA JUSTA ELEVATOR
TV. DO POÇO DA CIDADE
THE OLD PHARMACY
NOVA TERTULIA
9 HOTEL MERCY
RUA DA MISERICÓRDIA
RUTZ WALK IN CORK
BAIRRO ALTO NIGHTLIFE
100 MANEIRAS
MARISQUEIRA UMA
O FAIA
TASCA DO CHICO
ODD TRINDADE
O ARCO
RUA AUREA
MAJONG
To Taberna da Baixa
RESTAURANTE FIDALGO
BAIRRO ALTO
RUA DA ROSA
CORK & CO
RUA DO LORETO
ENTRETANTO ROOFTOP BAR
A BRASILEIRA
BERTRAND BOOKSTORE
BAIXA-CHIADO
CHIADO 44 GUEST HOUSE
SEA ME
HOTEL DO CHIADO
THE GEORGE PUB
A TABERNA DA RUA DAS FLORES
BAIRRO ALTO HOTEL
To National Museum of Contemporary Art and Cantinho do Avillez
© MOON.COM
0 100 yds
0 100 m

home to the Museu Arqueológico do Carmo, a museum with a collection of relics from dissolved monasteries, including sarcophagi and grisly but well-preserved Peruvian sacrificial mummies.

NATIONAL MUSEUM OF CONTEMPORARY ART
(Museu Nacional de Arte Contemporânea do Chiado: MNAC)

Rua Serpa Pinto 4, tel. 213 432 148, www. museuartecontemporanea.gov.pt, Tues.-Sun. 10am-6pm, €4.50, Metro Baixa-Chiado, Green/Blue Lines

Established by government decree in 1911, the National Museum of Contemporary Art—Museu do Chiado is housed in what was the old convent of São Francisco da Cidade. The convent was severely damaged by the 1755 Lisbon earthquake, and later by a huge fire in 1988; it was re-designed by French architect Jean-Michel Wilmotte and re-inaugurated in 1994. It specializes in 19th- and 20th-century Portuguese contemporary art, divided into temporary exhibitions and a permanent collection displaying thematic exhibitions that span Portuguese Romantic, naturalist, modern, and contemporary art.

Botanical Garden of Lisbon

SÃO ROQUE CHURCH AND MUSEUM
(Igreja e Museu de São Roque)

Largo Trindade Coelho, tel. 213 235 065 / 213 235 449, http://mais.scml.pt/museu-saoroque, Mon. 2pm-7pm, Tues., Weds., Fri.-Sun. 10am-7pm, Thurs. 10am-8pm, church free, museum €2.50 (children free), Sun. 10am-2pm free

As one of the first art museums to open in Portugal, the São Roque Museum was originally created to house an important collection of Italian art. Since its founding it has occupied a 17th-century cloister adjacent to the Church of São Roque, which had been donated to the Holy House of Mercy of Lisbon in 1768, after the expulsion of the Jesuits. Throughout the 20th century it was subject to a series of extensive refurbishments, allowing the museum to greatly expand its permanent exhibition area. Today comprising over 100 years of history, the São Roque Museum is said to be one of the most beautiful and complete museums of Portuguese religious artifacts and paintings.

The church itself is also a treat to visit. Its plain exterior belies the exquisiteness of its lavish gold-leaf interior and ornate embellishments. From the outside it may well be one of the city's least remarkable places of worship, but on the inside it is one of the most opulent—and said to be home to one of Europe's most expensive chapels (the fourth on the left, apparently). This church was also one of only a handful of buildings in Lisbon's westerly quarters to withstand the 1755 earthquake without major damage.

BOTANICAL GARDEN OF LISBON
(Jardim Botânico da Universidade de Lisboa)

Rua da Escola Politécnica 56/58, tel. 213 921 800, www.museus.ulisboa.pt/pt-pt/jardim-botanico-lisboa, daily 9am-7:30pm (9am-8pm Apr.-Sept.), €3, Metro Rato, Yellow Line

Once declared the finest botanical

THE 1755 EARTHQUAKE

On the morning of Saturday, November 1, 1755, the ground shook violently in Portugal. What followed was one of the most devastating and deadliest earthquakes Europe had seen. The 1755 earthquake—also referred to as the Great Lisbon Earthquake—destroyed not only vast swathes of Lisbon but also much of Portugal, and it triggered a tsunami that tore up the Tagus River, washing out most of Lisbon's downtown area. Portugal happened to be celebrating All Saints Day on the day of the quake; widespread fires were also caused after lit candles toppled in homes and churches.

With most of its buildings destroyed or greatly damaged, the decision was made to raze Lisbon's entire downtown quarter, or what was left of it, and rebuild with an orderly, spacious gridlike layout comprising large squares, large rectilinear avenues, and widened streets. This massive undertaking was spearheaded by Sebastião José de Carvalho e Melo, the 1st Marquis of Pombal and then a Minister of the Kingdom of Portugal, who was instrumental in rebuilding the city after the earthquake. As a tribute, his name was lent to the rebuild that today characterizes downtown Lisbon—the Pombaline style—hence, the *Baixa Pombalina*. This thorough renovation saw a revolutionary anti-seismic building method, centered on the *Gaiola Pombalina* (Pombaline cage), a masonry building reinforced with an internal wood-lattice cage that was both sturdy and earthquake-resistant. The innovative technique was among the earliest quake-proof constructions in Europe, and when coupled with the city's neat new layout, made Lisbon one of the first truly modern cities in the world. While the handsome Pombaline buildings continue to stand firm and proud, other landmarks still bear the scars of one of Portugal's darkest days.

- **Carmo Convent:** The naked bones of the roofless Carmo Convent are a stark reminder of the extent of the devastation caused by the 1755 earthquake. Built in 1389, the once magnificent Gothic building was left ruined beyond repair.

- **Augusta Triumphal Arch:** This majestic archway was built purposely after the 1755 earthquake to signal the rebirth of Lisbon city.

- **National Museum of Contemporary Art:** The National Museum of Contemporary Art is housed in the former São Francisco da Cidade convent, a complex of monastic buildings severely damaged by the earthquake. Later, in 1988, the area was again devastated by a raging fire; the museum was completely overhauled and re-inaugurated in 1994.

- **São Roque Church:** Home to "the world's most expensive chapel," São Roque Church was one of few buildings in the westerly quarters to survive the Great Lisbon Earthquake with only minor damage. It was given to the Lisbon Holy House of Mercy to replace their church and headquarters that had been destroyed by the quake.

garden in southern Europe, the Lisbon Botanical Garden is an enchanting oasis of cool and calm. Covering 10 acres on the Olivete Hill, on the northern fringe of Bairro Alto, it is resplendent with rare and exotic tree and plant species, comprising flora from all over the world. Created between 1858 and 1873, it is still home to one of the largest collections of subtropical vegetation in Europe. The Garden is particularly rich in tropical species from New Zealand, Australia, China, Japan, and South America, and it creates its own microclimate.

SÃO PEDRO DE ALCÂNTARA VIEWPOINT (Miradouro São Pedro de Alcântara)

A pretty, two-tiered garden embellishes this sprawling viewpoint.

Located next to the Glória Lift between Bairro Alto and the Baixa, the São Pedro de Alcântara viewpoint is one of the most popular. Visitors can often be heard gasping in awe at the sweeping vistas, and telescopes are on hand.

CAIS DO SODRÉ

Cais do Sodré has recently undergone a much-needed facelift that elevated the neighborhood from seedy to swanky. Gone are the days when swashbuckling sailors sought their thrills during layovers in Lisbon and fishermen told their colorful tales in the many tackle shops that dotted the area; nowadays the tackle shops have been converted into cool hangouts, brothels into trendy bars, and the hip Time Out Market is where new gastro trends are set.

BICA LIFT
(Ascensor da Bica)

Calçada da Bica Pequena 1, tel. 213 613 000, Mon.-Sat. 7am-9pm, Sun. and public holidays 9am-9pm, €3.80 (round-trip, purchased on-board)

Inaugurated in 1892, this funicular connects Lisbon's downtown to the Bica and Bairro Alto neighborhoods, running every 15 minutes between Rua de São Paulo, near Cais do Sodré's Time Out Market, and Largo do Calhariz (Calhariz Square). Its route takes passengers up one of Lisbon's steepest hills, Bica de Duarte Belo Street, on what is arguably one of the city's most picturesque funicular routes, passing quaint houses and traditional commerce. The funicular's traction system was originally powered by steam engines before being electrified in 1914. It was declared a National Monument in 2002 and is one of the city's most popular tourist

activities. Once up at the top, make sure to visit the Santa Catarina viewpoint, which offers stunning bird's-eye views of the city.

ESTRELA AND LAPA
ESTRELA BASÍLICA
(Basílica da Estrela)

Praça da Estrela, tel. 213 960 915, www.patrimoniocultural.gov.pt, daily 7:30am-8pm, free, tram 25 or 28

The neoclassical Estrela Basílica was built in the 18th century by order of Queen Maria I, whose tomb it houses. The interior walls and flooring are clad in swaths of yellow, pink, and gray marble in stunning geometric patterns. Twin bell towers stand atop the striking facade, while the dome provides views over the city. The Estrela Basílica was the first church in the world dedicated to the Sacred Heart of Jesus.

Estrela Basílica

ESTRELA GARDENS
(Jardim da Estrela)

The exquisitely landscaped Estrela Gardens is colloquially referred to as the Central Park of Lisbon, a tranquil, lush oasis in the heart of this affluent neighborhood, bordered by the main Rua da Estrela and Avenida Ávares Cabral, with the Estrela Basílica at the bottom and a statue of explorer Pedro

LISBON'S BEST VIEWS

Because Lisbon is laid out over seven hills, gorgeous views can be found throughout the city. Public viewing points (*miradouros*) offer views of the cityscape. Some are enhanced with cafés and restaurants, landscaped gardens, and even chic lounges. Best of all, they're free. Visit at sunset for a truly special experience.

- The famous **Miradouro São Pedro de Alcântara** (Rua São Pedro de Alcântara) provides panoramic views over São Jorge Castle and Alfama, as well as Lisbon Cathedral and the Tagus.

- The romantic **Miradouro da Nossa Senhora do Monte** (Largo Monte) is the highest viewpoint, offering bird's-eye views over the old quarters and castle all the way to the Tagus River.

- The **Miradouro Portas do Sol** (Largo Portas do Sol) overlooks the charismatic Alfama neighborhood.

- The **Miradouro da Graça** (Calçada da Graça) peers over São Jorge Castle.

Along with the *miradouros*, the **São Jorge Castle** has possibly the best views in the city. Panoramas can also be enjoyed from hotel rooftop bars, such as the **Hotel Mundial** (Praça Martim Moniz 2), where the Sunset Parties have a cult following.

Álvares Cabral at the top. Stroll past duck ponds, browse the library, and enjoy open-air concerts hosted in the wrought-iron bandstand on summer evenings.

NATIONAL MUSEUM OF ANCIENT ART
(Museu Nacional de Arte Antiga)

Rua das Janelas Verdes, tel. 213 912 800, www.museudearteantiga.pt, Tues.-Sun. 10am-6pm, €6

A 20-minute stroll south of the Estrela Gardens is the National Museum of Ancient Art. Housed in a former 17th-century palace on one of the city's toniest streets, the opulent museum is laden with artifacts that span the 12th to the 19th centuries. The collection includes paintings, sculptures, textiles, and furniture. Among the most celebrated pieces are the *Panels of St. Vincent,* which depict a cross-section of 15th-century Portuguese society gathered to venerate a saint. Take the Cascais-bound train or the Santos-o-Velho bus from Cais do Sodré to Santos.

PUPPET MUSEUM
(Museu da Marioneta)

Rua da Esperança 146, tel. 213 942 810, www.museudamarioneta.pt, Tues.-Sun. 10am-pm, €5, tram 25, 28

One of Lisbon's more unusual exhibited collections, the puppet museum is small but rather entertaining. It houses a colorful collection of marionettes from all over the world, which are odd and amusing in equal proportions. Check it out online in advance to see when live shows are on, and don't forget the obligatory puppet-selfie on your way out. Audio tour included in entry price, on request.

BRITISH CEMETERY
(Cemitério dos Ingleses)

Rua de São Jorge, 6, tel. 932 101 805, Mon.-Fri. 10:30am-1pm, Sun. 11am-1pm, closed Tues. and Thurs. in Aug., donation suggested, tram 25, 28 (stop at Estrela Basílica)

A cemetery might not be at the top of everyone's sightseeing list, but in this case it is a must. Despite having a thriving British community in the 1800s, during the Inquisition, Protestants were not allowed to be buried in Catholic cemeteries. However, thanks to an agreement between English political leader Oliver Cromwell and Portugal's King João IV, a plot of land was found in 1717 for Lisbon's British citizens to be buried in—hence the name. Located just around the corner from the grand Estrela Basílica, besides providing a slice of leafy, cool tranquility away from the city's throngs, the cemetery also has lovely lush gardens surrounding the 250+ years of history. Amid the gardens and gravestones, a raised tomb sits in tribute to novelist Henry Fielding, who died in Lisbon in 1754, although his exact final resting place remains unknown. The cemetery is also home to **St. George's Church,** a pretty, pink church that has an English-speaking Anglican service (Thursday 12:30pm, Sunday 11:30am).

ALCÂNTARA

25 DE ABRIL BRIDGE
(Ponte 25 de Abril)

tel. 212 947 920, www.lusoponte.pt, tolls €1.85-7.20 (northbound only)

Lisbon's iconic 25 de Abril Bridge dominates the skyline from most directions. Stand underneath it and the buzz of the vehicles whooshing above is hypnotic. Inaugurated in 1966, prior to the Carnation Revolution it was named the Salazar Bridge, after statesman António de Oliveira Salazar. Post-independence it was renamed the 25 de Abril Bridge, in tribute to the bloodless uprising that overthrew Salazar's dictatorial regime and gave Portugal independence and democracy, on April 25, 1974. Spanning 2,277 meters (1.4 miles) the bright red suspension bridge connects Lisbon to Almada, on the south bank of the

Tagus River. The upper deck carries six vehicle lanes, and the bottom deck is a double electrified rail track, added in 1999. Crossed by some 150,000 cars every day, for those who come into Lisbon over the bridge, it offers the most incredible views of the city.

The bridge is also home to one of Lisbon's newest tourist attractions, the **Pillar 7 Experience** (Avenida da Índia (N6 34), tel. 211 117 880, www.visitlisboa.com/en/places/pilar-7-bridge-experience, daily 10am-8pm, €6), an interactive museum that allows visitors to explore inside one of the famous bridge's pillars. Those with a head for heights can take an elevator to a 72-meter-high (236-foot-high) panoramic glass viewing platform adjacent to the pillar. Vertigo-sufferers be warned—the floor is glass too (but the views are worth the shaky legs)!

Christ the King statue

✪ CHRIST THE KING
(Cristo Rei)

Alto do Pragal, Av. Cristo Rei, tel. 212 751 000 or 212 721 270, www.cristorei.pt, daily 9:30am-6:30pm, €4

Dominating the skyline of the Tagus's south bank just across from the 25 de Abril Bridge is the *Christ the King* statue, standing with arms outstretched and epitomizing Portugal's Catholic faith. The idea to build the monument came after the Cardinal Patriarch of Lisbon visited Rio de Janeiro in 1934 and was impressed by its imposing *Christ the Redeemer* statue. Built on an isolated cliff top in the town of Almada, the statue stands 192 meters (630 feet) above the Tagus River. An express elevator whizzes visitors to a viewing platform at 82 meters (269 feet), which affords dazzling views over the city. At the statue's base is a chapel. The statue's interior contains a library, a large café, two halls, and another chapel.

BELÉM

✪ BELÉM TOWER
(Torre de Belém)

Av. Brasília, tel. 213 620 034, www. torrebelem.gov.pt, Tues.-Sun. 10am-5:30pm Oct.-Apr., Tues.-Sun. 10am-6:30pm May-Sept., €6

Jutting into the Tagus River, Belém Tower is Portugal's most famous monument and a UNESCO World Heritage Site due to its significance as a launchpad during the Age of Discoveries. Built in the early 16th century at the river mouth, the fortified tower was both functional and ornamental,

Belém Tower

defending Lisbon from sea raiders and also providing a ceremonial entrance to the city. The ornate white Manueline tower was the last and first sight sailors had of their homeland. The elaborate detail of the exterior belies the starkness of the interior.

Entering the tower over an ancient drawbridge, visitors access a bulwark housing artillery, in the middle of which is a small courtyard flanked by Gothic arches. Inside the tower are the Governor's Room, the King's Room, the Audience Room, and a chapel, all devoid of furnishings, showcasing only the bare stonework. The tower is built over five floors, connected by a narrow spiral staircase, each floor having lovely balconies, and topped by a viewing terrace. It's worth the climb to the top for views over the Tagus estuary and the Belém neighborhood's monuments.

NATIONAL COACH MUSEUM
(Museu Nacional dos Coches)

Av. da Índia 136, tel. 210 732 319, www. museudoscoches.pt, Tues.-Sun. 10am-6pm, €6

Before cars, there were horses and carriages, and Portugal has some fine examples of horse-drawn vehicles on permanent display at the National Coach Museum. From elaborately decorated Berlins that transported royalty to children's carriages and mail buses, the various collections of 16th- to 19th-century coaches are fascinating. Located on the fringe of the Afonso de Albuquerque Square (Praça Afonso de Albuquerque), the museum also hosts a number of collections of other stately items, such as ceremonial clothing, instruments, tapestries, and horse tack.

Jerónimos Monastery cloister

ⓞ JERÓNIMOS MONASTERY
(Mosteiro dos Jerónimos)

Praça do Império, tel. 213 620 034, www. mosteirojeronimos.gov.pt, Tues.-Sun. 10am-5pm Oct.-Apr., Tues.-Sun. 10am-6pm May-Sept., €10, ticket including the Maritime Museum and the Archaeology Museum €12, bus 727, 728, 729, 714, 751, tram 15, suburban train to Belém

Parallel to the Tagus River, with the stately Imperial Square Gardens sprawling in front of it, the exuberant Jerónimos Monastery is Belém's breathtaking centerpiece. A prime example of ornate Manueline architecture, it is also a UNESCO World Heritage Site. Construction on the impressive landmark began in 1501 on the order of King Manuel I, who wanted to honor the memory of explorer Henry the Navigator, as well as to demonstrate his own devotion to Saint Jerome. The vast building took 100 years to complete. Its several architectural styles include Renaissance and the lavishly ornate Spanish plateresque style. The magnificent riverside facade has a figure of Our Lady of Belém, while inside is the Latin-cross-shaped Church of Santa Maria, the final resting place of explorer Vasco da Gama and one of Portugal's greatest poets, Luís Vaz de Camões. Today the Monastery's long, regal wings also house the national naval museum.

Also located in the expansive wings of the Jerónimos Monastery is the National Archaeology Museum (Museu Nacional de Arqueologia) (€4, ticket including Jerónimos Monastery and the Maritime Museum €12), devoted to ancient Iberian art. Among its collections are ancient jewelry, busts, mosaics, and epigraphs, as well as metal artifacts, medals, and coins.

MARITIME MUSEUM
(Museu de Marinha)

€6.50, ticket including the Jerónimos Monastery and the Archaeology Museum €12

The Maritime Museum (Museu de Marinha), also often referred to as the Navy or Naval Museum, occupies the western wing of the Jerónimos Monastery as well as a modern annex to the north. It grew from a collection started by King Luís I (1838-1889), who had a keen interest in oceanographic studies and was an accomplished navigator. It currently comprises more than 17,000 pieces and is widely regarded as one of the most important maritime museums in Europe. Exhibits include historical paintings, archaeological items, and various scale models of ships, along with ancient instruments and maps, royal barges, the Fairey III *Santa Cruz* that made the first aerial crossing of the Atlantic in 1923, and the Portuguese Navy's first-ever aircraft, a flying boat. The museum also showcases Portugal's seafaring history as the pioneers of the Age of Discoveries, with the oldest exhibit—a real highlight—being a wooden figurine of the Archangel Raphael that Portuguese explorer Vasco da Gama is said to have taken with him on his expedition to India.

MONUMENT TO THE DISCOVERIES
(Padrão dos Descobrimentos)

Av. Brasília, tel. 213 031 950, www. padraodosdescobrimentos.pt, daily 10am-7pm Mar.-Sept., Tues.-Sun. 10am-6pm Oct.-Feb., €3

A short stroll from Belém Tower along the Tagus riverside is the Monument to the Discoveries. First erected in 1940 and made permanent in 1960 to mark 500 years since Henry the Navigator's death, the monument celebrates the Age of Discoveries in the 15th and 16th centuries with statues of Henry the Navigator, Pedro Álvares Cabral, and Vasco da Gama. Shaped

like a caravel—a small Portuguese sailing ship—it also houses an auditorium and a museum with changing exhibitions and has a viewing platform on top. In the square out front is the stunning **Compass Rose,** an elaborate decorative work of paving art shaped like a compass, 50 meters (164 feet) across, in black and red *lioz* limestone, in the center of which is a map of the world during the Age of Discoveries surrounded by decorative figures like mermaids, stars, and leaves.

Monument to the Discoveries

MAAT—MUSEUM OF ART, ARCHITECTURE AND TECHNOLOGY
(Museu de Arte, Arquitetura e Tecnologia)

Av. Brasília, tel. 210 028 130, www.maat.pt, Weds.-Mon. noon-8pm, €5

Inaugurated in 2016 in a contemporary building in stark contrast with its classical peers, MAAT is one of Lisbon's newest cultural additions. The building, by British architect Amanda Levete, has a curved design and white-tiled facade that juts out over the river like a low, gleaming spaceship. It hosts national and international exhibitions and collections of contemporary art, architecture, and technology, and is connected to the city by a footbridge. It is free to climb to the roof from outside for views over the Tagus at what has become an iconic location.

BERARDO COLLECTION MUSEUM
(Museu Colecção Berardo)

Praça do Império, tel. 213 612 878, www. museuberardo.pt, daily 10am-7pm, €5 (free entry on Saturdays), tram 15, bus 714, 728

Lisbon's most-visited museum is indeed a must-see for modern art lovers. Comprising a vast selection of carefully curated modern and contemporary art, spanning all genres from Cubism to Pop Art, the outstanding Berardo Collection Museum is a private collection that features iconic pieces by the greats—works by Mondrian, Picasso, Duchamp, Andy Warhol, Jackson Pollock, Salvador Dalí, and Francis Bacon can all be found here—as well as emerging artists. The permanent collection occupies the entire second floor, with rotating exhibitions on the lower floor.

CORDOARIA NACIONAL

Av. da Índia, tel. 213 637 635, www. patrimoniocultural.gov.pt, daily 10am-7pm (until 8pm weekends)

The Cordoaria Nacional is a former naval rope-making factory in Belém that now functions as an exhibition center. The original factory is believed to have been built on the order of the Marquis of Pombal circa 1771, being completed in 1779. Located on the main road running alongside the Tagus River, it produced sisal ropes, cables, sails, and other equipment for the Portuguese Navy and other ships. Widely revered as an outstanding example of 18th-century industrial architecture, it is now used as a space for rotating exhibitions, which have featured internationally acclaimed names such as Banksy.

PARK OF NATIONS
(Parque das Nações)

TOP EXPERIENCE

CABLE CARS

daily 11am-6pm, until 8pm in summer, closed in bad weather, €3.95 one-way, €5.90 round-trip

Cable cars run between the Oceanarium and the modern, 145-meter (476-foot) Vasco da Gama tower, gliding over the waterfront. To get to Park of Nations from downtown Lisbon, take the Metro from Baixa-Chiado (Green/Blue Lines) to Oriente on the Red Line.

Park of Nations

LISBON OCEANARIUM
(Oceanário de Lisboa)

Esplanada Dom Carlos I s/n, tel. 218 917 002,
www.oceanario.pt, daily 10am-8pm late
Mar.-Oct., daily 10am-7pm Nov.-mid-Mar.,
adults €16.20, children 4-12 €10.80
Inaugurated in 1998 for the World
Exposition, the Lisbon Oceanarium,
Europe's largest indoor aquarium, is
home to a huge assortment of marine
species, from seagulls to sea lions, sea
dragons, and surgeonfish. The star
attraction is a huge tank that houses
exotic sealife, including rays, sharks,
moray eels, barracudas, and sunfish.

VASCO DA GAMA BRIDGE
(Ponte Vasco da Gama)

tel. 212 328 200 (Mon.-Fri. 8:30am-6pm),
www.lusoponte.pt, tolls: €2.70–€11.70;
Southbound: toll free
Snaking across the Tagus River to link
eastern Lisbon to the South Bank, the
Vasco da Gama Bridge is Portugal and
Europe's longest bridge. Measuring
17.2 km (10.7 mi), it was purpose-
built for the 1998 Lisbon World Fair
Exposition (Expo '98), in the Park of
Nations area east of Lisbon city center.
Flanked by viaducts, the elegant and
sturdy cable-stayed bridge is a feat of
engineering and design. The six-lane
structure sees more than 62,000 vehicles cross it daily.

PAVILION OF KNOWLEDGE—
LIVING SCIENCE CENTER
Pavilhão do Conhecimento,
Centro Ciência Viva

Largo José Mariano Gago, tel. 218 917
100, www.pavconhecimento.pt, Mon.-Fri.
10am-6pm, weekends and holidays 11am-7pm
(closed Mon. Sept.-May), €9 (children €6-7),
Metro Gare do Oriente, Red Line
Children of all ages will enjoy spending a couple of hours at this highly
interactive and technologic center
dedicated to science. It comprises a

cable cars in Park of Nations

QUELUZ NATIONAL PALACE AND GARDENS

A commuter suburb about 20 minutes northwest of Lisbon, Queluz (keh-LOOZH) is home to the **Palácio Nacional de Queluz e Jardins** (Largo Palácio de Queluz, tel. 219 237 300, www.parquesdesintra.pt, daily 9am-6pm late Oct.-late Mar., daily 9am-7pm late Mar.-late Oct., last entry 1 hour before closing time, €10, audio guide €3), a fanciful royal palace and splendid gardens, making it a historic hot spot. This is a great place to visit if you'd like to see a spectacular palace but aren't quite ready to journey as far as Sintra yet.

Inside are the Corridor of *Azulejos* (tiles); the Throne Hall, dripping with shimmery mirrors and chandeliers; the Lantern Room, which houses the palace's biggest portrait; and the opulent Ambassadors' Hall, in which every square centimeter is gilded. Outside, visitors can wander gardens decorated with fountains and statues. **Corte em Queluz,** a two-hour reenactment of the 18th-century life inside the palace, is staged once a month (check dates beforehand; reservations required). The €10 fee includes entrance to the palace.

HISTORY OF THE PALACE

Built in the 18th century as a summer residence, Queluz National Palace soon became a royal favorite for leisure and entertaining. Portugal's royal family lived here permanently before fleeing to Brazil in 1807 to escape French invasions. The palace's extravagance is a heady blend of Baroque, neoclassical, and rococo styles, and its French-inspired gardens draw comparisons with the Palace of Versailles.

GETTING THERE

Queluz is a 20-minute drive, 14 kilometers (8.7 miles) north of Lisbon. Take the **N117** or the **A37** roads. A taxi will cost around €15 one way. From Lisbon's **Oriente** and **Rossio** stations, **CP trains** (tel. 707 210 220, www.cp.pt, €1.60) run on the Sintra Line every 10 minutes during the week and every half hour on the weekend. The journey to the **Queluz-Belas** or **Monte Abraão** station takes 20-25 minutes; both are about a 1-kilometer (0.6-mile) walk to the palace.

vast number of exhibitions and activities, covering wide-ranging themes that aim to be fun, stimulating, and educational at the same time. Located next to the Oceanarium, it offers a superb option for a rainy or really hot day. Main attractions include a suspended Skyline Bike Ride and robotics games.

WATER GARDENS (Jardins d'Água)

Ulisses boardwalk, open 24/7

Fronting the Park of Nations area are the attractive Water Gardens, which provide leafy cool refuge on a warm day. This peaceful oasis is a perfect complement to the neighborhood's contemporary feel and lends the built-up area some much-needed greenery. They comprise a number of pretty water features and offer splendid views over the Tagus and Vasco da Gama Bridge. The sculpted gardens hide several intriguing points of interest, such as the exotic plants and trees, large wind chimes, water volcano, and sculptures, and have plenty of seating, being the ideal spot to sit and enjoy a book with the calming sound of running water in the background. Just behind the gardens, set back from the riverfront, is a string of restaurants and bars that form the backbone of the Park of Nations' nightlife.

Sports and Recreation

TAGUS RIVER BOAT TOURS

A nice view of Lisbon is on approach from the opposite side of the Tagus River, and, given the nation's seafaring history, a boat trip offers a uniquely appropriate vantage point to see the city.

Lisbon by Boat

tel. 933 914 740, www.lisbonbyboat.com

Lisbon by Boat offers a variety of tours, from guided sightseeing trips to romantic sunset cruises, but all promise unforgettable views of the Portuguese capital. By motorboat or by yacht, trips range one to six hours, starting from around €35 pp for an hour-long historic Lisbon sightseeing cruise.

Yellow Boat Tour

www.yellowbustours.com, from €18

An alternative way to explore Lisbon is on the hop-on hop-off Yellow Boat Tour. Purchase a 24-hour ticket that allows access at points of interest on both sides of the Tagus. A nonstop circuit takes 1.5 hours, with a running commentary on sights in a number of languages, including English.

SEGWAY TOURS

Lisbon Segway Tours

www.lisbonsegwaytours.pt, from €35

Lisbon Segway Tours are a fun way to zip around the city and really get into its nooks and crannies. Tours visit different areas, including a riverside tour, a tour of Alfama, a city center tour, and a Belém tour. More unusual itineraries are a Lisbon by Night tour, a gastronomic tour to discover the city's foodie delights, and a three-hour super tour that covers most of the city's main spots.

WALKING TOURS

Personalized walking tours by locals have become popular in Lisbon, allowing you to explore the city at a leisurely pace. Guided tours are available in English, and many are free. From private tours to foodie tours, pub crawls, and even sunset tours, follow a local guide who knows the city and its secrets as only a native could. Tours take place rain or shine, and their duration can range from just over 1.5 hours to the full day. On free tours, payment is in the form of tips—a suggested tip is €5-12 pp. Specialist walking-tour companies include **Discover Walks Lisbon** (www.discoverwalks.com) and **Discover Lisbon** (tel. 932 060 800, www.discoverlisbon.org).

CYCLING

Gira

tel. 211 163 060,
www.gira-bicicletasdelisboa.pt

Lisbon City Hall has created an extensive shared-bicycle network and a web of cycle paths. The shared-bicycle scheme Gira comprises about 50 stations around the city, with 500 electric and standard bicycles. Download the app, buy a day pass for €2, and pedal away. Lisbon has more than 60 kilometers (37 miles) of bicycle lanes to explore.

Lisbon Bike Tour and Outdoors

Rua Presidente Arriaga 112, tel. 912 272 300, www.lisbonbiketour.com

Tour companies such as Lisbon Bike Tour and Outdoors have designed

a walking tour in Lisbon

exciting tours—all downhill—that cover key historic areas.

Rent-a-Fun

www.rent-a-fun.com

Rent-a-Fun includes some uphill climbs on its tours, but its bicycles are electric. Standard bike tours take three hours and cost €32 adults, €15 children. Rent-a-Fun also rents out electric, regular, and folding bicycles (daily 9am-9pm, €25), including delivery, a helmet, and a lock.

SOCCER (FOOTBALL)

Luz Stadium
(Estádio da Luz)

Av. Eusébio da Silva Ferreira, tel. 217 219 500, www.slbenfica.pt, Metro Colégio-Militar/Luz or Alto-dos-Moinhos, Blue Line

The 64,642-seat Luz Stadium (Estádio da Luz), the Stadium of Light, is the home of soccer team Benfica, one of the country's Big Three (along with cross-city rivals Sporting and northern team Porto). Architecturally impressive, its wavy roof of steel arches is designed to feel light and transparent. At the stadium there is a store, a museum, and 20-minute guided tours (daily 10am-6pm, €12.50, with museum €17.50). Game tickets start around €30.

José Alvalade Stadium
(Estádio José Alvalade)

Rua Professor Fernando da Fonseca, tel. 217 516 164, www.sporting.pt, Metro Campo Grande, Green Line

A short distance from Luz Stadium is José Alvalade Stadium (Estádio José Alvalade), or Lions' Stadium, home to the soccer team Sporting, "the lions." Predominantly green to echo its home team's colors, the stadium was designed by architect Tomás Taveira in a mall complex with a 12-screen movie theater, a health club, and a soccer museum. There are four guided tours daily of the stadium and museum (from €14). Game tickets start at €30.

Arts and Entertainment

OPERA

São Carlos National Theater (Teatro Nacional de São Carlos)

Rua Serpa Pinto, 9, tel. 213 253 000, see https://tnsc.bol.pt for program, Metro Baixa-Chiado, Green/Blue Lines

Portugal's national opera house, the São Carlos National Theater, was inaugurated on June 30, 1793, built by order of Queen Maria I to replace the Tejo Opera House in Comercio Square, which was destroyed by the 1755 earthquake. Inspired by Italy's grandiose La Scala theater in Milan and the San Carlo Theater in Naples, it is still today the only Portuguese theater that produces and showcases opera and choral and symphonic music. Classified a National Monument, the beautiful neoclassical building with ornate rococo touches has long been a centerpiece of the country's cultural scene.

CONCERT AND DANCE VENUES

Coliseu dos Recreios

Rua Portas de Santo Antão 96, tel. 213 240 580, www.coliseulisboa.com

Inaugurated in 1890, the famed Coliseu dos Recreios regularly welcomes international productions, traditionally from the realm of ballet, theater, and opera, as well as pop stars, circus troupes, and comedians. Architecturally, the Coliseu was ahead of its time with cutting-edge ironwork, seen in its spectacular German-made iron dome and iron roof.

Calouste Gulbenkian Foundation

Av. de Berna 45A, tel. 217 823 461, www.gulbenkian.pt

One of Lisbon's newer cultural venues, the Calouste Gulbenkian Foundation (Fundação Calouste Gulbenkian) has offerings beyond the world of art and exhibitions, with jazz, choral, and orchestral concerts, sometimes held in the lovely gardens.

Altice Arena

Rossio dos Olivais, tel. 218 918 409, http://arena.altice.pt

Huge Altice Arena, formerly known as the Meo Arena, is a futuristic-looking multipurpose venue on the Park of Nations riverside, hosting the biggest concerts and events, including in recent years U2, Beyoncé, Ariana Grande, Justin Bieber, Cirque du Soleil, and the 2018 Eurovision Song Contest.

Dona Maria II National Theater

THEATER

Dona Maria II National Theater (Teatro Nacional Dona Maria II)

Praça Dom Pedro IV, tel. 213 250 800, www.tndm.pt

Prestigious Dona Maria II National Theater (Teatro Nacional Dona Maria II) is a national jewel and cultural heavyweight on noble Rossio Square. Built between 1842 and 1846 in neoclassical style, it celebrates the performing arts with a full agenda of plays, shows, and concerts.

FESTIVALS AND EVENTS

Lisbon loves to party, and these annual events draw crowds. The Santo António festival is without a doubt Lisbon's main event, the biggest traditional religious celebration in the country. Lisbon hosts an array of summer music festivals and fairs and concerts by international artists throughout the year, mostly at Altice Arena in the Park of Nations.

SPRING
Carnival (Carnaval)
throughout Lisbon, mid-Feb.-early Mar.

Portugal goes into party mode for Carnival, and Lisbon has a succession of colorful floats and costumed dancers shimmying through the city's main avenues in a cloud of colorful confetti and streamers to the energetic rhythms of hot South American and popular Portuguese folk music, regardless of the weather. Carnival typically falls around mid-February or early March and lasts a number of days, during which concerts, masquerade balls, and street events are also held.

Lisbon Fish and Flavors (Peixe em Lisboa)
Carlos Lopes Pavilion, Av. Sidónio Pais 16, tel. 916 442 541, www.peixemlisboa.com, early Apr., €6-15

Discover the amazing flavors of the sea with gastronomic Lisbon Fish and Flavors, showcasing the best fish and seafood by innovative and well-known chefs and restaurants. The event takes place over 10 days and involves food and market stalls, cooking demonstrations, and discussions.

SUMMER
Santo António and June Festivities
throughout Lisbon, June

Dedicated to Saint Anthony, the city's patron, Santo António is Portugal's biggest traditional religious festival. Celebrations are staged throughout the capital for the whole month of June, reaching their peak on June 12, with jubilant parades and processions into the night. On June 13, the time-honored Casamentos de Santo António (Santo António weddings) are held. Established in 1958, these are a mass wedding of a dozen of the city's most impoverished couples, selected from hundreds of applicants. The entire ceremony, from the bridal outfits to the honeymoon, is funded by city hall and other sponsors. Over these two days, the city parties to pay homage to "matchmaker" Saint Anthony, from the afternoon through the early morning.

During Santo António, Lisbon is at its prettiest. Every garden and square is decked out with colorful trimmings and lights. Food and drink stalls, tables, and chairs are set up with small stages for local artists to perform traditional folk songs. Grilled sardines, sangria, and traditional *caldo verde* (potato and kale) soup are served from stalls to fuel the merriment. The neighborhoods of Alfama and Bica are the most popular for Santo António. Each neighborhood also designs a float and takes part in a grand procession along the city's main avenues in the pinnacle of the celebrations to decide which neighborhood wins. Santo António shouldn't be missed if you're in Portugal in June.

Shopping

Lisbon has a sophisticated shopping scene, from upscale stores along stylish Avenida da Liberdade to smaller boutiques and craft shops in the neighborhoods surrounding Baixa. It also has shopping centers galore and plenty of open-air markets.

Baixa itself, between Rossio Square and the riverside plazas and smaller boulevards, is the heart of commerce in Lisbon, where mainstream chain stores adjoin traditional grocery stores, boutiques, and souvenir shops. The two main shopping streets in the Baixa are **Rua da Prata** and **Rua Augusta,** parallel to each other from the main Comércio Square up to Rossio. However, for more unique souvenirs, you may want to venture further afield to neighborhoods like Alfama, Chiado, and Bairro Alto.

ALFAMA
TILES AND CERAMICS
Loja dos Descobrimentos

Rua dos Bacalhoeiros 14B, tel. 218 865 563, www.loja-descobrimentos.com, daily 9am-7pm

Loja dos Descobrimentos is a shop and workshop selling brightly colored hand-painted tiles and ceramics in styles from all over Portugal. Meet the artisans in the atelier and watch as they work on tiles, or paint your own.

Azulejos de Fachada

Beco do Mexias 1, tel. 966 176 953, www.azulejosdefachada.com, Mon.-Fri. 10:30am-12:30pm and 2pm-5:30pm

Another top place for authentic hand-painted tiles and ceramics with a bright modern twist, Azulejos de Fachada will also take custom orders and ship overseas.

SÃO VICENTE
MARKET
Feira da Ladra Flea Market

Tues. and Sat. 9am-6pm

Dating to the 12th century, the São Vicente Feira da Ladra Flea Market, which literally translates as "Thieves' Fair," is a chance to experience the sights and sounds of old-time Lisbon. With an eclectic mix of antiques and secondhand family heirlooms, vendors tout everything from jewels to junk. The vast market starts by the São Vicente Archway, near a stop for tram 28, and fills the streets around the Campo de Santa Clara square. While some of the traders have properly laid-out stalls, others simply pile their wares onto blankets on the ground.

Feira da Ladra Flea Market

✪ AVENIDA DA LIBERDADE

Lisbon's most famous avenue, and priciest real estate, Avenida da Liberdade has serious shopping. At 90 meters (295 feet) wide and more than 1 kilometer (0.6 mi) long, this fancy street—the busiest in Portugal—has fashion's biggest players, including **Louis Vuitton Lisbonne** (Av. da Liberdade 190, tel. 213 584 320, www. eu.louisvuitton.com, Mon.-Thurs. 10am-7:30pm, Fri.-Sat. 10am-8pm), **Prada** (Av. da Liberdade 206, tel. 213 199 490, Mon.-Sat. 10am-7:30pm), and **Gucci** (Av. da Liberdade 180, tel. 213 528 401, www.gucci.com, Mon.-Sat. 10am-7:30pm).

With exquisitely patterned cobblestone walkways and magnificent period architecture lining the stately boulevard, enhanced by cool, leafy gardens, it's often compared to Paris's Champs-Élysées. Most buildings along the avenue date from the 19th century, built after the devastating 1755 earthquake that razed most of Lisbon.

FOOD AND WINE
DeliDelux

Rua Alexandre Herculano 15A, tel. 213 141 474, www.delidelux.pt, Mon.-Fri. 8am-11pm, Sat.-Sun. 9am-11pm

Just off the Avenida da Liberdade at Rua Alexandre Herculano is the stylish DeliDelux, stocked with beautifully packaged gourmet products like wine, olive oil, and canned fish, which make great gifts.

CLOTHING AND ACCESSORIES
Luís Onofre

Av. da Liberdade 247, tel. 211 313 629, www. luisonofre.com, Mon.-Sat. 10am-7:30pm

Women's shoe designer Luís Onofre built his brand on generations of

family shoemaking history; the shoes are manufactured at a state-of-the art workshop in northern Portugal.

David Rosas

Av. da Liberdade 69A, tel. 213 243 870, www. davidrosas.com, Mon.-Sat. 10am-7pm

David Rosas is a family company that blends generations of craftsmanship in its fine jewelry. The design of this gorgeous store was overseen by acclaimed Portuguese architect Siza Vieira.

CHIADO AND BAIRRO ALTO
ARTS AND CRAFTS
Atelier 55

Rua António Maria Cardoso, 70-74, tel. 213 474 192, www.atelier55.blogspot.com, Mon.-Sat. 11am-7pm

A trove of authentic Portuguese arts and crafts, Atelier 55 brims with handmade ceramics, embroidery, and paintings from local artists.

BOOKS
Bertrand Bookstore (Livraria Bertrand)

Rua Garrett 73-75, tel. 213 476 122, www. bertrand.pt, daily 9am-10pm, Metro Baixa-Chiado, Green/Blue Lines

Distinguished by Guinness World Records as the oldest working bookshop in the world, the Bertrand Bookstore in Chiado is housed in a beautiful old building clad in traditional blue and white Portuguese *azulejo* tiles. Open since the mid-1730s, this wonderful bookshop has several rooms packed with literature from some of Portugal's greatest authors—including José Saramago, Eça de Queiroz, Almada Negreiros, Alexandre Herculano, and Sophia de Mello Breyner—as well as a cozy café where visitors are encouraged to "try before you buy" (the books, not the cakes or coffee!).

LISBON'S BEST SOUVENIRS: CORK AND *AZULEJOS*

cork souvenirs

Two of Portugal's most distinctive products are cork goods and beautiful *azulejo* tiles and ceramics. Once used to create only bottle stoppers for prestigious champagnes, today Portuguese cork has become fashionable for shoes, handbags, jewelry, and even clothing. **Bairro Alto** is the place to go cork-hunting, and **downtown Baixa-Chiado** brims with local arts and crafts.

Azulejo hand-painted tile plaques adorn walls throughout the city. Many smaller-size replicas of plaques and tiles are now produced as souvenirs. **Alfama** is the place to head for *azulejos,* with shops offering miniature versions of these ceramic squares.

CORK
Cork & Co
Rua das Salgadeiras 10,
tel. 216 090 231, www.corkandcompany.pt,
Mon.-Sat. 11am-8pm, Sun. 5pm-8pm
Everything at Cork & Co, from hats to shoes and all accessories, is made from natural cork.

Rutz Walk in Cork
Rua dos Sapateiros 181,
tel. 212 477 039, www.rutz.pt, daily
noon-8pm
Rutz Walk in Cork is a Portuguese brand specializing in shoes, bags, accessories, and gifts made from cork.

CAIS DO SODRÉ
ARTS AND CRAFTS
A Pequena Galeria
(The Little Art Gallery)
Avenida 24 de Julho, 4C, tel. 213 950 356,
www.apequenagaleria.com, Weds.-Sat.
5pm-7:30pm, free, Metro Cais do Sodré,
Blue Line
The Little Art Gallery is a collective project that occupies a snug space right on the riverside, aimed at exhibiting, informing about, and selling art. In the same vein as The Little Galleries of the Photo-Secession—later known as the 291 Art Gallery—in New York, this funky gathering place mainly focuses on photography.

ALCÂNTARA
ARTS AND CRAFTS
LX Factory

Rua Rodrigues de Faria 103, tel. 213 143 399, www.lxfactory.com, daily 6am-4am, free, tram 15

Less factory, more arty-hive, this historical industrial complex comprises more than 200 restaurants, shops, businesses, and offices under one roof. Converted from an old fabric-production plant spanning 23,000 square meters (248,000 square feet), today LX Factory is a hive of cool creativity and a rising tourist attraction. The LX Factory's first floor is entirely dedicated to an ethical market. There is also a food court, and open-plan workspaces allow visitors to see artisans in action. Enjoy the laid-back hipster vibe and grab a drink on one of the terraces overlooking the iconic 25 de Abril Bridge. Live music performances and other events are also staged on occasion—check the website.

PARK OF NATIONS
MALLS
Vasco da Gama Shopping Center

Av. Dom João II 40, tel. 218 930 601, www.centrovascodagama.pt, daily 9am-midnight, Metro Oriente, Red Line

Directly opposite the Oriente main transport hub in Park of Nations is the huge Vasco da Gama shopping center—one of the largest shopping malls in Portugal. The modern multilevel mall comprises more than 160 stores under its glass roof, housing all European high-street favorites plus a range of national specialty boutiques, movie theaters, and a vast food court. From here it is a short walk to all of Park of Nations' other main attractions, including the concert arena, riverfront gardens and bars, cable cars, Oceanarium, and Pavilion of Knowledge—Living Science Center. The Oriente Metro is also directly connected to Lisbon airport.

LX Factory

Food

Lisbon's food scene is a crossroads of traditional and contemporary, offering everything from street food and vegan restaurants to gourmet market stalls. One thing that sets Lisbon apart from other European capitals is value for money.

BAIXA

Bustling Baixa is a hub of restaurants, cafés, and bars, plenty of them arranged around the main Comércio Square, promising people-watching and alfresco dining.

PORTUGUESE
Restaurante Bastardo

Rua da Betesga 3, tel. 213 240 993, www.restaurantebastardo.com, daily noon-11pm, €15

Overlooking gorgeous Rossio Square, bohemian Restaurante Bastardo serves up classic Portuguese cuisine with an international twist, like codfish with kombu seaweed, along with fabulous cocktails. Have there ever been so many different types of chairs under one roof?

Taberna da Baixa

Rua dos Fanqueiros, 161-163, tel. 218 870 290 or 919 847 419, www.tabernadabaixa.pt, daily noon-3pm and 7pm-10:30pm, €15

This little gem is the perfect place to sample Lisbon's flavors. With a cozy, rustic-chic feel, the small restaurant showcases regional produce in the likes of shared cold platters paired with handpicked wines, and its signature dish, slow-cooked black pig cheeks in red wine. Live shows can also be enjoyed at the venue (check the website for dates).

Beer Museum & Restaurant (Museu da Cerveja)

Terreiro do Paço, East Wing 62-65, tel. 210 987 656, www.museudacerveja.pt, daily 11am-midnight, €20

Located in the Praça do Comércio, fashionable Museu da Cerveja showcases the finest beers produced in Portugal and Portuguese-speaking countries. A range of snacks and meals includes famous codfish cakes that complement the brews.

Restaurante Figus

Praça da Figueira 16, tel. 218 872 194, www.restaurantefigus.com, daily 11am-midnight, €20

Elegant and sophisticated Restaurante Figus is in the Beautique Hotel Figueira in Praça da Figueira downtown. It has a varied à la carte menu and a refined selection of wines. Favorites include a *chourciço* and *morcela* sausage platter, steak in Portuguese sauce, gourmet burgers, fish, and pasta dishes. Don't miss the fig cheesecake for dessert.

Restaurante Gambrinus

Rua das Portas de Santo Antão 23, tel. 213 421 466, www.restaurante-gambrinus.business.site, daily noon-1:30am, €20-40

Established in 1936, acclaimed Restaurante Gambrinus has a dedicated following for its tapas and seafood, served in a classic setting with polished dark wood and crisp white tablecloths.

Restaurante Cervejaria O Pinóquio

Praça dos Restauradores 79, tel. 213 465 106, www.restaurantepinoquio.pt, daily noon-midnight, €25

Café Nicola

The home cooking at Restaurante Cervejaria O Pinóquio is a legendary variety of quality tapas and entrées, specializing in excellent steak and seafood. The decor is sparse, but the outdoor terrace is charming. Although it's always busy, service is fast.

Varanda de Lisboa Restaurant

Praça Martim Moniz 2, tel. 218 842 000, www.hotel-mundial.pt, daily 6:30am-3pm and 7:30pm-10:30pm, €25

The name of Varanda de Lisboa Restaurant translates as "the veranda of Lisbon," referring to the views from its location at the top of the Mundial Hotel. It prepares accomplished dishes to match, like flambéed meats and *cataplanas* (seafood stews). There are weekly themed menus and three-course set menus.

Prado Restaurant

Travessa das Pedras Negras 2, tel. 210 534 649, www.pradorestaurante.com, Weds.-Sat. noon-3:30pm and 7pm-11pm, Sun. noon-5pm, €30

Spearheaded by rising young chef António Galapito, Prado takes clean, fresh flavors of the farm and the sea and magics them into contemporary dishes for the table. Housed in a lofty, bright former factory, the menu is a celebration of seasonal Portuguese produce, concocted into dishes such as black pork tenderloin with quinces and chocolate peppers and Barrosã beef sirloin steak and lettuce salad. Reservations are compulsory for groups of more than six.

CAFÉ
✪ Café Nicola

Praça Dom Pedro IV 24-25, tel. 213 460 579, daily 8am-midnight, €8

With a prime position on posh Rossio Square, the landmark Café Nicola epitomizes European coffee culture with its art deco interior, excellent coffees, and top-notch breakfasts. It was a favorite of poet Manuel du Bocage, who is memorialized in a statue out front. The celebrated café is excellent for people-watching, but prices are high.

65

APPETIZERS AREN'T FREE

As soon as you sit down at any table in Lisbon, waiters will almost immediately bring you an array of mouthwatering appetizers, such as a fresh bread basket, butter and pâtés, fritters, and olives and cheeses. Beware—these are not a complimentary welcome gift; the tab is totting up from the moment you butter that bread. Anything you don't want, don't be afraid to politely decline or send back. Always be clear on prices beforehand, as some cheeses and sausages can be pricy, and make sure you pay only for what you eat.

SEAFOOD
Solar 31 da Calçada
Calçada Garcia 31, tel. 218 863 374, www. solar31.com, Mon. 5pm-midnight, Tues.-Sat. 11:30am-11pm, €14

With simple and quaint decor that blends into its local neighborhood, Solar 31 da Calçada serves traditional Portuguese food with a focus on fresh fish and shellfish. Choose from a fantastic selection of starters and wines.

✪ Solar do Bacalhau
Rua do Jardim do Regedor 30, tel. 213 460 069, www.solardobacalhau.com, daily 10am-midnight, €20

Cod is king at charming Solar do Bacalhau, one of the best spots to enjoy the Portuguese specialty *bacalhau*. It also serves other meat and fish dishes in a setting with natural stone walls and elegantly laid tables.

Leão d'Ouro
Rua 1º de Dezembro 105, tel. 213 426 195, www.restauranteleaodouro.com.pt, daily noon-11pm, €20

At Leão d'Ouro, dark wood and traditional tiled walls provide an almost medieval complement to rich fish and shellfish dishes such as oven-baked cod.

Marisqueira Uma
Rua dos Sapateiros 177, tel. 213 427 425, Mon.-Sat. noon-3pm and 7-10pm, €20

This small and simple seafood joint is famous for its specialty, seafood rice—a rich, flavor-packed steel rice pot teeming with shrimp, crayfish, crab, and mussels.

✪ Cervejaria Ramiro
Av. Almirante Reis 1-H, tel. 218 851 024, www.cervejariaramiro.pt, Weds.-Mon. noon-12:30am, €20

Established in 1956, authentic beer house Cervejaria Ramiro is a famed institution featured on many travel programs. Expect long queues outside the restaurant. The rainbow of seafood includes prawns *al guilho*. The *prego no pão* is a steak sandwich with a cult following, which many eat at the end of meals in lieu of dessert. Wash it down with a chilled beer.

INTERNATIONAL
O Arco
Rua dos Sapateiros 161, tel. 213 463 280, Thurs.-Tues. noon-3pm and 7pm-11pm, €14

Hidden on a backstreet, bright, eclectically decorated O Arco serves up a selection of tasty Mediterranean favorites, from spicy chicken curry to flavorful prawn dishes.

Restaurante Cantinho do Aziz
Rua de São Lourenço 5, tel. 218 876 472, www.cantinhodoaziz.com, daily noon-11pm, €15

At popular, family-run Restaurante Cantinho do Aziz, savor exotic flavors from Mozambique in fare such as samosas, crab curry, and traditional Yuca Malaku and Yuca Miamba curries. The atmosphere is relaxed. Sit inside or on the long outdoor street terrace.

Tasca Kome

Rua da Madalena 57, tel. 211 340 117, www.kome-lisboa.com, Tues.-Thurs. noon-2:30pm and 7pm-10pm, Fri. noon-3pm and 7pm-10pm, Sat. 12:30pm-3pm and 7pm-10pm, €15

Established by powerhouse Japanese chef Yuko Yamamoto, whose Lisbon supper clubs were sell-out events, Tasca Kome is a Japanese tavern in the heart of the Baixa. Serving authentic Japanese fare, staples on the menu include miso soup, sushi and sashimi, plus house specials such as fried octopus balls, salmon zuke-don, and parmesan cheesecake.

ALFAMA

PORTUGUESE
CorkScrew Restaurant & Wine Bar

Rua dos Remédios 95, tel. 215 951 774, www.thecorkscrew.pt, Thurs.-Sat. noon-2am, Sun.-Weds. 1pm-midnight, €10

CorkScrew Restaurant & Wine Bar serves great Portuguese tapas of cheeses, cured meats, and fish preserves, accompanied by fantastic Portuguese wines.

✪ Chapitô à Mesa

Costa do Castelo 7, tel. 218 875 077, www.chapito.org, Mon.-Sat. noon-6pm and 7pm-1:30am, Sun. 7pm-1:30am, €25

Part of a famous circus arts school, Chapitô à Mesa offers fun, flamboyant cuisine alongside gorgeous views of Lisbon. Choose the snack bar, an alfresco grill terrace, or the elegant restaurant. Menu favorites include grilled shrimp with tropical fruit and pork cheeks with clams and sautéed potatoes.

Gosta do Castelo

Costa do Castelo 138, tel. 218 870 743, Weds.-Mon. noon-3:30pm and 7pm-11:30pm, €25

The traditional tiled facade enhances the cozy chic-vintage interior of Gosta do Castelo, which serves a lovely array of unusual takes on national staples, with a nice selection of wines. Try the Portuguese cheese platter with mango chutney. Entrées include duck magret with apple in port wine. Gosta do Castelo also has a brunch menu and a snack menu.

✪ Casa do Leão

Castelo de São Jorge, tel. 218 880 154, www.pousadas.pt, daily 12:30pm-3pm and 8pm-10:30pm, €28

Located inside the São Jorge Castle, Casa do Leão takes advantage of its architectural features, including a vaulted brick ceiling, to create an elegant atmosphere. Its culinary masterpieces are concocted from fresh seasonal ingredients. Seafood *cataplana* and Portuguese-style steak are highlights. Even more remarkable are the views from the terrace outside, overlooking the city.

Leopold

Pátio de Dom Fradique 12, tel. 218 861 697, Weds.-Sun. 7:30pm-11pm, tasting menu €40

Set in a charming former bakery, Leopold puts an innovative twist on classics in intimate surroundings, with just four tables and an open kitchen. The tasting menu includes fresh, inventive daily dishes like cornbread with lime-infused goat cheese and Azores beef with algae and mizuna. As there is no stove, everything is cooked sous vide.

CAFÉS
Mercearia Castello Café

Rua das Flores de Santa Cruz 2, tel. 218 876 111, daily 10am-8pm, €8

Tradition meets cool at Mercearia Castello Café, a funky little eatery and grocery store. Its wood-clad interior harks back to the old days, and its location at the top of the hill near the castle is second to none. The fresh homemade fare includes quiches, crêpes, and sandwiches made from quality regional products—it hits the spot after climbing to the castle.

Café Audrey

Rua Santiago 14, tel. 213 941 616, daily 7:30am-11pm, €12

Adjacent to the main entrance of the São Jorge Castle, Café Audrey is an eccentric little place with an eclectic menu, serving breakfast, lunch, and dinner dishes ranging from eggs Benedict to Goan curry.

SEAFOOD
Farol de Santa Luzia

Largo de Santa Luzia 5, tel. 218 863 884, Mon.-Sat. 5:30pm-11pm, €18

Rustic Farol de Santa Luzia is set in an 18th-century building directly opposite the Santa Luzia viewpoint, near São Jorge Castle. Menu favorites include octopus salad, shellfish *açorda* (a soupy bread dish), and pork *cataplana* with shrimp, clams, and *chouriça* sausage.

INTERNATIONAL
Restaurante Casanova

Av. Infante Dom Henrique Loja 7, tel. 218 877 532, www.pizzeriacasanova.pt, daily 12:30pm-1:30am, €10

Canteen-style Restaurante Casanova has a privileged riverside location with long tables conducive to sharing

authentic Italian food. Try the wood-oven-baked pizza.

Bica do Sapato

Av. Infante Dom Henrique Armazém B, Cais da Pedra, tel. 218 810 320, www.bicadosapato.com, Mon. 5pm-midnight, Tues.-Sat. noon-midnight, Sun. 12:30pm-4pm, €28

Located in an old port building on the Santa Apolónia docks, Bica do Sapato is a cool sushi bar that also specializes in contemporary and traditional Portuguese cuisine.

Zambeze

Calçada Marquês de Tancos, Edifício EMEL, Mercado Chão do Loureiro, tel. 218 877 056 or 925 200 631, www.zambezerestaurante.pt, daily 10am-11pm, €30

Situated in the historic heart of Alfama, Zambeze is housed in a restored historic marketplace. The clean and minimalistic interior accentuates the intriguing fusion of Euro-African flavors. An alfresco terrace boasts fantastic views over downtown Lisbon and the Tagus River. Set menu of chef's suggestions available for €19.50.

EXPERIMENTAL
Boi-Cavalo

Rua do Vigário 70 B, tel. 938 752 355, www.boi-cavalo.pt, Tues.-Sun. 8pm-2am, €40

Housed in an old butcher's shop, Boi-Cavalo (which translates literally as "Ox-Horse") is indeed a place of experimental fusions. It is where inventive chef Hugo Brito transfers his artistic talents to the ever-changing menu. Tasting menus change regularly, in accordance to the availability of seasonal ingredients, although the overriding focus is on quality national cuisine. Wine pairing available.

SÃO VICENTE

One of the city's oldest and more traditional areas, São Vicente has a more grown-up attitude that is reflected in its restaurants, which offer classic Portuguese and Mediterranean fare and cozy bistro-type eateries.

CAFÉ
Bistro Gato Pardo

Rua de São Vicente 10, tel. 934 696 871, Fri.-Tues. noon-10pm, €15

With its exposed stone wall and brick floor, hidden hole-in-the-wall Bistro Gato Pardo is inviting for a snack, coffee, or a cozy meal. Tasty lamb, risotto with fish, and shrimp dishes are favorites.

INTERNATIONAL
Damas

Rua da Voz do Operário 60, tel. 964 964 416, Tues.-Thurs. 6pm-2am, Fri. 5pm-4am, Sat. 7pm-4am, Sun. 5pm-midnight, €10

At no-frills hipster hangout Damas, craft beers and excellent food accompany live music. The menu is scribbled on the tile-clad wall and changes daily. Dishes from across the Mediterranean include smoked lamb, almond tagine with falafel, and seitan meatballs. On weekends, DJ sets and live concerts are held in a small back room.

Beco a Sério

Calçada de São Vicente 42, tel. 218 872 805, www.facebook.com/becoaserio, daily 1pm-4pm and 7pm-11pm, €20

A selective menu packed with simple, clean flavors is what Beco a Sério is all about. Choices are limited, but the menu includes tapas, vegetarian, salads, children's menu, vegan, gluten-free, and fish and meat entrées, with homemade starters and desserts.

Quality Portuguese dining in a small, family-friendly restaurant located up a quaint alley.

AVENIDA DA LIBERDADE

PORTUGUESE
Chafariz do Vinho

Rua da Mãe d'Água, tel. 213 422 079, www.chafarizdovinho.com, Tues.-Sat. 3pm-11pm, €25

Located in the Príncipe Real neighborhood just north of Baixa, between Rossio and Marquês de Pombal (near the Lisbon University Botanical Gardens), Chafariz do Vinho is a unique gem of a find. It is a fascinating wine and tapas bar housed in an ancient aqueduct with a vast wine cellar and tasty nibbles to accompany the drink.

MARKET
Food Market

Av. Fontes Pereira de Melo 6, tel. 210 199 258, daily 8am-10pm, from €5

Just off the Marquês do Pombal roundabout (northeast), Food Market covers breakfast, brunch, lunch, and dinner. The eclectic food hall's stalls tout everything from oysters to éclairs, grilled chicken to smoked fish, to eat in or take out.

SEAFOOD
O Cacho Dourado

Rua Eça de Queiroz 5, tel. 213 543 671, www.ocachodourado.com, Sun.-Fri. 7:30am-11:30pm, €15

Specializing in authentic Portuguese fish and seafood dishes, O Cacho Dourado is off the tourist track but always busy with regulars. If you visit on a Friday, try the famous codfish dish that has been served on Fridays only for nearly half a century.

INTERNATIONAL
The Great American Disaster
Praça Marquês de Pombal 1,
tel. 213 161 266, daily noon-midnight,
€12

Take a step back in time in this theatrical 1950s-America burger and fries joint—a slice of fun if you fancy a break from the local fare. The obligatory pink and black décor, red booths, and milkshakes are all here.

Unique Sushi Lab
Travessa do Enviado de Inglaterra 9,
tel. 910 509 675, www.uniquesushilab.pt,
Mon.-Fri. noon-2:30pm and 8pm-11:30pm
(Mon. till 11pm), Sat. 8pm-11:30pm, set
menus from €20

Experimental sushi at its best. That's what to expect at Unique Sushi Lab. Far from standard sushi, these colorful creations are exquisite works of food art that trigger a sensorial overload. Stunning to look at, tasty to eat.

CHIADO AND BAIRRO ALTO

Bohemian Bairro Alto might be better known for its nightlife, but it doesn't disappoint when it comes to restaurants, with a rainbow of international flavors.

PORTUGUESE
Cantinho Lusitano
Rua dos Prazeres 52, tel. 218 065 185,
www.cantinholusitano.com, Tues.-Sat.
7pm-11pm, €7

Located on the doorstep of Bairro Alto in the upscale Prince Real area, small and simple Cantinho Lusitano is a family-run joint serving up a colorful assortment of Portuguese tapas. The restaurant also serves as a café and wine bar.

A Taberna da Rua das Flores
Rua das Flores 103, tel. 213 479 418,
Tues.-Fri. noon-2:30pm and 5pm-11:30pm,
Sat. noon-11:30pm, €15

A long, narrow, typically Portuguese eatery located in an old greengrocer's store, retaining original vintage features such as its door and floor tiles. The cozy tavern is popular among locals and tourists alike, serving traditional tapas of yesteryear with a contemporary twist.

Restaurante Fidalgo
Rua da Barroca 27, tel. 213 422 900,
www.restaurantefidalgo.com, Mon.-Sat.
noon-3pm and 7pm-11pm, €20

A traditional, family-run Portuguese restaurant founded in 1972, Fidalgo serves good old-fashioned Portuguese food at reasonable prices. All the classics—rabbit stew, fresh fish, octopus and codfish dishes—are on the menu, along with homemade desserts and an excellent selection of national wines that line the walls of the cozy eatery.

Cantinho do Avillez
Rua Duques de Bragança 7, tel. 211 992
369, www.cantinhodoavillez.pt, Mon.-Fri.
12:30pm-3pm and 7pm-midnight, Sat.-Sun.
12:30pm-midnight, €40

Cantinho do Avillez is part of a chain of restaurants run by Michelin-star awarded chef José Avillez. Informal but up-market, it serves accomplished Portuguese cuisine.

SPECIALTY
Piglet & Co
Rua da Condessa 12, tel. 919 672 073, www.
pigletandco.pt, Tues.-Sat. noon-10pm, €15

Suckling pig is the specialty at this fun and funky little restaurant, available in a manner of styles from a simple roast

Ask anyone what Lisbon's most typical dishes are, and here's some of what you will hear:

- **Salted codfish (*bacalhau*),** for which the Portuguese claim to have a different recipe for each day of the year

- The ubiquitous ***pastel de nata* custard tart,** the national pastry; Pastéis de Belém bakery has its own recipe, which it calls *pastel de Belém*

- **Seafood** features heavily on menus throughout the city, with other popular dishes including *caldeirada* (fish stew), shellfish, and octopus creations

ginjinha cherry liqueur

- **Bite-size snacks** like codfish pasty (*pastéis de bacalhau*), green bean fritters (*peixinhos da horta*), and codfish fritters (*pataniscas de bacalhau*) are also popular, available at most restaurants and snack bars, to be washed down with a cold beer

- Try a ***ginjinha* cherry liqueur** at its home, the historic A Ginjinha bar in the Baixa's São Domingos Square

---

to pies, rissoles, and sandwiches. The menu is limited but also features savory snacks and homemade desserts.

100 Maneiras

Rua do Teixeira, tel. 910 918 181, www.100maneiras.com, Mon.-Sat. 7:30pm-2am, Sun. 7:30pm-midnight, €60

Owned by Bosnian celebrity chef Ljubomir Stanisic, refined and peaceful little 100 Maneiras serves a creative set nine-course tasting menu based on fresh seasonal produce and typical Portuguese flavors, heavily inspired by the sea. Reservations are recommended.

CAFÉ
A Brasileira

Rua Garrett 122, tel. 213 469 541, www.abrasileira.pt, daily 8am-2am, €5

The century-old A Brasileira café is one of the oldest and most famous cafés in Lisbon. The emblematic venue has an air of antique grandeur, with its art deco chandeliers, wooden booths, mirrored walls, and checkerboard floors. It is a time-honored meeting place for Lisbon's coffee-lovers and has a fascinating history, having once been frequented by the city's intellectuals, artists, writers, and free thinkers. A regular, allegedly, was famous Portuguese poet Fernando Pessoa, and a bronze statue of him sits permanently outside the busy café in tribute. Today it is a must-see tourist attraction, but the coffee is still as popular as it was when A Brazileira opened in the 19th century.

SEAFOOD
Sea Me

Rua do Loreto 21, tel. 213 461 564, www.peixariamoderna.com. Mon.-Thurs. 12:30pm-3:30pm and 7:30pm-midnight, Fri. 12:30pm-3pm and 7:30pm-1am, Sat. 12:30pm-1am, Sun. 12:30pm-midnight, €28

Modern, informal Sea Me pays homage to Lisbon's fishmongers with seafood purchased from the counter to be cooked in the kitchen, in a fusion of Japanese and Portuguese cuisines.

Aldeia

Travessa da Queimada 32, tel. 213 420 401, www.restaurantealdeia.com, Mon.-Sat. 1pm-2am, €30

With a focus on traditional national cuisine, this beautiful old-world Portuguese restaurant is a real find for those wanting to sample genuine flavors of Portugal. Aldeia specializes in seafood, although excellent meats and tasty tapas are also on the menu.

INTERNATIONAL
Flor de Laranja

Rua da Rosa 206, tel. 213 422 996, daily 7pm-11pm, €14

At welcoming and intimate Flor de Laranja, authentic Moroccan food is handmade by the Morocco-born chef, who is also the owner and the waiter. Reservations are required.

Bella Ciao

Rua de S. Julião 74-76, tel. 210 935 708, https://cantinabellaciao.wixsite.com/ bellaciao, Mon.-Thurs. noon-4pm and 7pm-midnight, Fri.-Sat. till 1am, €15

Quintessential Italian trattoria with the traditional red-and-white-checkered tablecloths and starched white napkins. Italian chef Marcello Di Salvatore brings genuine flavors of Italia to the heart of Lisbon, with homemade classics including spaghetti carbonara, risotto ai funghi, and tiramisu.

La Paparrucha

Rua Dom Pedro V 18-20, tel. 213 425 333, www.lapaparrucha.com, Mon.-Fri. noon-11:30pm, Sat.-Sun. 12:30pm-11:30pm, €25

Modern meets rustic and meat rules at

La Paparrucha, a firm favorite among locals. Almost everything is cooked on an authentic Argentinean grill.

BREWERY
✪ Cervejaria Trindade

Rua Nova da Trindade 20C, tel. 213 423 506, www.cervejariatrindade.pt, Sun.-Thurs. noon-midnight, Fri.-Sat. noon-1am, €28

One of Portugal's oldest and most beautiful breweries, bright and bold Cervejaria Trindade dates from the mid-1800s, when it was the choice for writers, poets, and politicians. Its huge medieval banquet rooms can accommodate groups of up to 200. National and international beers are accompanied by a different dish of the day, as well as typical Portuguese fish and meat dishes like steak in beer sauce.

CAIS DO SODRÉ

This waterfront wharf has shed its former seedy image and is now a cool place to eat, drink, and be merry. It's also the location of hip **Pink Street**, which makes it a convenient spot to spend an evening.

PORTUGUESE
Espumantaria do Cais

Rua Nova do Carvalho 39, tel. 213 470 466, daily 7pm-4am, €15

Located on Cais do Sodré's famous Pink Street, swanky and minimalistic Espumantaria do Cais is a marble-clad quayside tapas and Champagne bar. Pop open a bottle of bubbly, order a sharing platter like the popular cheeseboard or salmon tacos, and have a wonderful evening with some fizz.

Vestigius Wine & Gin Bar

Cais do Sodré 8, tel. 218 203 320, www. vestigius.pt, Sun.-Thurs. noon-7pm, Fri.-Sat. noon-1am, €22

Set in a lofty quayside warehouse,

Time Out Market Lisboa

shabby-chic Vestigius Wine & Gin Bar has huge windows and a terrace overlooking the water. A team of young chefs shape innovative flavors into bite-size tapas with Portuguese and Angolan influences. Dishes include calamari with aioli sauce, beef carpaccio, and beef osso buco.

MARKET
✪ Time Out Market Lisboa + Riverside Market (Mercado TimeOut + Mercado da Ribeira)

Avenida 24 de Julho 49, tel. 213 951 274, Sun.-Weds. 10am-midnight, Thurs.-Sat. 10am-2am, free, Metro Cais do Sodré, Blue Line

After its concession was taken over by the team behind the Lisbon edition of *Time Out* magazine, this landmark market hall—the historic Mercado da Ribeira, or Riverside Market, formerly one of Europe's most renowned markets—is today among the city's coolest hangouts. Despite being more than 100 years old (it first opened in the 1890s) this market is livelier than ever, with a huge, often chaotic food court that boasts a vast variety of gourmet stalls showcasing innovative and traditional Portuguese fare. The two-dozen-plus stands are allocated to chefs and restaurants handpicked by *Time Out*'s food writers. The eastern portion of the building still houses the traditional fruit and veg market, which also sells fresh fish, flowers, bread, and souvenirs. It operates between 6am and 2pm and offers early risers a glimpse of genuine Lisbon market trading. Live music adds to the ambience.

SEAFOOD
IBO

Compartimento 2, Cais do Sodré Armazem A, tel. 961 332 024, www.ibo-restaurante.pt, Tues.-Fri. 12:30pm-3pm and 7:30pm-11pm, Sat. 12:30pm-3:30pm and 7:30pm-1am, Sun. 12:30pm-3:30pm, €40

Set in a gleaming converted warehouse

on the riverside, at IBO, Portuguese seafood dishes and Mozambican curries go hand-in-hand. It's an upscale dining experience in a swish, modern setting. The views over the Tagus from the outdoor terrace are a bonus.

INTERNATIONAL
Las Ficheras
Rua dos Remolares 34, tel. 213 470 553, www.lasficheras.com, Sun.-Thurs. 11am-1am, Fri.-Sat. 11am-2am, €18

Hip and happening Las Ficheras provides five-star Mexican food with great cocktails in a warm, welcoming setting.

ESTRELA AND LAPA

Estrela's culinary scene follows the same feel as the neighborhood: refined and upscale with a pinch of cool.

PORTUGUESE
Flor da Estrela
Rua João de Deus 11, tel. 213 967 278, Mon.-Thurs. noon-10pm, Fri. noon-10:30pm, Sun. noon-3pm, €12

Behind the traditional tile-clad exterior with its decorative cobblestone paving, Flor da Estrela is another unassuming little eatery that serves honest home-cooked Portuguese fare.

Churrascaria o Lavrador
Calçada da Estrela 193, tel. 213 961 807, Tues.-Fri. 11am-3pm and 5pm-10pm, Sat. 11am-3pm, Sun. 11am-3pm and 5pm-9pm, €15

A proper local's favorite and aptly called "Farmer's Grill," this modest restaurant serves fresh meat and fish straight off the grill with hearty helpings of potatoes and salad.

XL
Calçada da Estrela 57, tel. 213 956 118, Tues.-Sun. 8pm-late, €25

Facing Parliament, chic XL attracts a well-heeled crowd with a fusion of international haute cuisine and old-fashioned Portuguese home cooking. Specialties include soufflés, steaks, and "the best cheeseburger on the planet."

MARKET
Mercado de Campo de Ourique
Rua Coelho da Rocha 104, tel. 211 323 701, Sun.-Thurs. 10am-11pm, Fri.-Sat. 10am-1am, €10-20

Lisboetas love to meet at trendy Mercado de Campo de Ourique, a neighborhood gastro market with a buzzing food court that feels both traditional and contemporary. Explore the many different stalls and choose what takes your fancy.

FINE DINING
Loco
Rua Navegantes 53, tel. 213 951 861, www.loco.pt, Tues.-Sat. 7pm-11pm, €85

Each meal at ultra-swanky Loco is a masterpiece. With two different tasting menus, this culinary experience is twice as nice.

BELÉM
PORTUGUESE
Prova - Enoteca
Rua Duarte Pacheco Pereira 9E, tel. 215 819 080, www.facebook.com/ProvaEnoteca, Tues.-Sat. 11am-10:30pm, €10

As the name of this trendy deli and wine bar indicates (it loosely translates as "try") the aim here is to sample excellent local produce with a good wine. Plates of cured cold meats and

PASTEL DE BELÉM VS. PASTEL DE NATA

It might look like Portugal's omnipresent *pastel de nata* (custard tart), it might even taste like the ubiquitous *pastel de nata*, but the *pastel de Belém* is a tart in its own right.

HISTORY
While the *pastel de nata* is found throughout Portugal, the *pastel de Belém* is found only in Belém. History has it that the *pastel de Belém's* secret recipe emerged in the 19th century from the Jerónimos Monastery.

In 1834, when all the monasteries and convents of Portugal were forced to close, the workers decided to start selling the sweet treats to make a living, in the same spot where the **Pastéis de Belém** bakery is today. The bakery was officially inaugurated in 1837.

pastel de Belém

TRYING *PASTEL DE BELÉM* TODAY
To this day the tarts are handmade following the same ancient original recipe that came from the Jerónimos Monastery. This recipe is a closely guarded secret, known only by a handful of master bakers at the Belém bakery, which has become one of the area's top tourist attractions.

There's an old saying that states going to Belém without trying a *pastel de Belém* is like going to Rome without seeing the Pope, and judging by the queues that form outside the bakery every day, there might be some truth in it.

cheeses, salads, veg platters, and fish tapas are all there for the taking, to be paired with a careful selection of great Portuguese wines.

Feitoria
Altis Belém Hotel & Spa, Doca do Bom Sucesso, tel. 210 400 208, www. restaurantefeitoria.com, Tues.-Sat. 7pm-11pm, €100

Enjoying on a prime position overlooking the Tagus River, Feitoria is a swish, cool, Michelin-star-awarded eatery renowned for its contemporary take on Portuguese classics. Located in the Altis Belém Hotel & Spa, it is an exciting choice for a special occasion.

BAKERY
✪ Pastéis de Belém
Rua Belém 84-92, tel. 213 637 423, www. pasteisdebelem.pt, daily 8am-midnight, €5

No visit to Lisbon is complete without a taste of the humble, iconic *pastel de nata* custard tart. It can be found throughout Portugal, but Belém is its birthplace. Pastéis de Belém started making the delectable tarts in 1837, following a secret recipe from the Jerónimos Monastery. The buttery pastry contains a creamy, eggy filling, slightly caramelized top, and a sprinkling of cinnamon. Other fresh-baked sweet and savory treats can be enjoyed in the large seating area, which is always packed full.

PARK OF NATIONS

The modern Park of Nations is home to eateries offering a kaleidoscope of cuisines, most located along the riverfront.

SEAFOOD
Restaurante D'Bacalhau

Rua da Pimenta 45, tel. 218 941 296 or 967 353 663, www.restaurantebacalhau.com, daily noon-4pm and 7pm-11pm, €20

As its name indicates, bright Restaurante D'Bacalhau specializes in codfish dishes from across the country, including a platter of four of the most traditional *bacalhau* concoctions; you can also enjoy a classic fish pasty.

INTERNATIONAL
Honorato Rio

Alameda dos Oceanos, Lote 2, Unit F/G, tel. 932 561 524 or 218 967 207, www.honorato.pt, Sun.-Thurs. noon-midnight, Fri.-Sat. noon-2am, €10

Chic fast-food joint Honorato Rio boasts the best handmade gourmet burgers in Lisbon.

Brasserie de l'Entrecôte

Alameda dos Oceanos 21101ª, tel. 218 962 220, www.brasserieentrecote.pt, daily noon-3:30pm and 7pm-midnight, €24

Next to Lisbon Casino, on the main Park of Nations Avenue, classy, contemporary Brasserie de l'Entrecôte specializes in delicious ribs.

FINE DINING
Fifty Seconds

Cais das Naus, Torre Vasco da Gama, tel. 211 525 380, www.fiftysecondsexperience.com, Tues.-Sat. 12:30pm-3pm and 7:30pm-11pm, €150

Located on the top floor of the Vasco da Gama Tower, Fifty Seconds is spearheaded by Spaniard Martín Berasategui, a multi-Michelin-star-awarded chef. An extraordinary culinary experience with mind-blowing 360-degree views over the Tagus, Fifty Seconds takes its name from the time it takes to climb the 120 meters (393 feet) to the restaurant in the elevator. Pricy, but an absolutely unique experience. Taster menus start from around €120.

Bars and Nightlife

Bohemian and cosmopolitan in equal measures, Lisbon's nightlife has a different vibe in each different part of the city, from giddy Bairro Alto and atmospheric Alfama to the funky Pink Street in Cais do Sodré and the trendy Park of Nations.

BAIXA

In comparison to other parts of Lisbon, and with the exception of peak seasons like summer and Christmas, nightlife in the Baixa is rather tame. It's more about having a quiet drink at the end of the day than a big night out.

BARS AND PUBS
A Ginjinha

Largo São Domingos 8, tel. 218 145 374, daily 9am-10pm

Home to Portugal's award-winning *ginjinha* cherry liqueur, A Ginjinha is a historic hole-in-the-wall serving tiny glasses of the sweet drink over its sticky slab of marble bar-top. *Ginjinha* is served as a shot, with a cherry in the glass if you ask. Soft drinks and beer are also available. This place is standing room only and crowded.

A Ginjinha

Hotel Mundial Rooftop Bar & Lounge

Praça Martim Moniz 2, tel. 218 842 000, www.hotel-mundial.pt, daily 6:30pm-12:30am

The swanky terrace of Hotel Mundial Rooftop Bar & Lounge has stunning views. During the warmer months, it is a fashionable in-crowd hangout, popular for sunset parties. The views over Lisbon's downtown are worth a visit, but drinks are pricy, and the terrace can get crowded.

The George Pub

Rua do Crucifixo 58-66, tel. 213 460 596, www.facebook.com/thegeorgelisbon, daily noon-2am

A good old-fashioned British pub in the heart of downtown Lisbon, the George is the kind of place where everyone knows your name (especially if you're an expat regular) and also has a

following for its famous eggs Benedict. Comfy couches and gleaming wooden surfaces lend original pub charm to this top spot for a refreshing pint and live sports.

Club Noir

Rua da Madalena 201, tel. 919 191 919, www.club-noir.wixsite.com/home, Fri.-Sat. 11pm-4am

Rock out at colorful Club Noir, an underground hangout that is a must for lovers of all genres of rock music—from post-punk, hard rock, and glam rock to heavy metal and indie rock. This trendy alternative venue is popular among Goths; don't miss the gorgeous brick-rimmed vaulted roof.

ALFAMA

Enjoy dinner and a show with spellbinding fado. Restaurants are intimate and offer traditional Portuguese dining. Many fado houses have a minimum fee that covers dinner and the show. It is customary for spectators to be silent while melodic fado is being sung, out of respect for the *fadista* (singer) and the accompanying musicians. With livelier songs, however, guests and even the staff join in. Reservations are strongly recommended.

FADO
Sr. Fado de Alfama

Rua dos Remédios 176, tel. 218 874 298, www.sr-fado.com, Weds.-Sun. 7:30pm-midnight, €35

Family-run Sr. Fado de Alfama belongs to *fadista* Ana Marina and is a cultural mainstay, with good traditional Portuguese food and a healthy dose of fado.

fado venue in Alfama

São Miguel d'Alfama

Largo de São Miguel, tel. 968 554 422, www.
saomigueldalfama.com, daily 7pm-midnight,
€25

Intimate, arabesque-styled São Miguel
d'Alfama is famous for its fado and
traditional Portuguese food.

Restaurante Dragão de Alfama

Rua de Guilherme Braga 8, tel. 218 867 737,
daily 7pm-2am, €20

Typical Portuguese food is served in a
cozy and informal setting with great
fado at Restaurante Dragão de Alfama,
near the Santo Estêvão viewpoint.

Clube de Fado

Rua de São João Praça 86-94, tel. 218
852 704, www.clube-de-fado.com, daily
8pm-2am, €40

In the heart of Alfama, behind an un-
remarkable exterior, famous Clube de
Fado serves excellent Portuguese cuisine to the sound of the Portuguese
guitar accompanying the *fadista*. It
has a warm, romantic, and almost
mystic atmosphere.

A Baiuca

Rua São Miguel 20, tel. 218 867 284,
Thurs.-Mon. 7:30pm-11:30pm, €25 minimum
pp includes dinner, drinks, and dessert

An authentic, classic fado dinner
haunt, tiny tavern A Baiuca serves
tasty home-cooked Portuguese fare
on long tables where patrons sit snugly
together. The convivial atmosphere is
conducive to a great evening enjoying
the magic of fado and new friends.

Parreirinha de Alfama

Beco do Espírito Santo 1, tel. 218 868 209,
www.parreirinhadealfama.com, Tues.-Sun.
8pm-1am, dinner until 10:30pm, €45, drinks
only thereafter (minimum consumption €15)

Small and atmospheric, Parreirinha is
one of Lisbon's oldest and most popular fado haunts. A legendary restaurant inextricably intertwined with
fado, it was established in 1939 and
is owned by acclaimed fado singer
Argentina Santos. Some of Portugal's
most famous fado singers have graced
the stage of Parreirinha over the years,
including the great Amália Rodrigues.

Its food is equally renowned, based on typical Portuguese flavors. Mains include monkish rice and roast kid. Fado is sung nightly.

✪ CHIADO AND BAIRRO ALTO

A quaint and traditional part of Lisbon that is sleepy during the day, bohemian Bairro Alto comes to life at night. The cobbled streets are packed with people and cool nightspots ranging from chic wine bars to historic fado houses and renowned jazz clubs.

BARS AND PUBS
Entretanto Rooftop Bar

Rua Nova do Almada 114, tel. 213 256 161, www.hoteldochiado.pt, daily 10:30pm-midnight

Perched on top of the Hotel do Chiado, Entretanto Rooftop Bar is a fab spot to enjoy a sundowner with bird's-eye views of the Baixa. It's small, so space can be limited.

ODD Trindade

Rua Nova da Trindade 9D, tel. 933 687 974, Mon.-Sat. 10pm-2am

Hidden away in the basement beneath the Trindade Theatre, groovy ODD Trindade is a must for beer lovers, being home to more than 170 brands of craft beer. It also has a vast selection of quality liquors, regular live music, and is the café-bar that serves the theater.

Toca Da Raposa Cocktail Bar

Rua da Condessa 45, tel. 965 463 262, www.facebook.com/Tocadaraposabar, Tues.-Sun. 6pm-2am

An ode to the art of mixology, stylish Toca da Raposa (the fox den) is a cocktail-lovers' paradise. Only fresh Portuguese ingredients are used to make the drinks, served on the solid marble bar.

Nova Tertulia

Rua do Diário de Notícias 60, tel. 918 505 655, Sun.-Thurs. 6pm-2am, Fri.-Sat. 6pm-3am

This popular meeting point in the heart of Bairro Alto is the place to be for shots and beers galore.

Majong

Rua da Atalaia 3, tel. 915 214 803, Mon.-Fri. 6pm-2am, Sat.-Sun. 6pm-3am

One of Bairro Alto's best-known bars, Majong is a favorite among the younger arty crowd, with a cool boho-chic interior where smoking is allowed.

Double 9

Rua da Misericórdia 78, tel. 212 481 480, daily afternoon-late

Classy cocktail bar Double 9, in a funky boutique hotel, is sophisticated yet laid-back.

Pavilhão Chinês

Rua Dom Pedro V 89, tel. 213 424 729, daily 6pm-2am

Take a trip back in time at Pavilhão Chinês, a sumptuously upholstered tearoom with a web of nooks and crannies spread over five rooms. The walls and cabinets of this popular hangout, converted from a grocery store, are filled with a vast private collection of shiny treasures and relics: mugs, plates, books, and ancient maps. Besides more than 40 different types of tea, the Pavilhão Chinês (which translates as "Chinese Pavilion") also serves wine, beers, cocktails, and liquors.

WINES OF PORTUGAL

Portugal has deservedly earned itself a spot among Europe's top producers of quality wines, alongside the likes of France, Spain, and Italy. While it produces a vast range of excellent reds and whites—even most of Portugal's table wines are perfectly drinkable—it is also producer of a number of unique, indigenous wines and spirits.

- **Vinho verde:** The so-called Green wine, which originated in the Minho region, is a slightly fizzy, fruity, crisp young wine that is actually a pale yellow in color, as opposed to green.

- **Port wine:** Exclusive to the Porto region, this sweet, warming fortified wine has a history as long and fascinating as Portugal's. Avilable in several varieties—ruby, tawny, white, and pink among them—no visit to Porto is complete without a tour of a port wine cellar in neighboring Vila Nova de Gaia.

- **Madeira wine:** A fortified wine from the subtropical island of Madeira, Madeira wine is baked to a thick, sweet consistency, giving it a distinct texture and flavor. It was hugely fashionable in 18th- and early-19th-century Europe and is today synonymous with Madeira Island.

- **Mateus Rosé:** Portugal is also the producer of one of the most famous rosé wines in the world—the acclaimed Mateus Rosé.

- *Ginjinha:* Though not a wine, this cherry liqueur has been enjoyed in Portugal for over a century. Made from the morello cherry, it is one of Lisbon and Óbidos's most traditional tipples, served with or without a cherry, sometimes chilled, with a squeeze of fresh lemon, or in little chocolate cups.

Among Portugal's main wine-producing regions are the **Douro Valley** (northern Portugal), **Dão** (central Portugal), the **Alentejo** (lower central Portugal), Lisbon, Tejo, and **Setúbal,** just south of Lisbon. Bairro Alto boasts some of Lisbon's best wine bars, such as the **Old Pharmacy, Artis,** and **Solar do Vinho do Porto.**

WINE BARS
The Old Pharmacy

Rua do Diário de Notícias 73,
tel. 920 230 989, daily 5:30pm-midnight

The Old Pharmacy is a quirky bar that offers a wide selection of wines by the glass or bottle. Wine bottles now fill the cabinets that were once stocked with medicines. Dim lighting and wine-barrel tables add to the allure.

Artis

Rua do Diário de Notícias 95, tel. 213 424 795, Sun. and Tues.-Thurs. 5:30pm-2am, Fri.-Sat. 5:30pm-3am

Iberian-rustic Artis is the ideal place for long conversations over wine, cheese, and tapas.

Solar do Vinho do Porto

Rua São Pedro de Alcântara 45, tel. 213 475 707, Mon.-Fri. 11am-midnight, Sat. 3pm-midnight, glasses from €2

Directly opposite the romantic São Pedro de Alcântara viewpoint and housed in an 18th-century palace, Solar do Vinho do Porto is run by the Port Wine Institute. It showcases more than 300 different types of port, many of which can be sampled by the glass, including rarer vintages that date as far back as 1937.

JAZZ CLUBS
Páginas Tantas

Rua do Diário de Notícias 85, tel. 966 249 005, Mon.-Thurs. 8:30am-2am, Fri.-Sat. 8:30am-3am, Sun. 8:30am-midnight

Partake in some foot-tapping at

Páginas Tantas, a popular jazz bar with live music. The instrument-themed decor and portraits of jazz greats give the club a colorful, contemporary vibe. Rising and established musicians jam live nightly on a little stage in the corner.

TOP EXPERIENCE

FADO
O Faia
Rua da Barroca 54-56, tel. 213 426 742, www.ofaia.com, Mon.-Sat. 8pm-2am, minimum €50

Founded in 1947, O Faia is a famed fado house with a cult following; it hosts nightly shows and has a restaurant that serves traditional Portuguese cuisine with a contemporary twist.

Tasca do Chico
Rua do Diario de Noticias 39, tel. 965 059 670 or 961 339 696, daily 7pm-3am, €15

Unlike other fado venues, Tasca do Chico is more of a fado bar than a restaurant. Dim lighting in this tiny tavern enhances the atmospheric experience. Drinks and typical Portuguese tapas, such as plates of cured meats, are served. There is no minimum consumption fee, but it's cash only.

CAIS DO SODRÉ

Created through a clever urban renewal program, the Pink Street project has taken a part of town that once was a red-light district and turned it into one of the hippest hangouts in Lisbon, with varying ambience along a short, colorful stretch.

BARS AND PUBS
Hennessy's
Cais do Sodré 32-38, tel. 213 462 467, Sun.-Thurs. 11am-2am, Fri.-Sat. 11am-4am

The traditional Irish pub Hennessy's offers live music and sports coverage in a warm and welcoming atmosphere.

Quero-te no Cais
Rua dos Remolares 41, tel. 213 425 309, Mon.-Fri. 8am-4am, Sat. 10pm-4am

Quero-te no Cais is small and friendly, with a big alfresco drinking area to enjoy.

Pensão Amor
Rua do Alecrim 19, tel. 213 143 399, www. pensaoamor.pt, Sun.-Weds. 2pm-3am, Thurs.-Sat. 2pm-4am

A former inn that once rented rooms to sailors and ladies of the night, Pensão Amor is now a lively and bohemian hangout.

Jamaica
Rua Nova do Carvalho 6, tel. 213 421 859, www.jamaica.com.pt, Tues.-Sat. midnight-6am, women free, men minimum about €8

Jamaica, one of Lisbon's best-known bars, is the place to go to drink and dance. It's not huge, so the dance floor can get crowded, but the DJs play a mix of '70s, '80s, rock, and current hits.

Vestigius
Cais do Sodré 8, tel. 218 203 320, www. vestigius.pt, daily 11am-late

A popular wine and gin bar (more than 100 gins on the menu!) with vintage retro décor and two outdoor waterfront esplanades.

ALCÂNTARA

Situated directly beneath the 25 de Abril Bridge, the Santo Amaro Docks, or Docas, have long been one of Lisbon's most popular nightlife spots. A long row of old port warehouses belonging to Lisbon Docks were renovated in 1995 and are enjoying a second lease on life as cool bars, restaurants, and clubs catering to a multitude of tastes—from Italian restaurants to Irish pubs and African-beat nightclubs—flanked by sports courts and street food to enjoy at sunrise. It overlooks a smart recreational marina, and the constant hum of traffic crossing the bridge overhead adds to the atmosphere. Take tram 15 or a train from Cais do Sodré to get there, getting off at Alcântara-Mar. Trains run every 20 minutes.

BARS AND PUBS
Irish & Co.

Edificio Topo Nascente, Doca de Santo Amaro, tel. 213 959 885, www.irishco.pt, daily 12:30pm-late

Popular among the expat community, Irish & Co. is a welcoming Irish bar with a relaxed feel and great *craic.* Reputedly the oldest Irish pub in Lisbon.

Hawaii

Warehouse 1, Doca Alcântara, tel. 213 900 010, daily 7pm-6am

A longstanding favorite on the Docas, especially among the younger crowds, Hawaii is the place to dance the night away. Good cocktails and open until dawn.

BELÉM
BARS AND PUBS
Bar 38° 41'

Avenida Brasília BP, tel. 210 400 210, www. altishotels.com, daily 11am-1am

Sit and watch the world sail by at this trendy dockside lounge-bar with guest DJs Thursday through Sunday in summer.

Casual Lounge Café

Rua Bartolomeu Dias 148b, tel. 213 019 024, www.facebook.com/casuallounge, Mon.-Sat. 4pm-2am

A laid-back, arty lounge in which to chill out with a cocktail, coffee, or a glass of wine.

PARK OF NATIONS

Enjoy dinner and a drink in style in this funky new part of town.

BARS AND PUBS
Irish & Co.

Rua Pimenta 57, tel. 218 940 558, www. grupodocadesanto.com.pt, noon-2am daily

For authentic Irish warmth and good *craic,* head to the traditional pub Irish & Co., where you'll find a friendly ambience with live music. With its vast open front on the riverside and a pub menu, it's a great place to spend a convivial few hours.

Me & You

Av. Dom João II, Lote 1.17.03, tel. 218 947 020, Mon.-Sat. 8am-2am, happy hour 6pm-8pm

Relaxed, informal café-bar Me & You is a quiet place for a light snack or to catch up on conversation over coffee.

Shisha Tea Food

Alameda dos Oceanos 44301M, tel. 215 940 508, www.shishateafood.pt, daily noon-2am

Shisha Tea Food is a funky Middle Eastern-inspired hookah bar and lounge with a warm Moroccan vibe and exotic *shisha* (water pipes) and great drinks, including teas and cocktails, and an alfresco esplanade.

CLUBS
Lux Discotheque

Av. Infante Don Henrique, Warehouse A, tel. 218 820 890, www.luxfragil.com, Thurs.-Sat. 11pm-6am, cover €10-20

Co-owned by actor John Malkovich, Lux Discotheque is one of Lisbon's most exuberant nightspots, renowned throughout Europe as the place to go to see and be seen. On two different levels, it regularly puts on live acts and DJs. Upstairs the music is mainstream, while the groove on the bottom floor is left to the resident or guest DJ. Outside is a huge terrace where you can watch the sun come up over the Tagus River.

Accommodations

Lisbon is awash with cool and interesting places to stay, from historic townhouses to converted palaces. The Baixa area is central and convenient. Lodging is generally pricy, but there are quality budget hostels and guesthouses.

BAIXA
UNDER €100
✪ Yes! Lisbon Hostel
Rua de São Julião 148, tel. 213 427 171, www. yeshostels.com, €32 dorm, €140 d with shared bath
Yes! Lisbon Hostel has it all: an excellent location, good service, and budget-friendly prices. Custom-made bunks ensure a good night's sleep, and reception is happy to provide tips on how to get the most out of your stay.

€100-200
✪ Hotel Mundial
Praça Martim Moniz 2, tel. 218 842 000, www.hotel-mundial.pt, €130-200 d
Despite its plain exterior, four-star Hotel Mundial is an institution because its rooftop has a great view. Decor is tasteful, beds are comfortable, and the location is second to none. A short walk from Rua do Comércio.

CR7 Pestana Lisboa
Rua do Comércio 54, tel. 210 401 710, www. pestanacr7.com, €150-200 d
The CR7 Pestana Lisboa was set up with Portuguese soccer superstar Cristiano Ronaldo. It has sporty decor and a great location in the heart of downtown.

Hotel Vincci Baixa
Rua do Comércio 32-38, tel. 218 803 190, www.vinccibaixa.com, €180-250 d
Square, elegant four-star Hotel Vincci Baixa embodies class and comfort in a prime location.

€200-300
Boutique Hotel Heritage Avenida da Liberdade
Av. da Liberdade 28, tel. 213 404 040, www.heritageavliberdade.com, €200-300 d
Set back from leafy Avenida da Liberdade, the stately Boutique Hotel Heritage Avenida da Liberdade is in an elegant 18th-century townhouse, a pleasant stroll from the Baixa area.

ALFAMA
€100-200
✪ Solar do Castelo
Rua das Cozinhas 2, tel. 218 806 050, www. solardocastelo.com, €160-200 d
Small, romantic Solar do Castelo is the only hotel within the walls of the São Jorge Castle. Converted from an 18th-century mansion, this eco-retreat with medieval and contemporary style even has specially commissioned furniture to enhance its uniqueness.

✪ Memmo Alfama Design Hotel

Travessa Merceeiras 27, tel. 210 495 660,
www.memmoalfama.com, €150-250 d

Cool and contemporary Memmo Alfama Design Hotel is a 44-room urban retreat fast earning a reputation for its chic, clean design, which blends well with the historic Alfama neighborhood.

€200-300
Santiago de Alfama Boutique Hotel

Rua de Santiago 10 a 14, tel. 213 941 616,
www.santiagodealfama.com, €200-300 d

A former 15th-century palace has been reborn as cosmopolitan Santiago de Alfama Boutique Hotel, which oozes authenticity from its tiled floors to its prime location in Alfama. It's one of Europe's most outstanding urban hotels.

SÃO VICENTE
€200-300
Casa dell'Arte Club House

Campo de Santa Clara 125, tel. 218 860 582,
www.casadellartelisbon.com, €200-300 d

Housed in an elegant 19th-century building with a typical *azulejo* facade, this upscale guesthouse overlooks the National Pantheon and combines traditional features with touches of glamour.

CHIADO AND BAIRRO ALTO
UNDER €100
Bairro Alto Hostel

Travessa da Cara 6, tel. 213 421 079,
www.bairroaltohostel.com, from €60 d with shared bath

Modern and clean Bairro Alto Hostel is in a historic 19th-century building. Private rooms and shared dorms are all equipped with free Wi-Fi; there's a communal lounge and kitchen facilities.

€100-200
Chiado 44 Guest House

Rua Horta Seca 44, tel. 930 544 457,
www.chiado44.pt, €120-200 d

Set in the heart of Chiado in a typical 19th-century building, Chiado 44 is a simple and relaxed three-star hotel with a cool, clean décor and river views.

9 Hotel Mercy

Rua da Misericórdia 78, tel. 212 481 480,
www.9-hotel-mercy-lisbon.pt, €130-200 d

Trendy little 9 Hotel Mercy offers contemporary class, a bohemian vibe, and panoramic views from its stylish rooftop bar.

Hotel do Chiado

Rua Nova do Almada, 114, tel. 213 256 100,
www.hoteldochiado.pt, €170-250 d

The charming Hotel do Chiado is housed in historic former warehouses that were renovated by leading Portuguese architect Siza Vieira following the catastrophic 1988 neighborhood fire. Famed for stunning city views from its seventh-floor rooftop terrace and its afternoon tea.

OVER €300
✪ Bairro Alto Hotel

Praça Luis de Camões 2, tel. 213 408 288,
www.bairroaltohotel.com, €350-400 d

Wedged between bohemian Bairro Alto and trendy Chiado, the five-star Bairro Alto Hotel enjoys a dominant position on the main square and has handsome 18th-century architecture. Within walking distance of shops, restaurants, and bars, the 55 rooms are twins, doubles, and suites.

CAIS DO SODRÉ

€100-200

LX Boutique Hotel

Rua do Alecrim 12, tel. 213 474 394,
www.lxboutiquehotel.com, €100-200 d
Overlooking the Tagus River, the decadently decorated LX Boutique Hotel is an atmospheric 19th-century hotel conveniently at the nexus of Chiado, Baixa, and Cais do Sodré.

✪ Hello Lisbon Cais do Sodré Apartments

Rua Nova do Carvalho 43,
tel. 937 770 007,
www.hello-lisbon.com, €100-200 d
Clean and comfortable self-catering Hello Lisbon Cais do Sodré Apartments reflect the youth and energy of their location on frenetic Pink Street. Edgy paintings provide a pop of color to the period architecture and smart interiors.

ESTRELA AND LAPA

€100-200

As Janelas Verdes Lisbon Hotel

Rua das Janelas Verdes 47,
tel. 213 968 143,
www.asjanelasverdes.com, €120-200 d
A night at the plush 18th-century As Janelas Verdes Lisbon Hotel feels like staying in someone's very grand home, with stunning views from the rooftop terrace.

Hotel da Estrela

Rua Saraiva de Carvalho 35,
tel. 211 900 100,
www.hoteldaestrela.com, €150-200 d
Occupying an old school building, the 19th-century Paraty Palace, the small Hotel da Estrela blends contemporary with quirky.

BELÉM

€100-200

✪ Hotel Palácio do Governador

Rua Bartolomeu Dias 117, tel. 212 467 800,
www.palaciogovernador.com, €150-250 d
Poised and polished five-star Hotel Palácio do Governador occupies the 16th-century Governor's Palace, carefully conserving its original features. With 60 rooms and two pools, it is a whitewashed and manicured oasis of tranquility in one of Lisbon's prettiest neighborhoods.

€200-300

Pestana Palace Hotel

Rua Jau 54, tel. 213 615 600,
www.pestana.com, €200-300 d
Feel like royalty with a stay at five-star Pestana Palace Hotel, in an exquisite 19th-century palace with gorgeous gardens.

OVER €300

Altis Belém Hotel & Spa

Doca do Bom Sucesso, tel. 210 400 200,
www.altishotels.com, €350-450 d
Along the river, the contemporary Altis Belém Hotel & Spa has a modern design inspired by the Age of Discoveries, with nautical themes in all of its 50 rooms, which include five suites.

PARK OF NATIONS

€100-200

✪ VIP Executive Arts

Av. Dom João II 47, tel. 210 020 400,
www.viphotels.com, €100-200d
The stylish and streamlined four-star VIP Executive Arts is within walking distance of the Oriente transport hub, the Vasco da Gama shopping center, the Altice Arena, and riverside nightlife.

Information and Services

VISITOR INFORMATION

"Ask Me" tourist information desks can be found throughout Lisbon, at the airport and major bus and train stations and monuments. Most are open daily about 9am-6pm. Also available are the main **Lisbon Tourism Visitors and Convention Bureau** (Rua do Arsenal 21, tel. 210 312 700, www.visitlisboa.com, Mon.-Fri. 9:30am-7pm) and the national tourist board, **Turismo de Portugal** (Rua Ivone Silva, Lote 6, tel. 211 140 200, www.visitportugal.com, www. turismodeportugal.pt, Mon.-Fri. 9am-1pm and 2:30pm-5:30pm).

EMBASSIES

- **United States:** Av. das Forças Armadas 133C, tel. 217 273 300, https://pt.usembassy.gov, Mon.-Fri. 8am-5pm
- **Canada:** Av. da Liberdade 196, tel. 213 164 600, www. canadainternational.gc.ca, Mon.-Fri. 9am-noon
- **United Kingdom:** Rua de São Bernardo 33, tel. 213 924 000, www.gov.uk, Mon., Weds., and Fri. 9:30am-2pm
- **Australia:** Av. da Liberdade 200, tel. 213 101 500, www.portugal.embassy. gov.au, Mon.-Fri. 10am-4pm

MONEY

In Lisbon, most hotels, currency exchanges, travel agencies, some banks, and even some shops have currency exchange facilities, or use your debit card to make a withdrawal from an ATM *(multibanco)*, which can be found throughout the city. The currency exchange company **Unicâmbio** (www.unicambio.pt) has more than 80 offices around the country, including the airports at Lisbon, Faro, and Madeira, the Rossio train station in central Lisbon, the Cais do Sodré station in Baixa, and El Corte Inglês shopping mall (Av. António Augusto de Aguiar 31).

HEALTH AND EMERGENCIES

- **European free emergency number:** 112
- **GNR Police Lisbon headquarters:** Largo do Carmo 27, tel. 213 217 000, www.gnr.pt
- **PSP Metropolitan Police Lisbon headquarters:** Av. Moscavide 88, tel. 217 654 242, www.psp.pt
- **PSP Tourist Police Lisbon:** Praça dos Restauradores, Palácio Foz, tel. 213 421 623
- **INEM medical emergency:** Rua Almirante Barroso 36, tel. 213 508 100, www.inem.pt
- **Lisbon Fire Brigade:** Av. Dom Carlos I, tel. 218 171 470, www.cm-lisboa.pt
- **CUF Private Hospital:** Travessa do Castro 3, tel. 213 926 100, www. saudecuf.pt
- **24-Hour pharmacy:** Farmácia Largo do Rato, Av. Alvares Cabral 1, tel. 213 863 044, www. farmaciasdeservico.net

Getting There and Around

GETTING THERE

AIR

Lisbon's **Humberto Delgado Airport** (LIS, Alameda das Comunidades Portuguesas, tel. 218 413 500, www.ana.pt) is Portugal's biggest and busiest international airport. European flights tend to be shorter than four hours and inexpensive. Portugal's national airline, **TAP-Air Portugal** (www.flytap.com), has expanded its operations to the United States and operates several direct daily flights between Portugal and U.S. cities. A number of U.S. airlines also fly to Lisbon.

Getting To and From the Airport

Lisbon's airport is 7 kilometers (4.3 mi) north of the city center. The **Metro** runs direct from the airport to Lisbon; the Red Line runs from just outside the airport's main entrance and connects with the Green Line at Alameda station, which runs to the Baixa and Cais do Sodré riverfront, and ends on the Blue Line, at the São Sebastião station. A journey to downtown Lisbon (€1.25) requires one transfer and takes 20 minutes. The **Aerobus** (www.aerobus.pt) shuttle bus runs regularly to the city center and to the financial district from outside the arrivals terminal (daily 7:30am-11pm, €3.15 one-way). Municipal bus company **Carris** (www.carris.pt, €1.85 one-way) runs five bus routes between Lisbon Airport and the city center. **Taxis** can be found outside the arrivals terminal; a trip to Lisbon city center should cost up to €15. Alternately, call an **Uber** (www.uber.com) ride-share.

The cheapest and easiest way to get around Lisbon is to buy a **7 Colinas/Viva Viagem card,** available at the airport from the newsagent on the second floor, or from main bus or Metro stations. The cards are prepaid and can be recharged. The card itself costs €0.50, and they are accepted on all local buses and Metro subways, trams, funiculars, and ferryboats. Most single trips on any mode cost €2-3. A one-day travel option has a flat rate of €6.

BUS

Eurolines (www.eurolines.com) operates regular international bus service between Lisbon and cities such as London, Madrid, and Paris. National intercity bus company **Rede Expressos** (tel. 707 223 344, www.rede-expressos.pt) operates express bus trips to Lisbon from most of the country's regions, including the Algarve and Porto, each around three hours' journey. Algarve bus company **Eva** (tel. 289 899 760, www.eva-bus.com) also runs daily routes between main bus stations in the Algarve and Lisbon.

The two main bus terminals in Lisbon are **Sete Rios** (Rua Professor Lima Basto 133, opposite Lisbon Zoo, tel. 707 223 344, ticket office 7am-11:30pm daily, Metro Jardim Zoológico, Blue Line), a Rede Expressos' hub, and the modern **Gare do Oriente** (Av. Dom João II, Park of Nations, tel. 218 956 972, Metro Oriente, Red Line), closest to the airport.

TRAIN

Getting to Portugal from other European countries by train isn't as straightforward as by air, and can sometimes be more expensive, usually involving passing through a hub such as Paris or Madrid, and a few transfers. There are two overnight sleeper trains from Spain: the **Lusitania Hotel Train** (www.cp.pt) from Madrid and the **Sud Expresso** (www.cp.pt) from San Sebastian. Traveling from Europe by train can make sense if you're using a rail pass such as the **Eurail** pass.

Trains run to Lisbon from most major towns across the country, and train travel can be a cheap and scenic option. The two types of trains for long-distance travel are the slower Intercidades (intercity) and the Alfa-Pendular (high-speed) train. All trains in Portugal have a first-class option and are operated by **Comboios de Portugal** (CP, tel. 707 210 220, www.cp.pt).

The four main railway stations in Lisbon are **Entrecampos** (Rua Dr. Eduardo Neves), **Oriente** (Av. Dom João II), **Sete Rios** (Rua Professor Lima Bastos), and **Santa Apolónia** (Av. Infante Dom Henrique). The Alfa-Pendular runs from Oriente, Santa Apolónia, and Entrecampos.

CAR

Two main motorways connect Lisbon to the country's extremities: the **A1** to the north (Porto) and the **A2** to the south (Algarve). The **A6** is the main motorway from the east. From outside Portugal, you'll cross the entire country from any border point to get to Lisbon. The scenery makes up for any potholes or wrong turns you might endure.

There are two crossings to Lisbon from the south over the Tagus River: the **25 de Abril Bridge,** to the western end of the city, or the newer **Vasco da Gama Bridge**—the longest in Europe—to the Park of Nations area. Both provide stunning views of the city on approach.

CRUISE SHIP

Lisbon has become a popular port-of-call for many transatlantic and European cruise itineraries and has a busy year-round docking schedule. There are two main cruise hubs; **Alcântara** (Alcântara Docks, Port of Lisbon, tel. 213 611 000, www.portodelisboa.pt), west of the main downtown area (Baixa) or **Santa Apolónia** (Avenida Infante Dom Henrique Warehouse B, Shop 8, tel. 213 611 000 (Port of Lisbon), www.portodelisboa.pt), east of the Baixa. Santa Apolónia, a brand-new, state-of-the-art-terminal, is slightly closer to the downtown (1.5 km/1 mi) and more convenient to explore on foot. If you only have a few hours, head straight to the Baixa (downtown) and medieval Alfama districts to see the sights there. Taxis will be readily available from both hubs. Day trips organized by the cruise company are good options to fit in as much as possible, but often expensive. A **hop-on hop-off bus** is always a good option to see the essential sights in a short time.

GETTING AROUND

Getting around Lisbon can be cheap and easy on public transport, or expensive if you opt for novelty transport like the city's mushrooming *tuk-tuks.*

LISBOA CARD

The Lisboa Card (www.lisboacard.org), Lisbon's official tourist pass, includes unlimited travel on public buses, trams, the Metro, elevators, and funiculars as well as travel on CP train lines to Sintra and Cascais; free

the famous tram 28

access to 26 museums, monuments, and UNESCO World Heritage Sites; and deals and discounts on tours, shopping, and nightlife. The cost is €20 for a 24-hour card, €34 for a 48-hour card, and €42 for a 72-hour card. Children's cards are half price. These cards can be purchased online, for which a voucher is given that can be exchanged at main tourist points such as the Lisboa Welcome Center, Foz Palace, and Lisbon Airport.

PUBLIC TRANSIT

Single trips on buses, trams, ferryboats, and the Metro generally cost under €1.50, and the rechargeable **7 Colinas/Viva Viagem card** can be bought at most newsagents and kiosks, stations, and terminals for €0.50. A **24-hour public transport pass** can be loaded onto the card; it costs €6 and covers all forms of local public transport (buses, trams, and Metro). Add ferryboat trips to the 24-hour pass and it costs €9, or €10 to also include trains to nearby Sintra

and Cascais. Some public transport timetables can vary depending on the season, with hours extended later in summer.

Bus

The capital has an efficient bus service, **Carris** (www.carris.pt), which also manages the city's tram system. It provides good coverage of the city, as well as service to neighboring towns and suburbs, and is inexpensive, with most trips under €2. Most buses run 6am-9pm daily, with the busiest lines running until midnight.

Tram

Carris (www.carris.pt) operates a network of historic trams and funiculars, a unique way to get into the city's backstreets. Five tram routes carry 60 trams, most of which are vintage vehicles. The star of the show is the famous **tram 28,** which circumnavigates Lisbon's historic neighborhoods Bairro Alto, Alfama, Baixa, and Chiado. A downside is that it is plagued by petty thieves, so stay alert. Trams and funiculars generally operate 6am-11pm daily.

Metro

Inaugurated in 1959, Lisbon's **Metro** (www.metrolisboa.pt) has consistently grown, including a stop beneath the airport, making travel fast and easy. The Metro has four main lines— Green, Yellow, Red, and Blue—and is simple to navigate, covering the city's important points. Trains run regularly and reliably. A 24-hour pass that also covers funiculars, trams, and buses costs €6. The Metro runs 6:30am-1am daily.

Ferry

Commuter ferries chug continuously across the Tagus River between Lisbon and Setúbal, operated by **Transtejo & Soflusa** (tel. 808 203 050, www.transtejo.pt) generally 5am or 6am to 1am daily, although crossings are more frequent on weekdays. Boats get busy during rush hours (before 9am and after 4:30pm weekdays) and depart from three terminals along Lisbon's riverside: Terreiro do Paço, Cais do Sodré, and Belém. The five stops on the Setúbal side are Montijo, Barreiro, Seixal, Cacilhas, and Porto Brandão-Trafaria. The Cais do Sodré-Cacilhas crossing is the busiest.

Commuter ferries are much cheaper than tourist boats, with single trips under €3. A charged 7 Colinas/Viva Viagem public transport card can be used to pay for tickets. Crossings provide awesome views of Lisbon's iconic 25 de Abril Bridge and of the city.

TAXI AND RIDE-SHARE

Taxis in Portugal are plentiful and easy to spot: beige or black with a minty green roof. Each is identified with a number, usually under the driver's side mirror. There are lots of taxi stands throughout the city at train and bus stations, central plazas, and near shopping malls. Hotel reception desks will call a taxi for you, or simply hail one on the street. The main taxi firms in Lisbon are **Taxis Lisboa** (tel. 218 119 000, www.taxislisboa.com), **Cooptaxis** (tel. 217 932 756, www.cooptaxis.pt), and **Teletaxis** (tel. 218 111 100, www.teletaxis.pt).

Uber cars are also now popular and widely available in Lisbon, giving taxi drivers a run for their money.

TUK-TUK

A novel way of exploring Lisbon is to jump on a *tuk-tuk*. These nifty little vehicles have taken the city by storm in recent years; it's rare to turn a street corner without hearing or seeing one of the colorful three-wheelers buzzing along. They have the advantage of fitting on streets and lanes where cars can't go, and they're cute and comfortable—but they are more expensive than public transport or taxis. *Tuk-tuk* operators include **Tuk Tuk Lisboa** (www.tuk-tuk-lisboa.pt), **City Tuk** (www.citytuk.pt), **Eco Tuk Tours** (www.ecotuktours.com), and **Tuga Tours Tuk Tuk** (www.tugatours.pt). Expect to pay €55-70 pp for an hour's tour of the sights.

CAR

Getting around Lisbon without a car is easy and convenient thanks to the comprehensive public transport network. A car is only necessary to visit outlying areas. Book one online and pick it up at the airport, or ask your hotel to help. In and around Lisbon Airport, the many vendors include **Europcar** (tel. 218 401 176, www.

europcar.com), **Hertz** (tel. 219 426 300, www.hertz.com), and **Budget** (tel. 808 252 627, www.budget.com.pt).

Driving in Lisbon can be fast, furious, and overwhelming. Main arteries such as the Segunda Circular ring road, which bypasses the airport, can become gridlocked during rush hour; signage is hit-and-miss (although it's slowly improving), and there are one-way roads to contend with. Lisbon's historic areas are a web of narrow, steep streets that can be daunting to drive, and finding parking, particularly in the busy city center, can be challenging. Most public parking spaces, including car parks, entail a hefty fee.

If you do rent a car to drive in Lisbon, check whether your hotel has private parking (which will entail additional cost), or find an underground car park that offers lower-cost "holiday fees," such as the one in Marquês de Pombal Square.

HOP-ON HOP-OFF BUS

Lisbon has various companies operating modern hop-on hop-off buses, which are an excellent way to see everything the city has to offer, in a relatively short amount of time. An audio guide is available onboard in various languages to provide an explanation of the city's history and main monuments—although the quality and sound of the narrative can be poor. Due to their—and Lisbon's—popularity, there can be long queues for the buses. A good tip is to first stay onboard for the entire circuit, and then get off at what interests you the second time around. There are three main companies operating hop-on hop-off tours; tickets start from around €20 for 24 hour-tickets on basic routes:

- **Yellow Bus – Carristur:** www.yellowbustours.com
- **Cityrama Gray Line:** www.cityrama.pt
- **City Sightseeing:** www.city-sightseeing.com

THE PORTUGUESE RIVIERA

The coastal area to the west of

Lisbon is often referred to as the Portuguese Riviera, as it includes the popular coastal towns of Estoril and Cascais, as well as the Boca do Inferno coastal beauty spot and the windswept Cabo da Roca, Europe's most westerly point. The Marginal Road, also known as the N6, is a popular Sunday drive from Lisbon along the Portuguese Riviera, and one of Portugal's most iconic routes. A very scenic drive, the N6 passes countless interesting sights en route, including museums and forts, gorgeous beaches, and parks.

HIGHLIGHTS

✪ **ESTORIL-CASCAIS BOARDWALK:** Spanning 3 km (2 mi), this scenic oceanfront boardwalk is one of the nicest ways to take in the sights, sounds, and smells of Lisbon's most famous coastal retreats (page 98).

✪ **BOCA DO INFERNO:** The unique shape of this cavernous chasm and the formidable force of the waves that carved it give it its dramatic name, Hell's Mouth (page 104).

✪ **CABO DA ROCA:** Make sure to take a photo when you stand on the windy cliffs of Cabo da Roca—mainland Europe's most western point (page 111).

The Marginal starts at Lisbon's Cais do Sodré docks and ends in Cascais, which at a leisurely drive takes between 45 minutes and 1 hour, depending on traffic. However, the road is generally busy; it is widely used by commuters and tourists, even more so on weekends when the locals head out of the city for a change of pace. As one of the main thoroughfares to the nearest beaches, it can become pretty congested in summer. Luckily, it's possible and very easy to take the train to most of the Portuguese Riviera's prettiest spot and avoid the traffic if needed.

ORIENTATION

Estoril and **Cascais** are located west of Lisbon; Estoril is approximately 25 km (16 mi) west, and Cascais a little further along, about 35 km (22 mi). The beautiful coastal retreats are popular among Lisbon locals and holidaymakers looking for an antithesis to the hustle and bustle of the capital. Many Lisboetas drive to Cascais and Estoril for a coffee and a stroll on a Sunday, and they flock to their **beaches** in summer.

One of the main attractions is the 3 km (2 mi) **seafront promenade** that runs between Estoril and Cascais. Other popular draws include **Tamariz beach** (right in front of **Estoril train station**); the natural pools along the promenade; the many majestic manor houses that dot the main thoroughfares between Estoril and Cascais, including the **Castelinho de São João e Estoril,** a spooky, castlelike house said to be one of the most haunted places in Portugal; and **Boca do Inferno,** an impressive rock formation a short walk northwest of Cascais town center.

Windswept and wild, **Guincho Beach,** a surfing hotspot, is a 15-minute (7 km/4 mi) drive northwest from Cascais, along the **N247 coastal road** or the inland **Rua Joaquim Ereira.** From Guincho, **Cabo da Roca,** mainland Europe's westernmost point, is another 15-minute drive north, continuing along the N247.

PLANNING YOUR TIME

One of Portugal's most scenic drives, the Marginal coastal road runs along Lisbon's southern hem, following the Tagus River west to where it opens into the Atlantic. The road stretches

The Portuguese Riviera

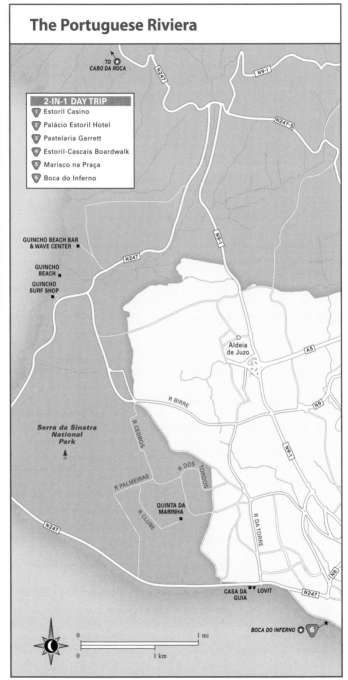

2-IN-1 DAY TRIP

1. Estoril Casino
2. Palácio Estoril Hotel
3. Pastelaria Garrett
4. Estoril-Cascais Boardwalk
5. Marisco na Praça
6. Boca do Inferno

TO CABO DA ROCA

GUINCHO BEACH BAR & WAVE CENTER

GUINCHO BEACH

GUINCHO SURF SHOP

N247

N9-1

N247-S

A5

N9

N9-1

N6

Áldeia de Juzo

R BIRRE

R CEDROS

Serra da Sinatra National Park

R PALMEIRAS

R DOS TORDOS

R CLUBE

QUINTA DA MARINHA

R DA TORRE

CASA DA GUIA LOVIT

N247

BOCA DO INFERNO 6

0   1 mi

0   1 km

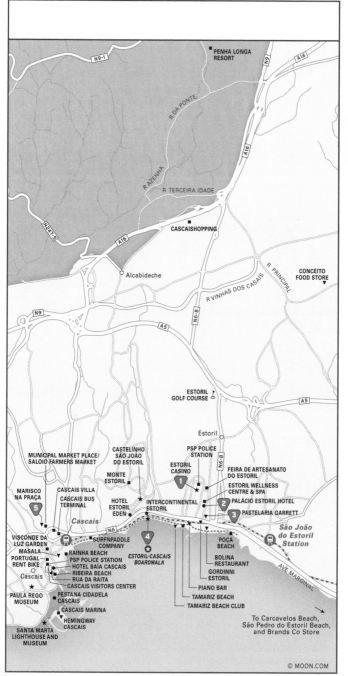

THE PORTUGUESE RIVIERA

PENHA LONGA RESORT

CASCAISHOPPING

Alcabideche

CONCEITO FOOD STORE

R VINHAS DOS CASAIS

ESTORIL GOLF COURSE

Estoril

MUNICIPAL MARKET PLACE/ SALOIO FARMERS MARKET

CASTELINHO SÃO JOÃO DO ESTORIL

PSP POLICE STATION

ESTORIL CASINO **1**

FEIRA DE ARTESANATO DO ESTORIL

MONTE ESTORIL

ESTORIL WELLNESS CENTRE & SPA

MARISCO NA PRAÇA **5**

CASCAIS VILLA

CASCAIS BUS TERMINAL

INTERCONTINENTAL ESTORIL

PALÁCIO ESTORIL HOTEL **2**

PASTELARIA GARRETT **3**

Cascais

HOTEL ESTORIL EDEN

São João do Estoril Station

VISCONDE DA LUZ GARDEN

SURFNPADDLE COMPANY

4

ESTORIL-CASCAIS BOARDWALK

POÇA BEACH

AVE MARGINAL

MASALA

PORTUGAL RENT BIKE

RAINHA BEACH

PSP POLICE STATION

HOTEL BAÍA CASCAIS

BOLINA RESTAURANT

GORDINNI ESTORIL

Cascais

RIBEIRA BEACH

RUA DA RAITA

PIANO BAR

CASCAIS VISITORS CENTER

PAULA REGO MUSEUM

PESTANA CIDADELA CASCAIS

TAMARIZ BEACH

TAMARIZ BEACH CLUB

CASCAIS MARINA

HEMINGWAY CASCAIS

SANTA MARTA LIGHTHOUSE AND MUSEUM

To Carcavelos Beach, São Pedro do Estoril Beach, and Brands Co Store

© MOON.COM

loosely between downtown Lisbon and the chic town of Cascais, passing ever-changing scenery, through charming neighborhoods such as Belém, Carcavelos, and Estoril. It takes drivers on a leisurely cruise past landmark sights, such as the 25 de Abril Bridge, the modern MAAT museum, iconic Belém Tower, the São Julião da Barra fort in Carcavelos, and the majestic Estoril Casino.

Allocate a full day to explore Estoril and Cascais. Due to their proximity to Lisbon, and to each other, it is possible to do both in one day—though Estoril is a popular holiday resort, making it perfect for an overnight stay. From Estoril, you can enjoy a leisurely stroll to nearby Cascais, while Cascais is the better day-trip option if you had to choose just one. Getting to these cities from Lisbon is easy and takes just under an hour by either car or train.

There are several main routes between Lisbon and Estoril and Cascais; by road, the A5 motorway is the fastest (tolls apply), while the Marginal (N6 coastal) Road is the most scenic. Both options can become congested due to the high number of commuters who use them. The Marginal Road is worth the patience and perseverance. It is likely most congested at peak commute times during the week (before 9am and after 5pm) and can also be busy on weekends when the weather is good, as *Lisboetas* head out of town to the beaches. However, an early morning drive or late night cruise of the Marginal offers a certain romantic quality, and should be less congested.

By train, the Cascais Line has frequent services between Cais do Sodré and Cascais, which run roughly every 30 to 40 minutes. A one-way ticket costs €2.25. Though the drive on the

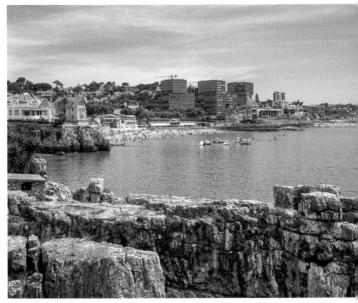

the vista from Cascais to Estoril

Marginal Road is scenic, it's often easier to take the train from Cais do Sodré; jump off at Estoril (or Cascais) and walk the boardwalk between the two.

Both towns are interesting to explore, but it's recommended to spend a couple of hours in Estoril first, in the morning, and to head to Cascais for lunch. Cascais has more to do and see and is a lovely place for a light meal and a spot of people-watching. If you have time to spend the night in the area, Estoril has a romantic vibe, perfect for a seafront sunset or dinner and a show in the casino, while Cascais has a lively town center filled with family-friendly restaurants and bars.

Itinerary Idea

2-IN-1 DAY TRIP

1 Take the train (or drive) from Lisbon to Estoril. From Estoril train station walk north, toward the extravagant Casino and its pretty gardens. Have a wander in the gardens and admire the fountains. There is parking available around the casino if you're driving.

2 Opposite the gardens to the east is the famous Palácio Estoril Hotel, a luxurious 1930s hotel once a popular haunt of spies and high society; head over and have a look inside, feel the glamour and intrigue.

3 Indulge in a coffee and a fresh-baked sweet treat at the famous Pastelaria Garrett, just down the road from Palácio Estoril.

4 Make your way south to the boardwalk and take the 25-minute walk along the seafront promenade to Cascais. Weather permitting, have a dip in the sea en route, or stop in one of the promenade's many restaurants for a cool drink. If you drove, you'll want to take your car.

5 Enjoy the freshest seafood lunch at Marisco na Praça in Cascais, and lounge the afternoon away on the beach and explore the city's chic boutiques.

6 In the late afternoon, burn off all the good food by taking a walk up to the Boca do Inferno rock formation (about 20-40 minutes), before taking the train (or driving) back to Lisbon.

Estoril

Glitzy São João do Estoril, better known as just Estoril (EEZH-too-reel), is a stylish seaside resort and home to the largest casino in Europe. Beaches are long and spacious, with a series of rocky outcrops and piers; calm, clean water; and a laid-back, romantic ambience. It is a popular escape for families and couples on weekends. Estoril is spread over a lengthy stretch of coastline fronted by a glorious promenade and a string of cosmopolitan restaurants and bars and dotted with intriguing historic properties and lush green spaces.

Estoril's heyday was in the mid-1900s, when it was a playground for the Portuguese aristocracy and European high society. During World War II, the resort's reputation as a hangout for spies gave it a sense of intrigue. This is where Ian Fleming wrote the first part of *Casino Royale,* which launched the James Bond series. Mainstream tourism has stripped Estoril of a little of its elitism, but it is still one of the most glamorous beach destinations in Portugal.

A 3-kilometer (2-mile) promenade connects Estoril and Cascais, and the views along the way are fantastic, with a long stretch of golden sand along a string of historic properties, restaurants, bars, and cafés. The promenade offers a safe alternative to the short drive and is well illuminated at night.

SIGHTS

ESTORIL CASINO

Av. Dr. Stanley Ho, tel. 214 667 700, www. casino-estoril.pt, daily 3pm-3am

The largest in Europe, Estoril Casino is in the heart of Estoril, separated from the coast by sprawling, manicured gardens that slope gently upward toward the glitzy casino building. During World War II, the casino was a convergence point for spies and dispossessed royals. Its colorful history also provided inspiration for Ian Fleming's James Bond 007 novel *Casino Royale.* With nightly entertainment and myriad slot machines, Estoril Casino is the ultimate place for dinner and a show. As well as the main games area, it has restaurants, bars, nightclubs, and a theater.

Estoril Casino

TOP EXPERIENCE

✪ ESTORIL-CASCAIS BOARDWALK

The Estoril-Cascais boardwalk is an enjoyable 3-km (2-mi) promenade that hems the beachfront between the two towns. Trimmed by bars and restaurants on one side and stunning beach views on the other, it is popular among exercise-loving locals who take advantage of its smooth, flat surface to jog and power-walk. The promenade is bookended by two train stations: the São João do Estoril station at the eastern end and the Cascais terminus at

Tamariz Beach

the western end. Along the route are interesting historical buildings and some of the finest beaches in the region, and it's is particularly wonderful on a balmy summer's evening.

CASTELINHO SÃO JOÃO DO ESTORIL

EN6, São João do Estoril seafront
Watch out for this quizzical cliff-top property, also known as the Little Castle, located along the main Marginal Road just before Estoril. Though not open to visitors, it's reputedly one of the most haunted places in Portugal, and it has an austere, gothic-like exterior that plays up its spooky reputation. Local legend has it that a childlike ghost holding a doll has been spotted roaming the grounds and cliff tops in front of the property. Urban stories say this is the ghost of a blind girl who fell from the cliffs to her death. With its patterned turrets and oversized pointy

battlements the property is incredibly theatrical and worth a photo. It is located on the seafront in the small town of São João do Estoril, just before Estoril proper.

SPORTS AND RECREATION

BEACHES

Tamariz Beach (Praia do Tamariz)

Avenida Marginal, directly in front of Estoril train station, no parking, open 24/7, lifeguards on duty during beach season, roughly May-Oct.
A medieval castle overlooks family-friendly Tamariz Beach (Praia do Tamariz), long, wide, calm, and clean but crowded in summer. Facilities include sun beds and umbrellas, lifeguards, public restrooms, and reasonably priced restaurants and bars. Adjacent to the beach is a saltwater pool, great for swimming when the waves get rough.

Poça Beach (São João do Estoril Beach)
(Praia da Poça/Praia de São João de Estoril)

Avenida Marginal, São João do Estoril, limited parking in vicinity, open 24/7, lifeguards on duty during beach season, roughly May-Oct.

Poça Beach (also known as São João do Estoril Beach) in São João do Estoril is a small, sandy beach smattered with rocky patches, along the back of which runs a pretty promenade lined with beach bars and cafés. It is delimited by two large cliffs on top of which stand a couple of old fortresses: Forte Velho, also known as Forte da Poça, at the one end, and the Forte de São Teodósio da Cadaveira at the other. This beach is located halfway between the São João do Estoril and the main Estoril train stations, so it's easily accessible by public transport and by car.

São Pedro do Estoril Beach
(Praia de São Pedro do Estoril)

Avenida Marginal, São Pedro do Estoril, open 24/7, lifeguards on duty during beach season, roughly May-Oct.

Conveniently located a short walk from the São Pedro do Estoril train station, this wide wedge of golden sand is not as big as some of its neighbors, but it is just as popular. It appeals to an array of visitors: The choppy surf attracts surfers, while the low tidepools are loved by families. Nestled between beautiful ravines, São Pedro do Estoril Beach is particularly popular among bodyboarders and very busy in summer.

Carcavelos Beach
(Praia de Carcavelos)

Avenida Marginal, 15-minute drive from Lisbon along Marginal Road, good parking, open 24/7, lifeguards on duty during beach season, roughly May-Oct.

Carcavelos Beach is a sprawling, popular beach, with plenty of parking on the doorstep, though it does fill up fast in the warmer months. A quick 20-minute train ride from Lisbon's Cais do Sodré station, exiting in Carcavelos, it is one of the largest beaches in the Lisbon region, with 1.5 km (0.9 mi) of soft, golden sands. Carcavelos Beach has excellent facilities, including plenty of sun beds and parasols, surf and sports equipment rentals, and restaurants. Carcavelos's array of sport and surf facilities attracts a young, active crowd, as well as families, thanks to its clean, safe waters. The waves are moderately sized for most of the year, except late autumn and winter, when the swells grow and the surf becomes rougher, making it popular among more experienced surfers. At the eastern end of the beach is the imposing São Julião da Barra fort, the largest and most impressive military defense complex in the Vauban style remaining in Portugal.

GOLF
Estoril Golf Course

Av. República, tel. 214 648 000, www.clubegolfestoril.com, greens fees from €50

Acclaimed 18-hole, par 69 Estoril Golf Course is nestled in the woods above the beach. It was designed by Jean Gassiat and Mackenzie Ross and opened in 1929.

SPAS
Estoril Wellness Center & Spa

Termas do Estoril, Rua Particular Hotel Palácio, tel. 214 658 600, www.estorilwellnesscenter.pt, daily 8am-9:30pm

The Estoril Wellness Center & Spa harnesses the natural properties of the local springs for soothing treatments, including whirlpools and massages.

Guincho Beach

SURFING

The number one spot in this area for all types of surfing is rugged, wind-swept **Guincho Beach** (page 110), a short drive from Cascais on Portugal's west coast. **Carcavelos Beach, São Pedro do Estoril Beach,** and **Bolina Beach** are also all popular with surfers of all capabilities, from learners to pros.

Brands Co Store

Rua Sacadura Cabral 40, tel. 215 879 869, www.brandsco.store, Mon.-Sat. 9am-7:30pm

Brands Co Store, a short stroll from the São Pedro do Estoril train station, provides surf equipment rentals as well as lessons through partner companies and a board repair service.

SurfnPaddle Company

Praia da Duquesa, tel. 933 258 114, www. surfnpaddle.com, daily 9am-7pm (may vary in winter)

In Estoril proper, the SurfnPaddle Company offers a variety of surf lessons, stand-up paddleboarding (SUP) classes, organized SUP and surf group parties, and gear rentals.

SHOPPING

Feira de Artesanato do Estoril

FIARTIL, Av. Amaral, tel. 214 677 019 or 912 590 249, weekdays 6pm-midnight, weekends 5pm-midnight, June-early Sept.

A nightly summer handicraft fair called Feira de Artesanato do Estoril is held behind the Estoril Casino, featuring about 300 artisans working on their wares plus food stands. The traditional Portuguese entertainment starts at around 9pm nightly.

FOOD

✪ Pastelaria Garrett

Av. Nice 54, tel. 214 680 365, Weds.-Mon. 8am-7pm, €5

Open since 1934, celebrated bakery and cake shop Pastelaria Garrett was once frequented by royalty and remains a popular haunt for Portuguese celebrities. Its displays are crammed with colorful sweet treats. It's busiest at lunchtime, and in December queues for traditional Christmas cakes spill into the street.

Gordinni Estoril

Av. Marginal 7191, tel. 214 672 205, www.gordinniestoril.com, Thurs.-Tues. noon-3:30pm and 7pm-11:30pm, €15

In the heart of Estoril with views over the bay, cozy Gordinni Estoril has a huge menu of freshly baked pizzas and pastas and is famous for its sangria and *caipirinha* cocktails.

Bolina Restaurant

Rua Olivença 151, tel. 214 687 821, www. bolina.fish, daily 10am-7pm, €20

With a prime position on the boardwalk, long-established Bolina Restaurant specializes in simple grilled fish, seafood, and meats—and sunset views.

NIGHTLIFE AND ENTERTAINMENT
Tamariz Beach Club

Av. Marginal 7669, tel. 919 573 899, Weds.-Sun. 11:30pm-4:30am

Fashionable Tamariz Beach Club is a popular place to be seen with a cocktail in hand. It has great views over the coast and gets lively after the sun goes down.

Piano Bar

Rua Olivença 6, tel. 939 103 654, Tues.-Sun. 10pm-4am

Atmospheric Piano Bar is a bluesy hangout with live music every night.

ACCOMMODATIONS
Hotel Estoril Eden

Av. de Saboia 209, Monte Estoril, tel. 214 667 600, www.hotelestorileden.pt; €188 d

A 200-meter (220-yard) walk from the beach, four-star Hotel Estoril Eden once hosted grand parties but is now a firm family favorite with

162 rooms. Most of its verandas offer nice views.

✪ Palácio Estoril Hotel

Rua Particular and Av. Biarritz, tel. 214 648 000, www.palacioestorilhotel.com, €270 d

Built in 1930, the storied Palácio Estoril Hotel was the refuge of choice for royalty fleeing World War II. Frequented by artists, writers, and spies, it later served as a set for the James Bond movie *On Her Majesty's Secret Service*. The hotel still retains many of its original features, decor, and beautiful gardens.

Intercontinental Estoril

Av. Marginal 8023, tel. 218 291 100, www. estorilintercontinental.com, €345 d

The imposing modern, glass-fronted Intercontinental Estoril stands out from the coastal landscape. All rooms have floor-to-ceiling sliding doors and private balconies, making the most of the views from its prime position midway between Estoril and Cascais.

INFORMATION AND SERVICES

- **PSP police station:** just behind Estoril Casino, tel. 214 646 700, www.psp.pt
- **Main post office:** Rua 9 de Abril 371, tel. 214 649 977

GETTING THERE AND AROUND

A lovely and safe 3-kilometer (2-mile) **seafront promenade** connects Estoril to Cascais, providing an enjoyable walk between the two. The town of Estoril is easily covered **on foot.**

CAR

Estoril is a 25-kilometer (16-mile) drive west of Lisbon. The easiest and fastest route (20 minutes) is the **A5** motorway, which has tolls. The scenic **Marginal coastal road (N6)** is toll-free but takes a little longer (about 45 minutes) and gets busy at commuter rush hours and on weekends.

TRAIN

CP trains (tel. 707 210 220, www.cp.pt) run about every half hour from **Lisbon's Cais do Sodré train station** 36 minutes along the coast to the **São João do Estoril Station** (€2.25 one way) and continue to Cascais. Trains are less frequent after dark.

There are four stations in Estoril: **São Pedro do Estoril, São João do Estoril, Estoril** (for the town, the casino, and Tamariz Beach), and **Monte Estoril** (halfway between Estoril and Cascais).

BUS

The local urban **Scotturb bus** (tel. 214 699 100, www.scotturb.com) runs between Estoril, **Cascais,** and Sintra, departing from outside Estoril train station. Lines 406, 407, 411, 412, and 416 run frequently between Cascais and Estoril (€3.35).

Cascais

Perched on the western tip of the coastline, cosmopolitan little Cascais (kash-KAIZH), with its picturesque bay and elegant marina, is one of Lisbon's wealthiest suburbs. King Luís I of Portugal made the seaside hamlet his summer home in the 1870s, and it has been a magnet for the rich and famous ever since. Despite hosting some of the most exclusive resorts in the country, Cascais maintains the charm of a fishing village.

On weekends, city dwellers drive the scenic Marginal coast road from Lisbon to Cascais to enjoy people-watching in its cafés and bars. Just north of town is windswept Guincho Beach, popular among surfers. A beachside promenade connects to nearby Estoril, perfect for an after-lunch or evening stroll.

SIGHTS

SANTA MARTA LIGHTHOUSE AND MUSEUM
(Farol Museu de Santa Marta)

Praceta Farol, tel. 214 815 328, www.cascais. pt, Tues.-Fri. 10am-5pm, Sat.-Sun. 10am-1pm and 2pm-5pm, €5

Built in 1868, the distinctive blue-and-white-striped Santa Marta lighthouse peers over Cascais Marina. Located to the south of Cascais center, it is a beacon for sailors around the bay. The quadrangular tower stands 8 meters (26 feet) tall and houses an interesting little museum in a neighboring building dedicated to lighthouse history. The views over Cascais from the top of the tower are fantastic, but it can be climbed only on Wednesdays.

PAULA REGO MUSEUM
(Casa das Histórias Paula Rego)

Avenida da República, 300, tel. 214 826 970, www.casadashistoriaspaularego.com, Tues.-Sun. 10am-6pm, €5

An intriguing building dedicated to one of Portugal's most famous and divisive current artists, the Paula Rego Museum was designed by acclaimed Portuguese architect Eduardo Souto de Moura at the artist's personal request. Paula Rego is a Portuguese-born visual artist best known for her thought-provoking storybook-based paintings and prints, whose descriptions range from disturbing to brilliant. Inaugurated in 2009, the ochre-red pyramidlike building sits in stark contrast with its azure, palm-tree-lined, Riviera-like surroundings. Consisting of four wings, comprising permanent collections and temporary exhibitions, it also has an auditorium, a café, and a gift shop; the collection includes 15 paintings by Rego's late husband, Victor Willing.

✪ BOCA DO INFERNO

1.5 km (1 mi) west of Cascais town

The dramatically named Boca do Inferno (Hell's Mouth) is a striking rock formation carved by relentless tides. After the ceaseless pounding caused the original cave to give way, it left behind an intriguing rock formation in the shape of a grotto and a large archway. Stunning coastal views can be enjoyed from the paths up and down the cliff. In summer, when the seas are calmer, the translucent turquoise water laps gently around the formation's base. In winter, huge waves lash the rock and cliffs—at times the spray from the crashing waves can dwarf the cliffs themselves. It's about 1.5 kilometers (1 mile) west of Cascais town, roughly a half-hour stroll along the coast. A scattering of cafés and market stalls selling souvenirs and gifts can be found here. You'll probably need around an hour to walk around the site, admire the views and the waves crashing against the cliffs, take a few photos, and enjoy a coffee or an ice cream from one of the nearby cafés.

There are a number of routes to walk from Cascais town center to

Boca do Inferno

The Cascais coastline has some of the most dramatic and inspiring scenery in the country, from romantic twinkling lights, sea and stars, to awe-inducing waves and cliffs.

- **Estoril-Cascais Promenade:** Join the locals for some power-walking or enjoy a romantic stroll as you take in the scenery of the stunning Estoril-Cascais coastline and beaches that stretch out along the boardwalk. This is a particularly lovely walk at dusk or dawn (page 98).

- **Boca do Inferno:** Admire the enormity of the coast and the vastness of the Atlantic from this uniquely shaped rock formation (page 104).

- **Guincho Beach:** The rugged dunes and rolling waves of wind-battered Guincho give this stretch of coast a formidable landscape, perfect for an invigorating stroll (page 110).

- **Cabo da Roca:** Who doesn't love the novelty of being able to say they have stood on the westernmost point of mainland Europe? And the coastal and ocean views are just as dramatic (page 111).

Boca do Inferno, which all generally take 20-40 minutes (depending on the pace). The most enjoyable is perhaps along the mostly flat **Avenida Rei Humberto II de Itália,** a seaside route that offers delightful ocean views as you walk past Cascais marina and lighthouse. You can also **bike** along the cycle path there, or take a **cab.**

CASA DA GUIA
(Guia House)

Avenida Nossa Senhora do Cabo 101, tel. 214 843 215, http://casadaguiacascais.com, 9am-2am daily, free

A 40-minute walk from Cascais town center, this 19th-century manor house is surrounded by 2 hectares (5 acres) of lovely gardens. Within the walls of the historic mansion are arts and crafts stalls, novelty shops, cafés and restaurants, and glorious ocean views, which altogether makes it worth spending an hour or two in Casa da Guia. There is limited parking on the road outside the mansion, which runs between Cascais and Guincho.

SPORTS AND RECREATION
BEACHES
Ribeira Beach
(Praia da Ribeira)

Cascais's main beach, Praia da Ribeira, also often referred to as Praia dos Pescadores, or Fishermen's Beach, is a charming little chunk of sand directly in front of the main town center. Overlooking Cascais's marina and docks, the beach can get pretty crowded in summer and on weekends, but there are plenty of parking lots in the vicinity. The water is very calm and cool, and the beach is just a short walk from Cascais train station.

Rainha Beach
(Praia da Rainha)

Just before Cascais's main Ribeira Beach, heading west from Estoril to Cascais, is Rainha Beach, a small, clean, bay-like beach with crystalline waters and soft sands studded with rock formations. Sun beds and umbrellas are available to the public to rent for around €20 per day. The beach is a 50-meter (150-foot) walk to Cascais high street.

Guincho Beach (Praia Grande do Guincho)
Guincho Road N247, open 24/7

Rugged, reedy, and windswept, Guincho Beach is a die-hard surfer's delight. Wild in winter and spacious in summer, vast Guincho faces straight out into the Atlantic, meaning waves and winds can be powerful and the water is significantly cooler than elsewhere along the Estoril-Cascais coast. The untamed beach is a popular location for international surfing competitions, plus there are a handful of surf rental outfits and excellent seafood restaurants on hand. It falls within Sintra-Cascais Natural Park, and Guincho's beautiful white sand dunes sit in stark contrast with the deep green carpet that covers the rolling hills of the Sintra mountain range. There is plenty of beachside parking, and a mostly flat cycle track runs 10 km (6 mi) between Cascais and Guincho. Guincho can also be reached by taking the train to Cascais, then the local BUSCAS bus service (www.mobicascais.pt) to Guincho Beach.

SAILING
Cascais Marina
Casa de São Bernardo, tel. 214 824 857, www.mymarinacascais.com

With a capacity for several hundred vessels, Cascais Marina regularly hosts sailing competitions and international events. It's also home to elegant restaurants and boutiques.

CYCLING
Portugal Rent Bike
Rua da Palmeira 39A, tel. 934 432 304, www.portugalrentbike.com, daily 9am-9pm

Enjoy one of Cascais' most popular bike rides, a 10-kilometer (6-mile) return trip along a flat and smooth purpose-made cycle path between Cascais and the stunning surfing beach of Praia de Guincho. It's an enjoyable half-day activity, taking in dramatic coastline, cliffs, beautiful beaches, and numerous interesting sights such as the **Boca do Inferno** and **Casa da Guia.** Stop at Guincho beach for a fresh seafood lunch at the swanky beach-shack-chic **Porto Santa Maria Restaurant** (Estrada do Guincho, tel. 214 879 450, www.portosantamaria.com, daily noon-11pm, €60).

GOLF
Penha Longa resort
Estrada da Lagoa Azul Sintra Linhó, tel. 219 249 031, www.penhalonga.com

The Penha Longa resort is home to one of Europe's top-30 golf courses, the 18-hole Atlantic Championship course (€74 per round) with rolling greens, world-class facilities, and the Sintra Mountains as a backdrop.

Quinta da Marinha
Rua do Clube, tel. 214 860 100, www.quintadamarinha.com, greens fees from €95

Quinta da Marinha is the site of an 18-hole, par 71 course designed by Robert Trent Jones, with a different challenge on every hole and amazing views over the mountains and the Atlantic.

SHOPPING

The lovely pedestrian street **Rua da Raita** is Cascais's main shopping street. It's a pleasant, pedestrianized, cobbled street with a distinctive black and white wavy pattern, lined with European fashion boutiques and the obligatory tourist souvenir shops.

Casa da Guia

MARKETS

Every Saturday and Sunday, **antiques and handicrafts fairs** are held in the **Visconde da Luz garden** in the heart of the town center and at nearby **Casa da Guia** (Av. Nossa Senhora do Cabo 101, tel. 214 843 215) in a 19th-century mansion on the road from Cascais to Guincho Beach, a 2-kilometer (1.25-mile) walk west of town that takes about 30 minutes.

Visconde da Luz Garden Antique Fair

Visconde da Luz Garden, Av. dos Combatentes da Grande Guerra, Weds. only 9am-8pm

Soak up the sights, sounds and smells of yesteryear at this bustling antique market brimming with interesting paraphernalia and collectors' items, from silverware to books and vinyl records.

Saloio Farmers Market/ Municipal Market Place

Rua Padre Moisés da Silva 29, Municipal Market Place, tel. 214 825 000, Weds. and Sat. 7am-1pm

Get your fill of tasty fresh produce or pack for a picnic at the Saloio Famers Market, which showcases the best regional delicacies like cured meats and cheeses.

MALLS
Cascais Villa

Avenida Dom Pedro, tel. 214 828 250, www.cascaisvilla.pt, daily 10am-10pm

Located on the road heading out of town toward Estoril, the Cascais Villa shopping center is small but perfectly formed, with its interesting blue glass feature front, a decent selection of shops and restaurants in the food court, and a supermarket.

CascaiShopping

Estrada Nacional 9, tel. 210 121 628, www.cascaishopping.pt, daily 10am-11pm daily

The larger of Cascais's shopping malls, CascaiShopping is a good place to bear in mind if the weather turns cool or rainy. Packed with trendy shops, from high street names to designer brands, and fun eateries, the mall also has wheelchairs and baby strollers available on request, a medical center, and a movie theater.

FOOD
Masala

Rua Frederico Arouca 288, tel. 214 865 334, www.restaurantemasala.pt, daily 10am-11pm, €13

Time-honored Indian restaurant Masala is a little jewel with vibrant decor to match the food.

✪ Marisco na Praça

Rua Padre Moisés da Silva 34, tel. 214 822 130, daily noon-midnight, €20

Don't miss the Marisco na Praça for old-fashioned seafood. In the town center, this no-frills *marisqueira* is both market stall and eatery, offering fresh catch. Have the seafood cooked here and served at the table.

Hemingway Cascais

Marina de Cascais 58, tel. 916 224 452,
www.hemingwaycascais.com, Thurs.-Tues.
7pm-late, €20

Romantic Hemingway Cascais, on Cascais Marina, is run by Pedro and Telma Vaz Moura, and its contemporary menu has cool twists on staples like fresh fish, steak, and risotto, complemented by extensive cocktail service until the wee hours. Take in a gorgeous sunset on the roof terrace.

LOVit

Av. Nossa Senhora do Cabo 101, Guincho,
tel. 214 862 230, www.restaurantelovit.com,
daily 12:30pm-11pm, €25

Trendy sushi restaurant LOVit has visually stunning delicacies served overlooking the sea from the Casa da Guia cliffs, a short stroll west of Cascais center.

Conceito Food Store

Rua Pequena, tel. 218 085 281, www.
conceitofoodstore.pt, Tues.-Sat.
noon-3:30pm and 7:45pm-11pm, Sun.
noon-3:30pm, €30

Traditional Portuguese cuisine is given a modern overhaul at Conceito Food Store, an in-demand restaurant with minimalist decor. Products from local suppliers are transformed into contemporary masterpieces. Taster menus add to the gastronomic experience.

BARS AND NIGHTLIFE

Cascais Jazz Club

Largo Cidade da Vitória 36, tel. 962 773
470, www.facebook.com/cascaisjazzclub,
Thurs.-Sun. 9:30pm-12:30am

This surprisingly agreeable little jazz house has live jazz sessions every Thursday, Friday, and Saturday night and Sunday afternoon.

O'Luain's Irish Pub

Rua da Palmeira 4, tel. 214 861 627,
daily noon-2am

There's always good *craic* at this typical Irish pub in the heart of old town Cascais, just back from the main beach. With live music on Fridays, Saturdays, and Sundays, it's a popular hangout among ex-pats and holidaymakers.

Shisha House

Rua Alexandre Herculano, 21,
tel. 210 176 925 / 925 724 165,
www.facebook.com/shishahousecascais,
open 6pm-3am Mon-Sat, closed Sun.

Exotic and funky, this is the place to head for a drink with a theme. Groovy colored lighting and mosaic tables give this Hookah Lounge a twist to complement the cocktails, teas, and shisha.

Iceberg Bar

Marina de Cascais, unit 19, first floor,
tel. 914 645 646, Thurs.-Sat. 7pm-3am,
7pm-2am Sun.-Weds.

On Cascais Marina, Iceberg Bar is a friendly place to get the night started. Karaoke and great drinks are the perfect recipe for a great start to a night on the town. The esplanade has lovely views over Cascais and the twinkling marina.

ACCOMMODATIONS

✪ Hotel Baía Cascais

Av. Marginal, tel. 214 831 033,
www.hotelbaia.com, €130 d

In the heart of Cascais, on the beachfront, the large three-star Hotel Baía Cascais offers a first-rate location at accessible prices. Ideal for families or groups, it has 113 rooms, 66 of which have sea-view verandas.

Pestana Cidadela Cascais

Av. Dom Carlos I, tel. 214 814 300, www.pestana.com, €291 d

Luxury hotel Pestana Cidadela Cascais, converted from a 16th-century fortress, is perched on an elevated citadel wall overlooking Cascais Marina. Its exterior is centuries old, but inside, the petite five-star hotel is chic and contemporary. A short walk into Cascais town center, it offers complimentary breakfast and round-the-clock room service.

INFORMATION AND SERVICES

- **PSP police station:** Rua Afonso Sanches 26, tel. 214 814 060, www.psp.pt
- **Cascais Visitors Center:** Praça 5 de Outubro, tel. 912 034 214, daily 9am-8pm
- **Main post office:** Av. Ultramar 2, tel. 214 827 281

GETTING THERE AND AROUND

Once you arrive, compact Cascais itself is easily covered on foot.

CAR

Cascais is 35 kilometers (22 miles) west of Lisbon's city center. The two main routes are the **A5** motorway, which has tolls, or the more scenic but often much busier **Marginal coastal road (N6)**, which runs parallel to the A5, passing pine-tree countryside, luxury villas, and old forts. On a good day, both routes take 30 minutes. With traffic, the Marginal can crawl, but the scenery is lovely. It's busiest at rush hour on weekdays and on weekends in good weather.

TRAIN

During the day, **CP trains** (tel. 707 210 220, www.cp.pt) run approximately every 30 minutes from the **Cais do Sodré** station in Lisbon along the coast to Cascais (€2.25 one way). The journey takes approximately 40 minutes. Trains are less frequent after dark but still run until around 1:30am. The **train station** in Cascais is on Largo da Estação, a 10-minute stroll east of the town center.

The CP train on the Lisbon-Cascais line runs frequently and is the quickest way to travel between Cascais and **Estoril's** seafront station. The journey takes just three minutes, and a one-way ticket (€1.30) can be bought at the station from machines or the ticket office. Cascais is also a pleasant 3-kilometer (2-mile) walk west from Estoril along a lovely flat seafront promenade with lots to see—tide pools, cafés and bars, and quirky old houses.

BUS

The local urban **Scotturb bus** (tel. 214 699 100, www.scotturb.com) runs between **Estoril**, Cascais, and Sintra. The main **bus terminal** in Cascais is beneath the **Cascais Villa shopping mall** (level 0), just north of the Cascais railway station and town center. From here, buses depart at least once an hour for the main destinations of **Guincho Beach, Cabo da Roca,** and Sintra. Lines 406, 407, 411, 412, and 416 run frequently between Cascais and Estoril, while line 418 runs between Cascais and Sintra. Line 403 passes Cabo da Roca, and lines 405 and 415 run to Guincho Beach.

Guincho Beach

Seven kilometers (4.3 miles) northwest of Cascais, windswept Guincho Beach (Praia do Guincho) is rugged and un-bridled, with vast coastal dunes that make the landscape almost desolate. It's located on the western fringe of the **Serra da Sintra National Park**, and the waves that roll in from the Atlantic make it popular for surfing, windsurf-ing, and kite-surfing, rather than for relaxation.

At 800 meters (half a mile) long, Guincho Beach and the surround-ing dunes are a prime spot for surfers, but there's not really much else to do or see here except surf and relax. But for those who are planning to spend a morning, afternoon, or even a full day here, the beach has good facilities, including public showers and toilets, beach bars, restaurants, and surf shops.

SURFING
Guincho Surf Shop
Praia do Guincho Estalagem Muchaxo,
tel. 214 850 286, www.guinchosurfshop.com,
daily 9am-6pm

Guincho Surf Shop, right on the beach, provides everything from lessons to equipment rentals.

Guincho Beach Bar & Wave Center
tel. 214 647 013 or 918 500 041, www.
bardoguincho.pt/en/wave-center, daily
9am-late

Situated just 50 meters (55 yards) from the beach, the Guincho Beach Bar & Wave Center covers a multitude of needs. It offers a range of facilities including lockers, board and equip-ment rentals, a surf school, a shop that stocks equipment and beach-wear, and changing rooms with hot showers.

GETTING THERE AND AROUND
CAR
Guincho is a 15-minute drive north-west from Cascais, following the Rua Joaquim Ereira road or the **N247** coastal road.

BUS
The local urban **Scotturb bus** (tel. 214 699 125, www.scotturb.com) lines 405 and 415 run between **Cascais** (from the main terminal beneath the Cascais Villa shopping center) and Guincho at least once an hour. Tickets cost about €2.

BIKE
Alternately, rent a **bicycle** in Cascais from a shop such as the **Portugal Rent Bike** (Rua da Palmeira 39A, tel. 934 432 304, www.portugalrentbike. com, daily 9am-9pm) to ride the scenic 5-kilometer (3-mile) cycle path from Cascais to Guincho.

✪ Cabo da Roca

For invigorating sea air, stand on mainland Europe's most westerly point at Cabo da Roca (www.cm-sintra.pt), flanked by gigantic granite boulders and dramatic vertical cliffs that drop 100 meters (328 feet) to the Atlantic. A solitary rock monument marks the spot with a crucifix and an engraved quote from Portugal's greatest poet, Luís de Camões, who declared in his epic *Os Lusíadas* that this is where "land ends and sea begins." A short walk away, Portugal's first purpose-built **lighthouse** has a **gift shop** that offers certificates confirming that visitors set foot on the western edge of Europe. Pack a jacket; this promontory is blustery and cold.

GETTING THERE AND AROUND

CAR
Cabo da Roca is 40 kilometers (25 miles) west of **Lisbon,** 15 kilometers (9.3 miles) north of **Cascais.** The drive takes around 25 minutes following the **N247** road.

BUS
The **Scotturb bus** (tel. 214 699 125, www.scotturb.com, €4) line 403, which runs from **Cascais** to Sintra, also stops here once an hour during the day, but services are irregular; check the schedule in advance.

Cabo da Roca lighthouse

SINTRA

If Sintra had to be summed up in just one word, it would be "magical"—a whimsical resort set into the picturesque, green foothills of the Sintra Mountains. Inland from windy Cabo da Roca and Guincho Beach, this fairytale forest town has a misty microclimate all its own, cooled by the Atlantic breeze that comes whooshing up the plains from the coast, made fragrant by the pine trees that cover the hills. This cooler climate made Sintra a popular spot for summer residences for Europe's aristocrats and wealthy artists, whose flamboyant mansions were

HIGHLIGHTS

✪ **PENA PALACE:** The Disney-like Pena Palace, high on a hill overlooking Sintra, is one of Portugal's most recognizable and popular attractions (page 116).

✪ **MOORISH CASTLE:** The ruins of sturdy Moorish Castle hark back to the stronghold's former glory days and offer breathtaking views over Sintra and beyond (page 117).

✪ **REGALEIRA ESTATE:** With its grand Gothic facade, gargoyles, mystic gardens, and secret passages, the Regaleira Estate is eerie and enthralling in equal measure (page 118).

inspired by the Romanticism of the era. Sintra's most famous attraction, the hilltop Pena Palace, is straight out of a Disney movie, while the town center's multihued historic mansions are swaddled by lush greenery. It's a little hub of theatrical extravagance. Other fascinating sights include the Gothic Sintra National Palace and the spooky Quinta da Regaleira (Regaleira Estate).

ORIENTATION

Most of Sintra's major sights are within **walking distance** the historic town center, albeit one or two entail steep-ish climbs: walking from the center to Pena Palace is recommended only for avid hikers.

Sintra National Palace is in the heart of Sintra's historic center; as such it is also often referred to as the "Town Palace." **Pena Palace,** the **Regaleira Estate,** and the **Moorish Castle** are all located in the hills west of the town center.

Quinta da Regaleira is the closest and easiest attraction to reach on foot from the town center, a 15-minute walk up a couple of small hills. Both Pena Palace and the Moorish Castle take around 50 minutes to reach on foot, up challenging climbs. The route

to Pena Palace involves a particularly steep hill, so taking the **434 tourist bus** from the **train station** to visit these two sights is recommended. The train station is located on the northeastern fringe of town, about 3 kilometers (2 miles) from Pena Palace.

Another tourist bus—the **435**—connects Sintra train station to the **Regaleira Estate** (a short walk from Sintra center), and **Monserrate Palace,** among others.

Most of the shops and restaurants in Sintra are clustered in the historic town center.

PLANNING YOUR TIME

Packed with elaborate mansions, grand monuments, and quirky attractions—and often much cooler than the rest of Lisbon (pack a windbreaker, just in case!)—Sintra a wonderful place that offers so many amazing vistas and experiences that it should definitely be top of the agenda when visiting Lisbon.

Deservedly popular, Sintra sadly has become victim of its own soaring popularity, and the town can often be packed with tourists and traffic, especially in peak season (July and

August), which means long queues and a lack of parking. Driving here is not recommended, even more so because public transport from Lisbon is cheap and easy. At least **a full day** should be allocated to really enjoy the essence of Sintra and see its top attractions, but there's enough to see and do here to justify spending a night, if you have the time. An **overnight stay** will allow you to visit the most popular monuments outside the usual day-tripper hours, when it might be quieter and queues shorter, as well as see some of Sintra's lesser-known attractions.

Sintra is located some 25 kilometers (15.5 miles) west of Lisbon; **trains** run regularly from Lisbon, with the journey taking just under an hour. From Sintra train station, the **434 tourist** bus runs a circular route from the station to the historic center, Pena Palace, Moorish Castle, and back to the station. There will also be plenty of **taxis** waiting outside the station.

The main sights—the **National Palace, Pena Palace, Moorish Castle,** and **Quinta da Regaleira**— are all within walking distance, but you'd be hard-pressed to see them all in a day, at least not at a leisurely pace. Staying the night allows you to go slightly further afield, for example to the **Montserrate Historic Park and Palace.**

Enjoy lunch at one of the many charming little restaurants that can be found in the historic center, but be aware: as with the monuments, they can be quite busy, especially during summer.

Itinerary Idea

ESSENTIAL SINTRA

Leave Lisbon for Sintra as early as possible to avoid the crowds; take the train from **Rossio** or **Oriente.** Trains run roughly between 6am and midnight. This itinerary can easily accommodate an **overnight** visit: Do everything up to the National Palace on Day 1, saving the Regaleira Estate for the next day and adding a stop at **Monserrate Palace.** This will give you a chance to beat the crowds, especially by taking advantage of the monuments' extended opening hours in summer.

1 Take the 434 bus from outside Sintra train station straight to **Pena Palace,** getting there as early as possible. Allow at least a few hours to see the palace, including its magnificent gardens.

2 Walk the 200 meters (220 yards) from the palace to the **Moorish Castle;** allocate another hour to explore this sturdy fortress nestled in the hills.

3 Take the 434 bus back down to the historic center for a spot of lunch at **Café Saudade.**

Sintra

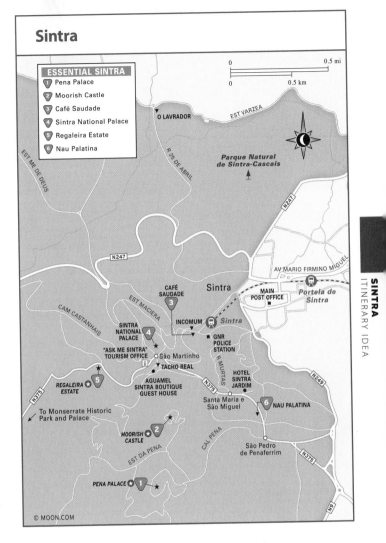

ESSENTIAL SINTRA
1. Pena Palace
2. Moorish Castle
3. Café Saudade
4. Sintra National Palace
5. Regaleira Estate
6. Nau Palatina

© MOON.COM

4 After lunch, head to the **National Palace** in the historic center.

5 Round off your day by strolling up to the **Regaleira Estate.**

6 Finish your day in Sintra with Mediterranean and Portuguese tapas at **Nau Palatina** before returning to Lisbon by train.

Sights

SINTRA NATIONAL PALACE
(Palácio Nacional de Sintra)

Largo Rainha Dona Amélia, tel. 219 237 300, www.parquesdesintra.pt, daily 9:30am-7pm late Mar.-late Oct., daily 9:30am-6pm late Oct.-late Mar., €10

In the town center, the Sintra National Palace was the residence of Portugal's royal families in the 15th to 19th centuries and today is the first stop for many visitors. Its white Gothic exterior, with some Manueline features, is minimalist, a counterpoint to the extravagance of the fanciful Pena Palace on the hilltop. The wow factor of the detailed interior makes up for the exterior. A bird motif is evident in the Magpie Room and the Swan Room, with its octagonal paneled ceiling. The rudimentary Moorish kitchen is topped with huge conical chimneys. Most splendid is the 16th-century Coats of Arms room, where the paneled ceiling contains the coats of arms of 72 aristocratic families. **Guided tours** (2:30pm daily, 90 minutes, €5) are available in Portuguese, English, and Spanish. Reservations and online discounts are available via the website.

TOP EXPERIENCE

✪ PENA PALACE
(Palácio Nacional da Pena)

Estrada da Pena, tel. 219 237 300, www.parquesdesintra.pt, daily 9:30am-8pm, €14, bus 434

Portugal's finest example of 19th-century Romantic architecture,

Pena Palace

SINTRA'S BEST VIEWS

- **Pena Palace:** Perched atop a steep hill on the outskirts of Sintra town, the vividly colorful Pena Palace offers a plethora of viewpoints, from all angles and fronts, giving bird's-eye views of the surrounding landscape (page 116).

- **Moorish Castle:** Magnificent panoramic views of Sintra can be enjoyed from the battlements of the Moorish Castle, which stands on a craggy hill high above Sintra town, swaddled by dense forest (page 117).

perched on a rocky peak often shrouded in clouds, the colorful, whimsical Pena Palace wouldn't look out of place in a Disney movie. Commissioned in 1838 by the young German-born King Ferdinand II for his wife, Portuguese Maria II, and built on the site of an abandoned 16th-century monastery, the project was entrusted to amateur architect Wilhelm Ludwig von Eschwege. The imitation medieval fortress that resulted includes a jumble of watchtowers, turrets, terraces, a tunnel, and even a drawbridge.

The bold pink, gray, and ocher can be seen for miles. The interior is just as eccentric, with stuccos, trompe-l'oeil murals, and *azulejo* plaques. Note the exquisite carved chairs and vaulted ceiling in the Royal Dining Room, the rich upholstery in the Noble Room, and the orchestra of brass pots and pans in the kitchen. The Queen's Terrace and a clock tower offer the best views. **Guided tours** (2:30pm daily, 90 minutes, €5) are available in Portuguese, English, and Spanish, and require prior booking. Reservations and online discounts are available via the website.

✪ MOORISH CASTLE
(Castelo de Mouros)

Estrada da Pena, Parque de Monserrate, tel. 219 237 300, www.parquesdesintra. pt, daily 9:30am-8pm late Mar.-late Oct., daily 9:30am-7pm late Oct.-late Mar., €8, bus 434

Surrounded by lush forest, the crumbling old Moorish Castle provides excellent views from its towering stone walls and extensive ramparts. Built in the 9th century during Moorish occupation, the castle fell into disrepair after the Christian reconquests but was later restored in the 19th century by Ferdinand II, who incorporated it into the vast gardens surrounding Pena Palace. As one of Portugal's most recognizable landmarks, the hilltop Pena Palace is a feast of architectural geniality, one of the most remarkable examples of 19th century Romanticist castles in the country as well as one of its most unique and theatrical tourist attractions. A series of ornately decorated rooms, fanciful details, and stunning views await those who make their way to this fairy-tale palace.

Moorish Castle

✪ REGALEIRA ESTATE
(Quinta da Regaleira)

Rua Barbosa do Bocage 5, tel. 219 106 650, www.regaleira.pt, daily 9:30am-5pm, €6, bus 435

If the Pena Palace is a fairy tale, the sprawling Regaleira Estate, near the town center, is out of a scary movie, a spooky Gothic palace awash with gargoyles and spiky pinnacles and topped with a striking octagonal tower. Inside, a warren of hallways and stairways lead to rooms spread over five floors. The lush surroundings have hidden passages and secret spots with lakes, grottoes, wells, and fountains. The estate once belonged to the Viscountess of Regaleira, who was from a wealthy merchant family in Porto. The current building was completed in 1910.

MONSERRATE HISTORIC PARK AND PALACE
(Parque e Palácio de Monserrate)

Rua Visconde de Monserrate, tel. 219 237 300, www.parquesdesintra.pt, park daily 9:30am-8pm late Mar.-late Oct., daily 9:30am-7pm late Oct.-late Mar., palace daily 9:30am-7pm late Mar.-late Oct., daily 9:30am-6pm late Oct.-late Mar., €8, bus 435

The award-winning gardens are the main attraction at the 19th-century Monserrate Historic Park and Palace, 4 kilometers (2.5 miles) west of Sintra town. The flora ranges from romantic to wild to exotic, with species from around the world. The estate was bought in 1856 by wealthy English textile magnate Francis Cook, who commissioned architect James Knowles to design the small palace with Gothic, Indian, and Moorish influences.

Monserrate is part of the **Sintra-Cascais Natural Park** (tel. 219 247 200, www.cm-cascais.pt), which covers a third of the Cascais region, from Sintra to Cabo da Roca. It's a popular place for hiking, biking, horseback riding, and even zip-lining.

Food

Strong meaty flavors and delicious sweets are staples in this part of Portugal. Typical is *vitela à Sintrense*, a slow-roasted veal dish served with roast potatoes. The traditional *queijadas de Sintra* is a decadent sweet treat, with a creamy filling of fresh cheese and cinnamon wrapped in delicate, crisp pastry.

including regional specialties like pork cheeks, traditional Alentejo delicacies, and many vegetarian-friendly options.

Nau Palatina

Calçada de S. Pedro 18, tel. 219 240 962, Tues.-Sat. 6pm-midnight, €10

Nau Palatina is a cute little place with scrumptious Mediterranean and Portuguese haute-rustic tapas,

Café Saudade

Av. Doutor Miguel Bombarda 6, tel. 212 428 804, daily 8am-8pm, €10

The Portuguese word *saudade* roughly means "longing." This pretty eatery across from the train station fulfills longings for tasty meals and treats with an extensive menu that includes sandwiches, fresh soups and salads, coffee, and freshly baked pastries and snacks.

outdoor dining in Sintra

O Lavrador

Rua 25 de Abril 36, tel. 219 241 488,
http://restaurantelavrador.business.site,
Tues.-Sat. noon-3pm and 7:30pm-10pm, Sun.
noon-3pm, €20

Small, traditional Portuguese restaurant O Lavrador, on the main 25 de Abril road out of Sintra, has specialties that include *naco de carne na pedra* (chunks of beef on hot stone) and prawn and bacon skewers. Don't miss the Portuguese pottery hanging overhead.

Tacho Real

Rua Ferraria, 4, tel. 219 235 277,
Facebook/RestauranteTachoReal,
daily noon-3pm and 7:30pm-11pm, €20

A delightful little eatery serving typical Portuguese dishes in a historic building, complete with vaulted ceiling, *azulejo*-clad walls, a cobblestone patio, and echoes of Portuguese guitar strumming in the background.

Incomum

Rua Dr. Alfredo da Costa 22, tel. 219 243
719, www.incomumbyluissantos.pt, Sun.-Fri.
noon-midnight, Sat. 4:30pm-midnight, €30

Contemporary cuisine in the historic heart of Sintra. An exciting fusion of traditional Portuguese and modern Mediterranean fare that has taken the local culinary scene by storm.

Bars and Nightlife

Fonte da Pipa

Rua Fonte da Pipa, 11-13,
tel. 219 234 437, daily 12:30pm-2am

A popular meeting place for young people and locals, Fonte da Pipa, in Sintra's town center, is a lively, down-to-earth drinking hole with a selection of Portuguese beer and wines.

Bar Saloon Sintra

Avenida do Movimento das Forcas Armadas
N 5, tel. 914 462 761, Mon.-Fri. 8pm-2am and
Sat.-Sun. 3pm-2am

Boasting a huge range of spirits, crafts beers, and cocktails, Bar Saloon Sintra, on the southern outskirts of town, is a quirky little bar with something for everyone, good music, and nibbles.

Accommodations

Hotel Sintra Jardim

Travessa dos Avelares 12,

tel. 219 230 738,

www.hotelsintrajardim.pt, €95 d

Built from a quirky mid-19th-century building overlooking the Moors' castle, Hotel Sintra Jardim is a convenient short walk from the train station and Sintra's historic center. Its 15 classically decorated rooms overlook lush gardens and a pool, a welcome oasis after a day of exploring.

✪ Aguamel Sintra Boutique Guest House

Escadinhas da Fonte da Pipa 3, tel. 219 243 628, www.aguamelsintra.com, €120 d

In the heart of the historic center, family-run Aguamel Sintra Boutique Guest House offers a deluxe home-away-from-home experience. Contemporary on the inside, this cozy 19th-century property is a slice of history with a superb location in the town center.

Information and Services

- **GNR police station:** Rua João de Deus 6, tel. 213 252 620, www.gnr.pt
- **"Ask Me Sintra" tourism office:** Praça República 23, tel. 219 231 157, daily 9:30am-6pm
- **Main post office:** Praça Dom Afonso Henriques 7, tel. 219 241 623

Getting There and Around

GETTING THERE

CAR

Sintra is 25 kilometers (15.5 miles) west of **Lisbon** on the main **A16** motorway, a 30-minute drive. Taking the train is strongly recommended over driving to Sintra—the train is frequent, cost-efficient, and convenient. Parking is limited in the town center, restricted to residents, city buses, emergency services, commercial vehicles, and taxis. There are a few **parking lots** on the outskirts, a couple of which offer free parking, within walking distance of the historic center (www.cm-sintra.pt/car-parking-in-sintra). The roads to and in Sintra are rather narrow, and the center can become heavily congested, particularly in summer when the flux of traffic and tourists buses is at its peak.

TRAIN

CP trains (tel. 707 210 220, www.cp.pt) to Sintra run from **Lisbon's Rossio station** many times daily, roughly every half hour. A one-way ticket costs €2.25 and takes about 40 minutes. **Sintra train station** (Avenida Dr. Miguel Bombarda, tel. 707 210

220, ticket office Mon.-Fri. 6:45am-8:30pm, Sat., Sun., and public holidays 7am-8:30pm) is approximately 1.5 kilometers (1 mile) from town (about a 20-minute walk), but the **434 and 435 Sintra tourist buses** connect the station, the town center, and the main attractions such as Pena Palace.

GETTING AROUND

Sintra's compact town center can be covered **on foot**, but most sights are farther afield. The hop-on hop-off **Scotturb tourist buses** (tel. 214 699 125, www.scotturb.com) connect all the main sights.

TOURIST BUS

The **434 route** (€6.90 hop-on hop-off, €3.90 one-way) includes stops at Sintra train station, the historic town center, Pena Palace, and Moorish Castle. The **435 route** (€5 hop-on hop-off) goes to the Regaleira and Monserrate palaces. A full-day pass for all lines costs €15. Other fun ways to explore Sintra include a tourist train and *tuk-tuks,* both found in the main town center.

TUK-TUK

Operated by a number of private companies, such as **Turislua Tourist Entertainment** (tel. 219 243 881), the *tuk-tuks* can be rented for a single trip or for a full day's sightseeing—but this is a costly alternative to the bus, at around €30/hour. *Tuk-tuks* can be found near the train station and in the town center.

TOURIST TRAIN

The Sintra tourist train (tel. 918 258 001, www.comboiodesintra.pt) also takes visitors on a leisurely (and at times bumpy, thanks to the cobblestone roads) trip around the town and its attractions. It does a tour of the most emblematic locales in Sintra, including the National Palace, Quinta da Regaleira, Moorish Castle, and Pena Palace. The starting point is in the **old town center** (a two-minute walk south from the National Palace), and there's a stop on Estrada da Pena for Pena Palace visitors. The complete tour lasts 45 minutes and costs €8 (€5 children age 6-12). It takes passengers on a figure-eight loop from the historic center, north along Volta Duche (the scenic main road between the historic town center and Sintra train station), back around clockwise to the center, before climbing counterclockwise past the Regaleira Estate, Moorish Castle, and Pena Palace, and back down into town again.

MAFRA AND ERICEIRA

Mafra and Ericeira are day trips

from Lisbon with a difference. Distinct from each other and located just under an hour from the capital (there are direct buses to both), their proximity means they can be combined into one day. Steeped in heritage, Mafra, some 40 kilometers (25 miles) northwest of Lisbon in the Central Portugal region, is regal—a beautiful little town with one very big tourist attraction. The gargantuan Mafra National Palace is widely considered the most important example of Baroque architecture in Portugal, and the Tapada Nacional de

HIGHLIGHTS

✪ **MAFRA NATIONAL PALACE:** One of the most extravagant examples of Baroque architecture in Portugal, the massive 18th-century Mafra National Palace complex rolls a palace, a monastery, and a basilica all into one outstanding package (page 127).

✪ **MAFRA NATIONAL PARK:** The Tapado Nacional de Mafra is a magical forest teeming with wildlife; once a popular spot for royal recreation, nowadays it's frequented by active families (page 128).

✪ **ERICEIRA'S BEACHES:** A world surf reserve, this quaint fishermen's village has a life that revolves around the waves, the beach, and the local village square. Oh, and the "sea hedgehogs" (page 130).

Mafra hunting reserve, the sprawling palace grounds, is open for visits too.

Ericeira, a 15-minute drive down the road from Mafra, is a laid-back surfy seaside town; it's a whitewashed suntrap piled on sheer cliffs that is famous for stunning ocean views and fresh seafood, not to mention world-class surfing. Attracting calm-seeking weekenders and wave-worshipers in droves, Ericeira is a barefoot beach retreat with a year-round summery vibe.

PLANNING YOUR TIME

Because of their proximity to Lisbon and direct public transport, **Mafra** and **Ericeira** can be combined into one day, especially if traveling by car.

Mafra—about 40 km (25 mi) northwest of **Lisbon** on the **A8** motorway—has just the one major attraction (its **palace** and **national park**), but they are outstanding; set aside a full morning to explore them, with at least 1.5 hours for the palace.

Move on to Ericeira—15 minutes northwest from Mafra—for a seafood lunch. Spend the afternoon strolling the quaint streets and lazing on a beautiful beach, soaking up the surfy vibes. If you have the time, spend a night in Ericeira, especially if visiting during summer when the village really comes alive after sundown, to allow time for a spot of surfing, or catch the last bus back to Lisbon (which leaves around 9:45pm).

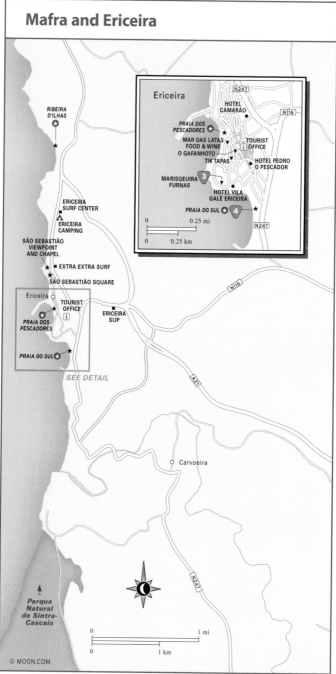

Mafra and Ericeira

RIBEIRA D'ILHAS

Ericeira

HOTEL CAMARÃO

N247

N116

PRAIA DOS PESCADORES

TOURIST OFFICE

MAR DAS LATAS FOOD & WINE
O GAFANHOTO
TIK TAPAS

HOTEL PEDRO O PESCADOR

MARISQEUIRA FURNAS

3

HOTEL VILA GALÉ ERICEIRA

PRAIA DO SUL

4

N247

0   0.25 mi

0   0.25 km

ERICEIRA SURF CENTER

ERICEIRA CAMPING

SÃO SEBASTIÃO VIEWPOINT AND CHAPEL

EXTRA EXTRA SURF

SÃO SEBASTIÃO SQUARE

Ericeira

TOURIST OFFICE

PRAIA DOS PESCADORES

ERICEIRA SUP

PRAIA DO SUL

SEE DETAIL

N116

A21

Carvoeira

N247

Parque Natural de Sintra-Cascais

0   1 mi

0   1 km

© MOON.COM

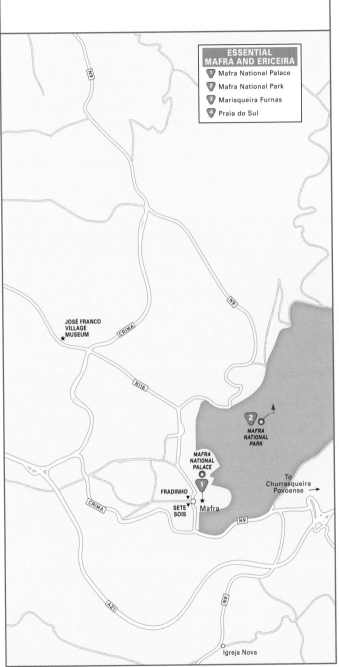

Itinerary Idea

ESSENTIAL MAFRA AND ERICEIRA

Leave Lisbon as early as possible for Mafra. Buses depart about hourly from the **Campo Grande station** (www.mafrense.pt), or it's a 40-minute drive on the A8.

1 In Mafra, head straight for the vast **Mafra National Palace.** Don't miss the impressive library.

2 If traveling by car, after visiting the palace head to **Mafra National Park,** where there are several hikes to choose from, or you can do as the royals did with a bit of horseback riding, archery, or falconry.

3 Catch the bus (or drive) the short distance (just under 10 km/6 mi) from Mafra to Ericeira, where you can enjoy a fresh seafood lunch at **Marisqueira Furnas.** Try the local specialty *ouriço-do-mar* (sea hedgehog).

4 Amble the quaint streets, admire the whitewashed fishermen's cottages, and make your way to **Praia do Sul** beach for rest and relaxation before making your way back to Lisbon.

Mafra

Just under 40 kilometers (25 miles) northwest of Lisbon, Mafra is famous as the home of a large, extravagant palace, which makes it a popular stop between the capital and coastal surfing mecca Ericeira. The small rural town boomed in popularity as a commuter suburb after the completion of the A8 motorway in the 1990s. Mafra usually hums with a steady stream of page-turning tourists who stop there solely to take in the outstanding Mafra National Palace and Mafra National Park. The charming town center has plenty of little cafés and restaurants. Besides that, there is little else for visitors to do and see in Mafra, but the sheer size and sumptuousness of the palace and its park more than justify a visit to the town.

ORIENTATION

The main motorway to Mafra is the A8—tolls (approximately €4) apply, and can be paid in cash or with a card. Mafra's main attraction, the National Palace, is located in the **town center. Buses** from Lisbon conveniently stop right in front of the palace. The **Tapada Nacional** is best visited by car, as it would take over 1.5 hours to walk from the palace. It is a 10-minute drive north along the N9-2 road, or take a **taxi/Uber** from Mafra town.

SIGHTS

✪ MAFRA NATIONAL PALACE
(Palácio Nacional de Mafra)

Terreiro Dom João V, tel. 261 817 550,
www.palaciomafra.gov.pt, Weds.-Mon.
9am-6pm, €6

On a hilltop above the town center, the monumental Mafra National Palace is the finest example of 18th-century Baroque architecture in Portugal, built during the reign of John V (Dom João V) to fulfill a promise he made that if his wife bore him children, he would build a convent. The first stone was laid in 1717, and it took 13 years and 52,000 workers to complete it. The original plan was a monastery for 13 monks, but the project grew to immense proportions, eventually housing 300 monks and including a basilica and a royal palace. The sprawling monument's limestone facade measures 220 meters (722 feet). Painted in sunny yellow, its beautiful exterior features twin bell towers that frame the central basilica. The lavish interior comprises 1,200 rooms and 5,000 windows and doors. The Old Library is a trove of 36,000 ancient books, and the basilica has no fewer than six organs. Outside, a lovely courtyard is frequented by wild birds, and the vast decorative patio creates a border between this national monument and the town. Guided tours of the palace are available with prior booking.

JOSÉ FRANCO VILLAGE MUSEUM
(Aldeia Tipica de José Franco)

N116, tel. 281 815 420, www.cm-mafra.pt,
Mon.-Sat. 9am-1pm and 2pm-5pm, donation

Just 3.2 kilometers (2 miles) north of Mafra town, in the village of Sobreiro, the José Franco Village Museum is a detailed miniature replica of a typical Portuguese village from the turn of the 20th century. This tribute to the local

Mafra National Palace

people and their customs is the vision of renowned potter José Franco, who began building it in the 1960s. Among the miniature buildings are a windmill, cottages, and a schoolroom. The wood oven-baked *chouriça* sausage bread made on-site is worth the visit.

SPORTS AND RECREATION

✪ Mafra National Park (Tapada Nacional de Mafra)

Portão do Codeçal, tel. 261 817 050, www. tapadademafra.pt, daily 9:30am-6pm

A 10-minute drive northeast of Mafra town on the N9-2 road, the 8-square-kilometer (3-square-mile) Mafra National Park is a sprawling royal game reserve created for the Mafra National Palace. Today it is still verdant and varied habitat for free-roaming deer, wild boars, wolves, foxes, badgers, and birds of prey. Activities include hiking, mountain biking, horseback riding, archery, and falconry, staged mostly on weekends. For more information on how and where to join these activities, enquire at the main ticket office at the entrance (tel. 261 814 240, 9:30am-6pm) or see the park website.

There are four different hiking routes of varying lengths between 4 km and 8.5 km (2.5 to 5.3 mi). The longer routes take hikers to further-flung corners of the reserve, where spotting wild animals is more likely. Each route is marked out with a different color (blue, green, red, or yellow) in accordance with their respective length, level of difficulty, and slopes encountered. Maps are available at the main ticket office or online. Guided Footpath Tours are also available.

BTT (all-terrain mountain bike) routes are open from 9am till 4pm. There are three designated routes: white (8 km/5 mi), yellow (15 km/9.3 mi), and red (25 km/15.5 mi), which can be downloaded in advance from

deer in Mafra National Park

the Tapada de Mafra website (http://tapadademafra.pt/wp-content/uploads/2016/09/Percursos-BTT.zip). Rental bikes are available only for the white route and can be found at the trailhead (€7 children, €10 adult).

There is no fixed entry fee to the Tapada as prices are by activity. All entries pass through the main ticket office/visitors center. Hikes are €4 weekdays, €6.50 weekends. Other activities, such as **running** in the forest and a modern-day **geocaching** treasure hunt, also cost €4 per participant. Another exciting activity is the Tapada's tree climbing circuit, **Canopy Adventure,** which comprises 13 activities and obstacles, among them suspended bridges, ropes, nets, tunnels, and a slide, and costs €7 per person (participants must be over 6 years of age and under 100 kg/200 lbs). To simply sit back and enjoy the view, the **Enchanted Circuit train** (1 hour, adults €12, children €9) runs around the park, starting from just outside the main entrance.

FOOD
Fradinho
Praça da República, no. 28/30, tel. 261 815 738, www.pastelariafradinho.com, daily 7am-8pm, €5

If it's a quick snack or a sugar boost you want, then this is the place to go. The Fradinho pastry shop and café has a wide selection of freshly baked regional sweets and delicacies, savory snacks, and sandwiches.

Churrasqueira Povoense
Rua 10 de Maio 2, Povoa da Galega, tel. 219 856 080, Mon.-Weds. noon-3pm, Thurs.-Sat. noon-3pm and 7:30pm-10pm, €8

Superb, unpretentious Churrasqueira Povoense specializes in grilled meats like the famous *tirinhas de porco,* delicious thin strips of pork grilled on charcoal and served with fries and salad.

Sete Sois
Largo Conde Ferreira 1, tel. 261 811 161, https://sete-sois.eatbu.com, Mon.-Sat. noon-3pm and 7pm-10pm, Sun. noon-3pm, €20

Straight across the road from the National Palace the cozy, elegant restaurant Sete Sois has a lovely little alfresco courtyard right in the middle of the town's action. It specializes in tasty grilled fish and meat dishes as well as local game specialties.

GETTING THERE
CAR
Mafra is 40 kilometers (25 miles) northwest of **Lisbon,** about a 40-minute drive. Follow the **A8** motorway from Lisbon, taking **junction 5** and then heading west on the **A21.** There is a spacious paid **parking lot** just next to the Mafra Palace (parking costs a couple of euros for a few hours) and also a large parking lot just outside the Tapada that is free for paying visitors.

BUS
Mafrense buses (tel. 707 201 371, www.mafrense.pt) run hourly from Lisbon's **Campo Grande main bus station,** stopping in front of **Mafra National Palace.** The trip takes one hour each way and costs €4.30. Buses are less frequent on weekends.

GETTING AROUND
It is not recommended to walk between the Mafra National Palace and the Tapada; **drive,** or take an **Uber/taxi,** which should cost €7-15 one-way. The **palace** is located in the charming town center of Mafra.

Ericeira

On the coast, around 35 kilometers (22 miles) north of Lisbon, the fishing village of Ericeira attracts surfers and big-name surfing competitions. The Save the Waves Coalition has even declared it a World Surfing Reserve, only the second in the world and the only one in Europe. Laid-back Ericeira is a little gem, not especially picturesque but with stunning ocean vistas and beautiful beaches. A jumble of whitewashed fishermen's cottages piled atop high-backed cliffs that encircle the covelike main beach and harbor, it is a place where you can walk around barefoot and carefree.

What Ericeira lacks in picturesqueness it makes up for with vibrant nightlife and excellent seafood. Be sure to try the local specialty, the curiously named *ouriço-do-mar* (which literally translates as "sea hedgehog" but is better known as the sea urchin). Still not quite on the mass tourism radar, Ericeira has managed to strike the perfect balance between traditional and cool, which makes for a fun and heady combination that keeps visitors coming back.

ORIENTATION

Life in Ericeira centers around the **Praça da República** square, a cobbled hub fringed with lovely cafés and cake shops, set back off the main **Praia dos Pescadores (Fishermen's Beach)**. **Rua Dr. Eduardo Burnay** is the buzzing main street that runs south from the square to South Beach (**Praia do Sul**), lined with bars and seafood restaurants. At the northern end of the village is the **São Sebastião Square**, where the scenic São Sebastião **viewpoint** and **chapel** can be found.

The **bus terminal** is toward the top end of the village, opposite **North Beach** and the **Praia dos Pescadores**. Praça da República square is a 3-minute walk south from the bus terminal. Traversing the entire village is the main **N247 road,** which runs along the seafront. Most sights in Ericeira are within walking distance, and covering the entire length of the village—from São Sebastião viewpoint to South Beach—takes around 20 minutes (1.5 km/1 mi).

SIGHTS
SÃO SEBASTIÃO VIEWPOINT AND CHAPEL
Praia de São Sebastião

Peering over a beach that goes by the same name, the São Sebastião chapel is a small and simple whitewashed hermitage on the northern fringe of town. Its cliff-top setting offers panoramic views out to sea that are particularly spectacular at sunset.

✪ BEACHES
Pescadores Beach (Praia dos Pescadores)
Largo das Ribas

Backed by a not-so-attractive high cement wall, Ericeira's Pescadores Beach is the town's most central beach. Besides the droves of beachgoers who flock here, it is also a busy working harbor, a hive of activity for the local fishermen and their boats. Praia dos Pescadores's claim to fame is that it was from here that King Manuel II and his family fled on fishing boats to meet the royal yacht out at sea on October 5, 1910. Their departure into permanent exile signaled

Praia dos Pescadores

the end of the monarchy and the beginning of the Portuguese republic. **Parking** anywhere near here is virtually impossible.

South Beach
(Praia do Sul)

Short walk south from the village center

Praia do Sul, near the village center, is the most popular beach in Ericeira. It is a crescent-shaped swath of golden sand sheltered by high cliffs, with clean seawater and mild waves, making it appropriate for sunbathing and swimming.

Ribeira d'Ilhas

3 km (2 mi) north of village center

One of the top surfing spots in the region is Ribeira d'Ilhas, a regular fixture on the World Surf League Championship Tour, 3 kilometers (2 miles) north of Ericeira town, a short eight-minute drive on the N247 road. It has strong surf most of the year and is where most of the local surfers head.

SPORTS AND RECREATION

SURFING

Ericeira has good surfing conditions year-round, with spots for beginners to experts. Dozens of different surf spots can be found on a relatively short stretch of coastline; if one doesn't suit you, you can find another. The **Ericeira Surf Center** (Estrada Nacional 247, tel. 261 864 547, www.boardculturesurfcenter. com) and **eXtra eXtra Surf** (Av. São Sebastião 14I, tel. 261 867 771, www. extraextrasurf.com) are two well-established local companies that have boards, wetsuits, and other gear for rent. They also provide **lessons** and a wealth of information. Surfboard rentals start from €15 for a half-day; group lessons are €30-35 pp.

SUP

Stand-up paddleboarding (SUP) is popular in Ericeira and a nice alternative for non-surfers. The nooks and crannies of the coastline along Ericeira, a World Surfing Reserve, is perfect to explore by SUP.

Ericeira SUP

Rua dos Pocinhos, Rosa dos Ventos building, tel. 916 009 498, www.ericeirasup.com

Local company Ericeira SUP organizes SUP excursions for paddlers of all levels of expertise, on the flat water of Ericeira harbor, the ocean, and along the bays and rock pools of the Ericeira World Surfing Reserve (coastline), as well as tours to nearby rivers and dams. Prices start from €40 and include paddleboard, paddle, wetsuit, and insurance.

FOOD

O Gafanhoto

Rua da Conceição 8, tel. 261 864 514, https://brunomata17.wixsite.com/gafanhoto, Weds.-Mon. 11am-3pm and 7pm-10:30pm, €10

In the town center, O Gafanhoto (The Grasshopper) is typically Portuguese on the outside, with its *azulejo* tiles and sky-blue trim, and typically Portuguese on the inside, with a menu that features good old-fashioned favorites like *Cozido à Portuguesa* (Portuguese stew), Portuguese-style liver, and the Transmontana bean stew. Daily special menus are available in full or half portions.

Tik Tapas

Rua do Ericeira 15, tel. 261 869 235, Tues.-Thurs. 7pm-midnight, Sat.-Sun. 12:30pm-3pm and 7pm-midnight, €10

A rainbow of tasty meat, fish, and vegetarian tapas is served in this vibrant little eatery, with its bright-blue bar and tables and burnt-orange walls.

Marisqueira Furnas

Rus das Furnas 3, tel. 261 867 914, www.marisqueirafurnasericeira.com, daily noon-10pm, €20

The oceanfront Furnas restaurant specializes in the freshest fish and seafood and is famous for its continual all-you-can-eat *rodizio*.

Mar das Latas Food & Wine

Rua Capitão João Lopes 24A, tel. 912 218 423, www.facebook.com/mar.das.latas, Thurs.-Tues. 7pm-midnight, €30

This classy, modern-traditional eatery is a great place to head for fine wine, accomplished cuisine based on fresh local ingredients, and sunset drinks with a view. From the kitchen of a talented young chef come tasty starters such as ceviche, fried squid, and tuna tartar, while entrées range from delectable leg of lamb to cod curry, beetroot risotto, and Wagyu beef.

ACCOMMODATIONS

Hotel Pedro o Pescador

Rua Dr. Eduardo Burnay 22, tel. 261 869 121, www.hotelpedropescador.com, €30-70 d

Quirkily named Pedro o Pescador (Peter the Fisherman) Hotel is a small, whitewashed hotel offering modest and affordable accommodation with refurbished rooms in the center of town, just 300 meters (330 yards) from the beach.

Hotel Camarão

Tv. Espírito Santo 1, tel. 261 862 665, www.hotelcamarao.com, €50-100 d

A short walk from Fisherman's Beach, Hotel Camarão (Shrimp) is a simple, bright, and relaxed hotel with clean, comfortable rooms. Open February through November.

Hotel Vila Galé Ericeira

Largo dos Navegantes 1,
tel. 261 869 900, www.vilagale.com,
€100-200 d

A large, grand dame-style hotel on the Ericeira cliffs, facing South Beach on the southern edge of town. Vila Galé Ericeira has comfortable rooms and two pools, one of which is saltwater, both overlooking the ocean.

Ericeira Camping

Estrada Nacional 247, tel. 261 862 706,
www.ericeiracamping.com, 2 people + 1
tent approx. €20 pp/night high season
(July-Aug.), classic 4-person bungalow €110
pp/night (July-Aug.)

Free your inner adventurer and stay at the modern and well-equipped Ericeira Camping park. It offers traditional camping among shady trees as well as bungalows and mobile homes for accommodation, catering, and a surf school right next door.

INFORMATION AND SERVICES

- **GNR police station:** Largo Domingos Fernandes 7, tel. 261 860 710, www.gnr.pt
- **Tourist office:** Rua Dr. Eduardo Burnay 46, tel. 261 863 122, daily 10am-6pm
- **Main post office:** Rua do Paço 2, tel. 261 860 501

GETTING THERE

CAR

Ericeira is 50 kilometers (31 miles) northwest of **Lisbon**, 9.5 kilometers (5.9 miles) west of **Mafra.** The quickest and easiest way to Ericeira from Lisbon is by car along the **A8** motorway, then the **A21** road west to the coast. It's about a 45-minute drive, and 15 minutes from Mafra, also on the A21.

BUS

Regular bus services operated by **Mafrense** (tel. 707 201 371, www.mafrense.com) run throughout the day between Lisbon's **Campo Grande terminal** and Ericeira (€6.25 one-way). Buses leave Campo Grande hourly, and the journey takes an hour; the bus drops off at the **Mafrense terminal,** 250 meters (275 yards) north of Ericeira town center. Buses are less frequent on weekends.

GETTING AROUND

Getting around Ericeira is easy—most main beaches and amenities are within walking distance of the village center and bus terminal. **Parking,** however, is limited. Ericeira's streets are narrow and can get very crowded, especially during summer. But there is plenty of parking in **free parking lots** set back from the main beachfront, or limited paid parking within the village.

COSTA DA CAPARICA

Located just south of Lisbon, on the other side of the Tagus River, Costa da Caparica is a modern sun-and-fun destination geared largely toward Portuguese tourists. Born from a traditional fishing village, it is still very much a working fishermen's town, and colorful little fishing boats can be seen going out to sea and coming in with their loads on a daily basis. Being a more recent resort, Costa da Caparica lacks some of the traditional charm and character that other popular beach resorts like Cascais and

HIGHLIGHTS

✪ **CAPARICA PROMENADE:** Walk off the ice cream with a scenic stroll along the seafront promenade that hems Costa da Caparica town (page 138).

✪ **PRAIA FONTE DA TELHA:** Make like a hippo and wallow in the restorative muddy waters of Fonte da Telha Beach (page 140).

✪ **TRANSPRAIA MINI TOURIST TRAIN:** See the best of Costa da Caparica's many beaches on this fun little tourist train (page 143).

Estoril offer but makes up for it with space and competitive prices.

Famous for its beaches, Caparica has the longest continuous stretch of sand in Europe, a 30-kilometer (19-mile) strip of coastline that extends along the entire western fringe of the Setúbal Peninsula. Popular with seaside loving *Lisboetas*, Costa da Caparica is still relatively undiscovered by foreign tourists. In summer, the resort area comes alive with cool sunset parties at busy beach bars. Luxury villas sit alongside neat apartment blocks, hotels, and traditional fishermen's huts. With its consistent rolling waves and Portugal's original nudist beach (Meco), Costa da Caparica is a hip melting pot of families, in-crowds, surfers, and free-spirits. The further south you head, the wilder and more rugged the scenery becomes.

ORIENTATION

Costa da Caparica is a knife-shaped strip of coast that extends from the top of the Setúbal Peninsula, narrowing off toward Meco Beach at the bottom. The resort's **town**, the heart of Costa da Caparica, with its shops, bars, restaurants, and hotels, is located toward the top of the coastal strip. The **bus** **station** is located about 1 kilometer (0.6 mile) southeast of the main town center, and 500 meters (0.3 mile) from the beachfront. A 2 km (1.2 mi) **promenade** runs along the seafront. Toward the bottom end of the promenade is the **Bairro dos Pescadores,** the old fishermen's quarters, where the local fishermen go about their daily lives in their whitewashed houses. In peak season the little **Transpraia** beach train connects 15 different stops along a 9 km (5.5 mi) stretch of coast. It departs from **Nova Praia,** the beach in front of the fishermen's quarters, and runs to **Fonte da Telha.**

The busy north end of Costa da Caparica is family-friendly and developed for tourism. Farther south, you'll find vast, spacious stretches of sand where nudism becomes the norm. At the far southern end, the beaches are pristine, fringed by rugged reedy dunes and accessible only by **car** or by the **tourist train.** Also along this stretch of coast is the **Costa da Caparica Fossil Cliff Protected Landscape** (Paisagem Protegida da Arriba Fossil da Costa da Caparica)—around 10 kilometers (6 miles) south of Costa da Caparica town, reachable by walking from **Fonte da Telha** village—a nature preserve rich in ancient fossils and rocks. Blanketing the cliffs that shelter the southern beaches, this natural area is a protected zone that sprawls over 1,000 hectares (2,500 acres). It is rich in ancient fossils and rocks, some of which are more than 15 million years old.

The N377-2 is the main road that runs through the town and along the seafront.

PLANNING YOUR TIME

A 20-minute drive from Lisbon (17 km/10.5 mi), the Caparica Coast is a great place to head—especially in summer—for a few hours at the beach or a fun weekend away from the flurry of the city. It is easy to reach by car from Lisbon, over the 25 de Abril Bridge, and there is regular and inexpensive public transport between Lisbon and Costa da Caparica. A direct bus is one option, while taking the ferry from Cais do Sodré to Cacilhas, and from there an express bus to Costa da Caparica, is another. In summer Costa da Caparica will be busy but seldom feels crowded or overrun.

Itinerary Idea

ESSENTIAL COSTA DA CAPARICA

Make your way from Lisbon to Costa da Caparica after breakfast, by either driving over the 25 de Abril Bridge or taking public transport. If driving, you can park in the northern end of town, in the parking lots near the Inatel campsite and Praia do Norte beach. It's a good idea to pack towels and swimsuits for a trip to Costa da Caparica, but don't worry too much if you forget—there's no shortage of shops selling such paraphernalia in town. There are also plenty of beach concessions with sun beds and parasols for rent for around €7-10 a day.

1 Spend a few hours people-watching and soaking up the sun on the Praia do Norte.

2 For a waterfront lunch, sample freshly caught seafood at Borda d'Agua.

3 Walk lunch off with a stroll along the promenade, admiring the fishing boats, hotels, and vistas en route.

4 Head to the Fishermen's Quarters to explore this traditional neighborhood with its typical shacklike houses, characterful inhabitants, and fishing equipment strewn along the streets.

5 Jump on the Transpraia train to see Costa da Caparica's southern beaches, such as Fonte da Telha, famed for its healing mud.

6 Return to town on the Transpraia just in time for a sunset dinner at Sentido do Mar before heading back to Lisbon.

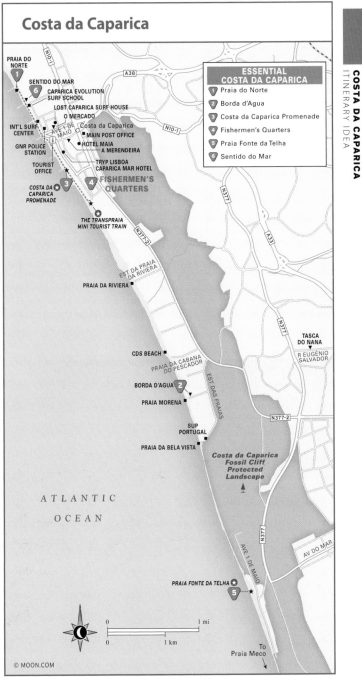

Costa da Caparica

**ESSENTIAL
COSTA DA CAPARICA**

1 Praia do Norte
2 Borda d'Agua
3 Costa da Caparica Promenade
4 Fishermen's Quarters
5 Praia Fonte da Telha
6 Sentido do Mar

PRAIA DO NORTE

SENTIDO DO MAR

CAPARICA EVOLUTION SURF SCHOOL

LOST CAPARICA SURF HOUSE

O MERCADO

INT'L SURF CENTER

Costa da Caparica

MAIN POST OFFICE

GNR POLICE STATION

HOTEL MAIA

A MERENDEIRA

TOURIST OFFICE

TRYP LISBOA CAPARICA MAR HOTEL

COSTA DA CAPARICA PROMENADE

FISHERMEN'S QUARTERS

THE TRANSPRAIA MINI TOURIST TRAIN

EST DA PRAIA DA RIVIERA

PRAIA DA RIVIERA

CDS BEACH

PRAIA DA CABANA DO PESCADOR

BORDA D'AGUA

PRAIA MORENA

EST DAS PRAIAS

SUP PORTUGAL

PRAIA DA BELA VISTA

Costa da Caparica Fossil Cliff Protected Landscape

ATLANTIC OCEAN

TASCA DO NANA

R EUGÉNIO SALVADOR

PRAIA FONTE DA TELHA

AVE 1 DE MAIO

AV DO MAR

0   1 mi

0   1 km

To Praia Meco

© MOON.COM

Sights

✪ COSTA DA CAPARICA PROMENADE

*Avenida General Humberto Delgado;
limited parking along this strip*

Costa da Caparica's long promenade is the perfect spot for a refreshing stroll any time of year. It runs north to south, parallel with the beach and the main coastal through-road, Avenida General Humberto Delgado. Soak up the sun and the sea breeze as you walk along the seafront, past colorful beach shacks and hip bars; make way for the rollerbladers and cyclists and joggers. It's about a half-hour stroll (2.6 km/1.6 mi) from North Beach at the top end of town to the Fishermen's Quarters and beach train at the bottom.

FISHERMEN'S QUARTERS
(Bairro dos Pescadores)

*Rua Parque de Campsimo de Almada,
on-street parking*

This part of town is not as easy on the eye as Costa da Caparica's beautiful beaches, but it is an important piece of the local fabric and history. Built to house the town's traditional fishing families, the Fishermen's Quarters is a raw and authentic government-funded social housing neighborhood, located next to a campsite that is more reminiscent of a migrant settlement. Its inhabitants still live off the sea and are mostly active fisher-folk. Their neighborhood is a mish-mash of different sized boxy buildings, with corrugated

Costa da Caparica's promenade

iron trimmings, colorful clothing flying from washing lines, authentic characters in the street, and fishing paraphernalia strewn in the yards.

COSTA DA CAPARICA FOSSIL CLIFF PROTECTED LANDSCAPE
(Paisagem Protegida da Arriba Fossil da Costa da Caparica)

Rua Dom João V, 17, Aroeira, Estrada Florestal da Costa de Caparica - Praia da Rainha

Costa da Caparica Fossil Cliff

This protected area, about 12 kilometers (7.5 miles) south of Costa da Caparica town and covering 1,570 hectares (3,880 acres), centers on a ridge of unusually shaped cliffs, rich in fossil fauna. A marked nature trail runs along the foot of the cliffs, which are swaddled by a blanket of woodland, scrubland, and pine trees that form the basis of a botanical reserve. It was designated a protected landscape in 1984 for the purpose of preserving its geomorphological and geological characteristics. Dating back some 10 million years, these cliffs and their surroundings are among the most important examples of their kind in Europe.

Sports and Recreation

BEACHES

Costa da Caparica is famous for its beaches, and with good reason. Boasting a coastline of golden sandy shore that stretches over 30 kilometers (19 miles), it has an entire spectrum of beaches for all purposes and ambiences: surfing, naturist, families, gay, you name it, Costa da Caparica has a beach for it. A lively resort in summer and peaceful but still popular in winter, its beaches are sought by sunlovers and surfers alike. The sea here is cool, and waves can be powerful and of a good size but not on the same scale as in Nazaré or Peniche. Most of these beaches will have some form of beach bar or restaurant providing service, and usually a concession with beds and parasols, while parking is generally available along the roads leading to the beaches or in dusty parking lots.

There are more than a dozen beaches making up the Costa da Caparica coast, starting with the northernmost, the aptly named **Praia do Norte** (North Beach). The stretch of sand immediately fronting the Costa da Caparica resort is segmented by tidal piers to protect the coastline from rough tides. This creates a series of small beaches, locally named after the bars that serve them. From there a long stretch of beach extends over 24 kilometers (15 miles) to the southernmost Caparica beach, **Meco**, which is Portugal's original and most famous nudist beach. The best-known beaches along the coast are usually sought-after for their easy access and space. Most will have a lifeguard on duty during the main beach months, loosely May/June to September. The adorable **Transpraia beach train** connects over a dozen of the beaches, starting in Costa da Caparica town near Praia do Norte.

North Beach
(Praia do Norte)

Rua Manuel Agro Ferreira 1, off Costa da Caparica main town; parking lots available nearby

A thin sliver of sand at the top end of Costa da Caparica, Praia do Norte is one of the busier beaches, frequented by locals, tourists, working fishermen and surfers. Flanked by two pontoons, when the tide is high this strip of beach all but disappears.

Morena Beach
(Praia Morena)

6 km (3.7 mi) south of Costa da Caparica town
Just before Bela Vista Beach, Morena Beach is renowned for being a quiet, tranquil beach with plenty of space, easy parking, and translucent, calm waters that make it ideal for stand-up paddleboarding.

Bela Vista Beach
(Praia da Bela Vista)

7 km (4.3 mi) south of Costa da Caparica town
An official nudist beach, Praia da Bela Vista is a wide, peaceful beach of fine white sand, flanked by cliffs and dunes. It is accessed by a dirt road and has its own parking lot.

✪ Fonte da Telha Beach
(Praia Fonte da Telha)

10 km (6 mi) south of Costa da Caparica town

Fonte da Telha Beach is famous for its mud; it's not uncommon to see people caked head to toe in the restorative sludge.

Meco Beach
(Praia Meco)

30 km (18.6 mi) south of Costa da Caparica town
Wide and rugged, Meco, the Costa's original and most famous nudist beach, is at the southernmost extremity.

SURFING AND STAND-UP PADDLEBOARDING

surfing off Costa da Caparica

Waves along this stretch are consistent but not in the same category as Guincho or Ericeira, which makes Costa da Caparica perfect for less-experienced surfers. Top spots for surfing are **CDS Beach** (Costa da Caparica town, off the main avenue) and **Praia da Riviera** (2 km/1.2 mi south of CDS Beach).

Caparica Evolution Surf School

Estrada da Muralha, Marcelino Beach-K bar, tel. 939 124 758, www.kevolutionsurf.com, daily 9am-8pm May-Oct., daily 10am-6pm Nov.-Apr.

Local surf schools, shops, and guesthouses have flourished in the vicinity, including the Caparica Evolution Surf School. Board plus wetsuit rental is around €15 for a half-day; lessons are around €15.

International Surf Center

Rua Praia do CDS, Apoio Praia 11, tel. 912 530 689, www.caparicasurf.com, daily 9am-6pm

Located on Costa da Caparica's main town beachfront, the International Surf Center organizes lessons, rentals, and repairs of all surf equipment.

SUP Portugal

Praia da bela vista, tel. 967 697 039, www. sup-portugal.com, daily 10am-7pm

Located on Bela Vista beach, SUP Portugal is a stand-up paddleboard school that runs courses, tours, and board rentals that start from around €15 per hour.

Food

Costa da Caparica excels in seafood. *Canja de carapau* (mackerel soup) is a local specialty.

A Merendeira

Rua dos Pescadores 20, tel. 212 904 527, www.amerendeira.com, Sun.-Thurs. 10am-1am, Fri.-Sat. 10am-2am, €6

A Merendeira's wholesome soups, freshly baked *chouriço* rolls, and traditional puddings make it the perfect pit stop for a quick lunch.

Tasca do Nana

Rua Eugénio Salvador 23, tel. 933 240 178, www.nanapetiscos.pt, Tues.-Sun. 5pm-midnight, €8

Typical *tasca* (simple, small Portuguese eatery) Tasca do Nana serves a rainbow of *petiscos*, fish and meat snacks perfect for sharing.

Sentido Do Mar

Rua Muralha da Praia, Apoio 7, Praia do Norte 278, tel. 212 900 473, Mon.-Sat. noon-11pm, €10

For seafood, funky modern Sentido do Mar has menus covering sushi to grilled fresh fish, complemented with fantastic sunset views.

Borda d'Agua

Praia da Morena s/n, tel. 212 975 213, www. bordadagua.com.pt, daily 10am-midnight, €15

The name of Borda d'Agua translates as "waterside," and it makes the most of its beachside location, with a large deck for al fresco dining as well as enclosed indoor seating for breezier days. It's a must-visit for delicious fresh fish with a sea breeze.

O Mercado

Avenida 1° de Maio 36D, tel. 218 235 099, www.facebook.com/pg/omercadocc, Tues.-Sat. 12:30pm-3pm and 7:30pm-10pm, €15

A rustic-chic gastropub in the center of Costa da Caparica that serves typical Portuguese fare made from the freshest market produce, with a contemporary international flourish; don't miss the octopus tempura.

Accommodations

Lost Caparica Surf House

Rua Dr. Barros de Castro 17, tel. 917 552 202, www.lostcaparica.com, €35 pp shared, €65 d

Surfers will love Lost Caparica Surf House, whose accommodations range from a shared six-bed room to a private family studio with a small bath. An added bonus is the on-site surf school.

Hotel Maia

Av. Dr. Aresta Branco 22, tel. 212 904 948, www.hotelmaia.com, €100 d

Set a few streets back from the beach, small, simple Hotel Maia is unfussy and clean, with a good breakfast included in the rates.

✪ Tryp Lisboa Caparica Mar Hotel

Av. Gen. Humberto Delgado 47, tel. 212 918 900, www.tryplisboacaparica.com, from €138 d

Hotels in Costa da Caparica are varied and cheaper than most in central Lisbon. The ultimate beachfront hotel, four-star Hotel Costa da Caparica is family-friendly, with a nice swimming pool. Some of the 354 rooms over seven floors have views over the Atlantic.

Information and Services

- **GNR police station:** Rua Pedro Álvares Cabral 29, tel. 265 242 590, www.gnr.pt
- **Tourist office:** Av. da República 18, tel. 212 900 071, Mon.-Sat. 9:30am-1pm and 2pm-5:30pm
- **Main post office:** Praça de 9 de Julho

Getting There and Around

GETTING THERE

CAR

Costa da Caparica is roughly 16 kilometers (10 miles) from downtown **Lisbon.** From Lisbon, take the **A8** motorway over the **25 de Abril Bridge** southbound, before heading west on the **A38** to Costa da Caparica. This is the fastest road route between Lisbon and Costa da Caparica and takes around 20 minutes if traffic is flowing normally.

BUS

There are two ways of getting from Lisbon to Costa da Caparica by public transport. The most direct is by taking the **161 bus** operated by **Transportes Sul do Tejo** (TST, www.tsuldotejo.pt) from **Praca do Areeiro** (Metro Green line). There two departures every hour between 8am and 7pm, and at 15 and 45 minutes past the hour on weekends. Monday to Friday, departures are on the hour and 30 minutes past the hour. A one-way ticket costs €3.20 (buy from the driver) and the journey takes 40-60 minutes, depending on traffic. The 161 bus goes straight to the **Costa da Caparica terminal**, in **Praça Padre Manuel Bernardes**, around 500 meters (550 yards) from the beach and 1 km (0.6 mi) south of the town center,

Alternately, take the **ferry** from **Cais do Sodré** (Metro Green line) to Cacilhas, and catch the express bus from **Cacilhas** to Costa da Caparica. The ferry costs €1.25 one-way and terminates at the Cacilhas main transport hub. From there take the express bus (**TST 135** or **124**) to Costa da Caparica. The TST 135 bus runs once or twice per hour and is the faster, more direct service at 20 minutes. The 124 runs three or four times per hour and takes around 40 minutes. Both cost €2.40

and can be purchased straight from the driver. There is also a direct service between Cacilhas and **Fonte da Telha Beach** and village, the TST **127**.

GETTING AROUND

✪ Transpraia Mini Tourist Train

Rua Parque Infantil, www.transpraia.pt, tel. 212 900 706, daily 9am-8pm June-Sept.

The Transpraia mini tourist train carries beachgoers from one end of Costa da Caparica to the other. It's a bumpy but scenic way to discover Costa's best beach spots. It runs 9 kilometers (5.6 miles) from Caparica town to Fonte da Telha, which takes around 25 minutes, with four little stations and 15 stops en route. The track is divided into **zone 1** (€5 round-trip) and **zone 2** (€8 round-trip). The train operates only in high season (June-September). There are two departures per hour from each end, one on the hour and the other at half past. In Caparica, the Transpraia train leaves from in front of the children's beachside play park in the main town center.

Costa da Caparica's main sights—the main beach and town center, **Fishermen's Quarter**, and **tourist train**—are all within walking distance.

Transpraia train

SETÚBAL PENINSULA

Comprising several municipalities and cities, the Setúbal Peninsula is an enthralling, underexplored region just a stone's throw from Lisbon. An hour's drive south from the capital, it is home to a dolphin-inhabited estuary, famed natural landscapes, and a folklore-infused cape where dinosaurs once roamed. Its golden beaches and freshest seafood are the cherry on top.

Wedged between the Arrábida Natural Park and the Sado Estuary Natural Reserve, the main city, Setúbal, a 50-minute drive south of Lisbon, is an industrialized working port, home to the

HIGHLIGHTS

✪ **DOLPHIN-WATCHING IN SADO ESTUARY:** Enjoy one of Setúbal's most unique and popular attractions with a boat trip to meet the Sado Estuary's friendly community of wild bottlenose dolphins (page 150).

✪ **SEAFOOD IN SESIMBRA:** Sesimbra's seafood isn't famed for nothing; tuck into heaped platters of the freshest delicacies straight from the Atlantic Ocean at a picturesque port-side restaurant—make sure to try the local specialty, grilled black scabbard fish (page 156).

✪ **CABO ESPICHEL PROMONTORY AND LIGHTHOUSE:** There's something alluringly eerie about the barren Espichel Cape with its abandoned sanctuary, dinosaur footprints embedded in the cliff tops, and the tiny chapel sat solemnly overlooking the endless Atlantic (page 158).

country's largest fish market. Setúbal makes no apologies for its unrefined, unpolished character, but the unbridled natural beauty that surrounds the city eclipses what it lacks in airs and graces. A few kilometers west of Setúbal city is the sprawling Arrábida Natural Park, where wild birds of prey soar over dramatic coastal scenery. Farther on, toward the western tip of the Arrábida Park, are charming fishing town Sesimbra and the vertiginous Espichel Cape. But one of the major draws to Setúbal is its estuary, one of few water inlets in Europe to be inhabited by wild dolphins, which happily make appearances for eager tourists.

ORIENTATION

Setúbal city is situated 54 kilometers (33.5 miles) south of Lisbon, across the **Tagus River.** It is sandwiched by two expansive natural beauty spots: **Arrábida Natural Park** to the west and **Sado Estuary Natural Reserve** to the east. Heading west, through the Arrábida Park, you reach **Sesimbra,** and further on still, at the very westernmost tip of the peninsula, is **Cabo Espichel,** the Espichel Cape. The

region's most popular tourist activity, **dolphin-watching trips** depart from Setúbal waterfront and Sesimbra's little port.

PLANNING YOUR TIME

A day trip to Setúbal is highly recommended to see a rawer, unadulterated side of Portugal's seafaring soul, and the Sado dolphins never fail to bring a smile to those who catch one of the many boat trips that run from the city. **Setúbal** is an easy 50-minute drive (54 km/33.5 mi) south of Lisbon, following either the main **A2** or **A12** motorways. Allow a full day to explore its attractions; the **dolphin trips** usually take around three hours. **Book trips online beforehand** to secure places.

Also set aside a couple of hours to explore the **Arrábida Natural Park,** just west of Setúbal. While all this and more can be done in one day, spending a night in quaint **Sesimbra,** a short drive west of Setúbal, is highly recommended. There you can enjoy a romantic seafood dinner and a trip to **Espichel Cape.**

Itinerary Ideas

OUTDOOR ESCAPADES

DAY 1

Leaving Lisbon for Setúbal in your rental car, take either the **A2** motorway over the **25 de Abril Bridge** or the **A12** over the newer **Vasco da Gama Bridge**.

1 In Setúbal, head straight to the waterfront for a morning Sado Estuary dolphin-watching trip with **Vertigem Azul**; book your tickets in advance.

2 Enjoy lunch at **Batareo**, one of Setúbal's many great seafood restaurants.

3 Walk around the town center, taking in such sights as the recently re-vamped waterfront and the **Monastery of Jesus of Setúbal**.

4 Jump in the car and head 2.5 km (1.5 mi) west to the Arrábida Natural Park, spending a couple of hours exploring this beautiful area with a hike and visiting the **Our Lady of Arrábida fort**.

5 Keep heading west along the N3791-1 coastal road toward Sesimbra, stopping at the **Arrábida Monastery** en route.

6 Enjoy more fresh seafood at **Lobo do Mar** and spend the night in this charming seaside town.

DAY 2

1 The next morning, keep driving west along Av. 25 de Abril toward Cabo Espichel, the westernmost point of the Setúbal Peninsula. Stroll around the blustery **Cabo Espichel Promontory** toward the **lighthouse.**

2 Explore the ghost town **Our Lady of the Cape Sanctuary.**

3 Walk along the cliffs over to the **dinosaur footprints** before driving back to Lisbon in time for lunch.

Setúbal Peninsula

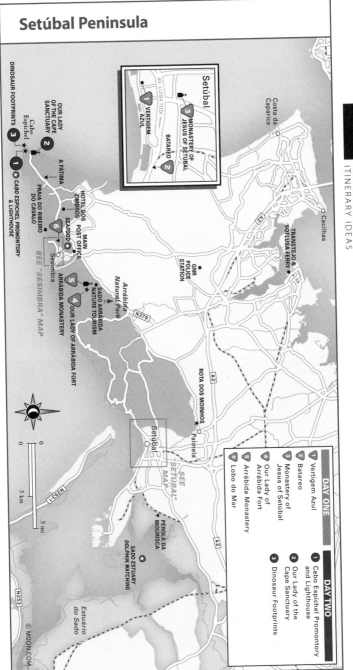

Setúbal
- 1 VERTIGEM AZUL
- 3 MONASTERY OF JESUS OF SETÚBAL
- 2 BATAREO

- 3 DINOSAUR FOOTPRINTS
- 2 OUR LADY OF THE CAPE SANCTUARY
- 1 CABO ESPICHEL PROMONTORY & LIGHTHOUSE
- Cabo Espichel
- A FÁTIMA
- PRAIA DO RIBEIRO DO CAVALO
- 6 SEAFOOD
- HOTEL DOS ZIMBROS
- MAIN POST OFFICE
- Sesimbra
- 5 ARRÁBIDA MONASTERY
- 4 OUR LADY OF ARRÁBIDA FORT
- SADO ARRÁBIDA NATURE TOURISM
- Arrábida Natural Park
- GNR POLICE STATION
- TRANSTEJO & SOFLUSA FERRY
- Cacilhas
- Costa da Caparica
- N379
- ROTA DOS MOINHOS
- Palmela
- Setúbal
- SEE "SETÚBAL" MAP
- SEE "SESIMBRA" MAP
- A2
- N253-1
- N253
- PÉROLA DA MOURISCA
- SADO ESTUARY DOLPHIN WATCHING
- Estuário do Sado
- 0   5 km
- 0   5 mi
- © MOON.COM

DAY ONE
- 1 Vertigem Azul
- 2 Batareo
- 3 Monastery of Jesus of Setúbal
- 4 Our Lady of Arrábida Fort
- 5 Arrábida Monastery
- 6 Lobo do Mar

DAY TWO
- 1 Cabo Espichel Promontory and Lighthouse
- 2 Our Lady of the Cape Sanctuary
- 3 Dinosaur Footprints

Setúbal and the Sado Estuary

The unpolished port town of Setúbal is divisive. Many are charmed by its lovely old town square, busy waterfront, and unrepentant lack of pretension; others are unable to see past its gritty industrial facade. Colorful fishing boats and commuter ferries run beside leisure vessels, a sure sign that tourism is buoying the city. With good hotels and restaurants, Setúbal is well placed as a base for exploring the wildlife-heavy Sado Estuary.

Originating in the deep Alentejo, in the Vigia mountain range, the Sado River flows into the sea south of Setúbal. The humid and fertile Sado Estuary Natural Reserve covers 23,000 hectares (89 square miles) of rich wetlands. It is a protected nature reserve, one of 30 officially protected areas in the country, where mirrorlike wetlands and surrounding banks and thickets host more than 200 bird species, including white storks and pink flamingos. Once one of the most important salt-producing areas in the country, it is a hot spot for bird- and dolphin-watching. A pod of bottlenose dolphins has long resided in the estuary's calm waters, a phenomenon unique in Portugal and rare in the world.

ORIENTATION

Sustained by the Sado River, Setúbal formed on the river's bay-like western bank, an industrious, underrated port city that is surprisingly appealing once you scratch past its unpolished surface. It sits on the southern fringe of the Setúbal Peninsula, wedged between the

town center of Setúbal

Setúbal

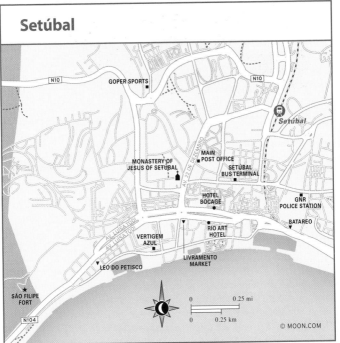

Arrábida Natural Park and the **Sado Estuary.** Located along the waterfront is the **ferry terminal,** and set back from the waterfront is the historic **old town** and its maze of quaint cobbled streets dotted with hip boutiques and eateries. Setúbal's main **bus terminal** is set a few streets back from the waterfront, about 150 meters (500 feet) from the city center, while the **train station** is just under a kilometer (half a mile) north of the center. Most of Setúbal's main sights can be easily reached on foot from the pedestrianized center.

SIGHTS
MONASTERY OF JESUS OF SETÚBAL
(Convento e Igreja de Jesus)

Rua Acácio Barradas 2, tel. 265 537 890, www.mun-setubal.pt, Tues.-Sat. 10am-6pm, Sun. 2pm-6pm, free

Designed in 1494 by architect Diogo de Boitaca (best known for his work on Lisbon's emblematic Jerónimos Monastery), the austere gray Monastery of Jesus of Setúbal is one of the earliest examples of Manueline architecture in Portugal. Among its distinguishing features are soaring spiral granite pillars and typical *azulejo* murals. Outside, gargoyles and twisted pinnacles perforate an otherwise plain facade. Inside, an intricate ribbed vaulted ceiling in the main chapel and twisted-rope columns of pink and beige Arrábida stone are highlights.

SÃO FILIPE FORT
(Fortaleza de São Filipe)

Estrada Castelo de São Filipe, tel. 265 545 010, www.sintracascaissesimbra.com/setubal/Setubal-castle-Forte-Sao-Filipe.html, open 24/7

Sitting atop a swollen mound on the western skirts of the city center, the

149

a dolphin-watching cruise on the Sado Estuary

16th-century São Filipe (Saint Phillip) Fort (also referred to as Setúbal Castle) is one of Setúbal's top attractions. Peering over the city, its fishing port, and the Sado beyond, it is an imposing sight, with its austere, sturdy ramparts and solid battlements. It's a 30-minute hike up from the town, but the persistent are rewarded with stunning sights and a quaint little chapel with a fascinating *azulejo* wall. Currently housing a luxury hotel, the battlements and grounds are open to the public.

SPORTS AND RECREATION

TOP EXPERIENCE

✪ DOLPHIN-WATCHING IN SADO ESTUARY

Dolphin-watching cruises (3 hours, from €30) are available from companies including **Vertigem Azul** (tel. 265 238 000, www.vertigemazul.com), **Portugal Sport and Adventure** (tel. 910 668 600, www.portugal-sport-and-adventure.com), and **Sado Arrábida**

Nature Tourism (tel. 265 490 406 or 915 560 342, www.sadoarrabida.pt).

Galleon Sal Sado Trips

tel. 265 227 685, www.sal.pt, 3 hours, €25

A different way to explore the Sado is aboard a historic *sal* (salt) galleon. These wooden ships were converted from small fishing vessels, first used to transport salt and later used for fishing and cargo. The restored boats are now used for coastal and estuary cruises. **Sal Cruises** runs cruises on the Sado, Tagus, and Zêzere rivers.

Tourists cruise the Sado aboard a restored *sal* galleon.

FOOD

You'll often see locals sitting al fresco, sharing a plate of local specialty *choco frito* (fried squid) with a cold beer.

Livramento Market (Mercado do Livramento)

Avenida Luísa Todi 163, tel. 265 545 392, Tues.-Sun.7am-2pm

One of the most famous markets in Portugal, lively Mercado do Livramento bursts with fantastic fresh produce and buzzes with activity. Regional cheeses, the freshest fish and seafood, and fruit and vegetables galore are all in their finest glory to be seen and sampled. Originally inaugurated in 1876, it houses a diversity and character that visitors would be hard-pressed to find elsewhere in Portugal. Widely considered one of Portugal's best markets, it is also one of the biggest.

✪ Leo do Petisco

Rua da Cordoaria 33, tel. 265 228 340, Mon.-Sat. noon-3pm and 7pm-10pm, €8

Head for the simple café-snack bar Leo do Petisco in Setúbal's town center to try local delicacy *choco frito* served on a plate or—interestingly—in a sandwich.

Pérola da Mourisca

Rua da Baía do Sado 9, tel. 265 793 689, Weds.-Sun. 7:30pm-10:30pm, €10

With the best sea and river produce, down-to-earth Pérola da Mourisca is best known for its shellfish tapas but also cooks seafood-based rice and pasta dishes.

Batareo

Rua das Fontainhas 64, tel. 265 234 548, Tues.-Sun. noon-3:30pm, €15

Small, simple dockside Batareo does only fish and shellfish. Fish move straight off the boat and into the glass display case.

ACCOMMODATIONS

Hotels in Setúbal are located in and around the town center and the port.

Hotel Bocage

Rua de São Cristóvão 14, tel. 265 543 080, www.hoteisbocage.com, €80-100 d

Just off Setúbal's main drag, Avenida Luísa Todi, in the heart of the historic part of town, two-star Hotel Bocage provides an unfussy, comfortable stay. Its sister, Bocage Guest House, is on a side street just around the corner.

Rio Art Hotel

Av. Luísa Todi 117, tel. 965 801 988, www.rioarthotel.pt, €100-150 d

In the heart of Setúbal, the Rio Art Hotel retains some original features of its historic exterior. The renovated interior is gleaming and contemporary, with 23 colorful, spacious rooms and vintage-chic touches.

INFORMATION AND SERVICES

- **GNR police station:** Av. Jaime Cortesão, tel. 265 242 500, www.gnr.pt
- **Tourist office:** Travessa Frei Gaspar 10, tel. 265 539 120, daily 10am-7pm
- **Main post office:** Av. Mariano Carvalho s/n, tel. 265 528 621

GETTING THERE AND AROUND

Setúbal's downtown area, with the main sights, attractions, and restaurants, can easily be explored on foot. The main bus terminal (Avenida 5 Outubro / Av. Dr. Manuel de Arriaga 2, tel. 265 525 051, www.tsuldotejo.pt) is closer to the old town center than the **train station** (Praça do Brasil, tel. 707 210 220, www.cp.pt), which is to the north of the city, about 1 kilometer (0.6 miles), a 14-minute walk, to Praça de Bocage, Setúbal's main square, or 1.3 kilometers (0.8 miles) to the waterfront **ferry terminal.**

The **Sado Natural Reserve** is located approximately 90 kilometers (56 miles) south of Lisbon; it envelops the immediate fringes of Setúbal, and is about 38 kilometers (24 miles) east from Sesimbra. The best way to explore the protected wetlands is with an **excursion** from Setúbal or Sesimbra, and most people plan on staying and eating in Setúbal or Sesimbra.

CAR
Located 50 kilometers (31 miles) southeast of Lisbon Airport, Setúbal is a 45-minute drive from Lisbon. By car the main route is over the **25 de Abril Bridge,** following the **A2** motorway.

TRAIN
There is direct public transport between Lisbon and Setúbal. **CP trains** (tel. 707 210 220, www.cp.pt) run every hour from Lisbon's **Santa Apolónia** and **Cais do Sodré stations** and take around two hours. Single-trip tickets cost €11.20. The train station is about 1 km (0.6 mi) east of the main town center in **Praça do Quebrado** (Quebrado Square), near the main bus stops on **Avenida 5 de Outubro.**

FERRY
Alternately, take the **Transtejo & Soflusa ferry** (tel. 808 203 050, www.transtejo.pt) from Lisbon's **Terreiro do Paço** terminal to **Barreiro** (€2.40), with up to seven crossings per hour; then catch a CP train from the station next to the ferry terminal to **Praça do Quebrado** in Setúbal (twice per hour, 30 minutes, €2.25).

the ferry in Setúbal

BUS
Transportes Sul do Tejo express buses (tel. 707 508 509, www.tsuldotejo.pt) also run directly from Lisbon's Praça da Espanha (lines 561 and 563) and Gare do Oriente (lines 562 and 563) stations, departing once an hour; the trip takes 50 minutes and costs €4.45 one-way. National express-bus company **Rede Expressos** (tel. 707 223 344, www.rede-expressos.pt) operates a dozen buses per day between Lisbon's Sete Rios terminal and Setúbal (45 minutes, €6).

Arrábida Natural Park

Blanketing a chunk of coastline between the city of Setúbal and the village of Sesimbra, the Arrábida Natural Park (Parque Natural da Arrábida, www.natural.pt) covers 16,500 hectares (64 square miles). A rugged belt of deep green, the Serra da Arrábida mountain range is separated from the Atlantic by thin, white-gold beaches. Its tallest peak stands 499 meters (1,637 feet), and the chalky Arrábida massif is covered by a thick rug of plant life, including rare species like rockroses and purple star thistle as well as typical Mediterranean *maquis* and *garigue* scrubland. To protect the vegetation, some areas can only be accessed with an authorized guide.

Opt for a leisurely activity such as biking or hiking, or join certified guides who lead mountain climbing, caving, and diving excursions. For information, contact the **park office** (Praça da República, Setúbal, tel. 265 541 140).

SIGHTS

OUR LADY OF ARRÁBIDA FORT
(Forte de Santa Maria da Arrábida)

Portinho da Arrábida, tel. 212 189 791, Tues.-Fri. 10am-4pm, Sat. 3pm-6pm, €3.50; access to the fort is via the Park's narrow, winding roads; roadside parking available in the vicinity of the fort

Perched above translucent seawater and overlooking one of the prettiest beaches in the region, Portinho da Arrábida, the Arrábida Fort was built

Arrábida Monastery in the Arrábida Natural Park

in 1676 as part of a strategic coastal defense line. An **oceanographic museum** now occupies the historic cliff-foot Fort. Inside, make sure to visit the chapel and its stone image of Our Lady, then take a refreshing dip in the sea below.

ARRÁBIDA MONASTERY (Convento da Arrábida)

tel. 212 180 520, www.foriente.pt, on-site parking

The park is also home to the enigmatic Arrábida Monastery (Convento da Arrábida). This 16th-century complex is situated higher in the hills above the fort, amid 25 hectares (62 acres) of dense shrubbery. The cluster of religious buildings includes two former convents, chapels, a garden, and a sanctuary. It can be **toured** (Weds. and Sat.-Sun., €5) if you reserve in advance.

SPORTS AND RECREATION

Blanketed with thick, verdant indigenous vegetation, the Arrábida Natural Park's rugged coastal terrain and its stunning views are conducive to a menu of physical outdoor activities that range from leisurely **hikes** to radical sports. The translucent turquoise waters along the jagged coast are also perfect for **SUP, kayaking, and canoeing.**

Several accredited companies organize more radical activities in the park, such as coasteering, diving, and mountain climbing. Certain areas of the park are accessible only when accompanied by an official guide. For more information, contact the **main park headquarters** (Praça da República, Setúbal, tel. 265 541 140).

A number of companies in both Setúbal and Sesimbra, such as **Dive Club Cipreia** (Sesimbra, tel. 917 255 072, www.diveclubcipreia.com), **Vertente Natural** (Sesimbra, tel. 210 848 919, www.vertentenatural.com), and **Goper Sports** (Setúbal, tel. 265 501 621, www.bikeexperience.pt), organize guided activity excursions in the park and along its coastline, as well as equipment rentals.

HIKING

The park itself is crossed by signposted footpaths, tailored to varying degrees of physical aptitude. There are three main hikes.

Formosinho Peak

This is a demanding 3-kilometer (2-mile) trail to the highest point of the Arrábida mountain range, Formosinho Peak (500 meters/1,640 feet), which takes around two hours there and back, starting at the Convento da Arrábida.

Serra do Risco (Risk Point)

Another scenic route also popular with mountain bikers is the roughly 4-kilometer (2.5-mile) trail from the Mina de Brecha da Arrábida viewpoint to Serra do Risco (Risk Point).

Rota dos Moinhos

A longer, well-signed 13 km (8 mi) route, the Rota dos Moinhos (Windmill Path) takes hikers from the village of Palmela along a path dotted with traditional windmills. Allow 5-6 hours for the entirety of this hike.

INFORMATION AND SERVICES

Arrábida Park Office

Praça da República, Setúbal, tel. 265 541 140

Contact the park office for more information on attraction opening times, hiking and cycling routes, and other park activities.

GETTING THERE AND AROUND

Arrábida Natural Park is 2.5 kilometers (1.6 miles) west of **Setúbal,** a five-minute drive along the **Avenida General Daniel de Sousa** and the **N10 road.** A taxi from Setúbal should cost around €13.

From **Sesimbra,** the 10-kilometer (6.2-mile) drive east takes about 20 minutes on the N378 road and Avenida 25 de Abril. A taxi should cost €18.

Public transport is infrequent; the best way to reach the Arrábida Natural Park is **by car,** or by asking at your hotel or the local **tourist office** what excursions are available.

The Arrábida Natural Park is located approximately 40 kilometers (25 miles) south of **Lisbon;** the fastest route is following the **A2** motorway over the **25 de Abril Bridge** (50 minutes).

Sesimbra

At the foot of the Arrábida Mountain Range (Serra da Arrábida) in a protected bay, the authentic fishing town of Sesimbra (seh-ZEEM-brah) has marvelous beaches but remains largely undiscovered, allowing its genuine seaside charm to shine. It's also located at the western edge of the Arrábida Natural Park, making it a gateway to unspoiled natural beauty.

ORIENTATION

Sesimbra is a small seaside town nestled at the foothills of the Arrábida mountain range. The outskirts of town step down toward the **main center,** which is centered on the **beach.** At the western tip of town is the small **fishing port** and its authentic **fresh fish restaurants,** while at the opposite end are a couple of swanky modern hotels. The two ends are bound by a sweep of golden sand and a pretty seafront road and promenade, **Avenida dos Naufrágios,** with all the other main hotels, bars, and restaurants found in between them. The small, open-air bus terminal is on **Avenida da Liberdade,** one of the main avenues that run down into Sesimbra, perpendicular to the beachfront. It is approximately 350 meters (385 yards) to the beach.

SPORTS AND RECREATION

BEACHES

With fine sand and crystalline waters, Sesimbra's beaches are glorious.

Ouro Beach (Praia do Ouro)
Avenida dos Náufragos

Praia do Ouro (just west of the town center) is a generous strand of golden

Praia do Ouro

Sesimbra

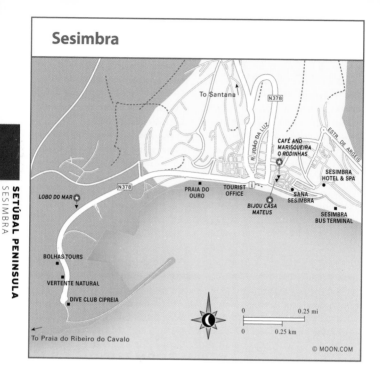

sand sloping gently toward calm, clear water, along Sesimbra's main seaside avenue. Find comforts like sun beds, beach bars, and a children's play area.

Ribeiro do Cavalo Beach (Praia do Ribeiro do Cavalo)

Rua Baía de Sesimbra

Smaller Praia do Ribeiro do Cavalo is on a cove with rocky beds teeming with sea life, making it perfect for diving or snorkeling. There are no diving outfitters on the beach, so bring your own gear. It's a 3-kilometer (2-mile) drive west of town, but you can reach it by **boat** from Sesimbra's port for €10 round-trip.

FISHING

Fishing trips are the main excursions in Sesimbra, and deep-sea fishing is the most popular. Tours vary but generally last around five hours and are suitable for the whole family.

Bolhas Tours—Follow Sensations

*tel. 910 658 555 or 916 205 429, www.
bolhastours.com*

Bolhas Tours—Follow Sensations operates from Sesimbra Marina with sightseeing boat trips, fishing trips, and dolphin-watching as well as boat rentals and diving. Prices start around €35.

✪ FOOD

Sesimbra's gastronomy is all about the sea. Local specialties include *arroz de marisco* (a rich, well-sauced rice stew packed with gently boiled seafood and spices) and *peixe-espada preto* (black scabbard fish).

✪ Café and Marisqueira O Rodinhas

Rua Marques de Pombal 25, tel. 212 231 557,
www.marisqueiraorodinhas.pt, Thurs.-Tues.
noon-10:30pm, €12

Unpretentious Café and Marisqueira O Rodinhas serves seafood delights in a cozy and casual interior.

Café and Marisqueira O Rodinhas

Bijou Casa Mateus

Largo Anselmo Braamcamp 4, tel. 963 650 939, www.casamateus.pt, Tues.-Sun. noon-3:30pm and 7pm-11pm, €15

With its charming worn tile facade and simple wooden tables, acclaimed Bijou Casa Mateus puts all the focus on the seafood. Offerings include *caldeirada* (fish stew) and *arroz de marisco,* along with seafood delicacies such as razor clams, Sesimbra lobster, and cockles.

✪ Lobo do Mar

Av. dos Náufragos, Porto de Abrigo, tel. 212 235 233, www.lobodomar.com, Tues.-Sun. noon-4pm and 7pm-10pm, €15

Simple seaside Lobo do Mar is famous for its grilled fish.

ACCOMMODATIONS

Sesimbra has only a handful of hotels, including newish middle-size units and charming guesthouses.

Sana Sesimbra

Av. 25 de Abril, tel. 212 289 000,
www.sesimbra.sanahotels.com,
€100-200 d

On the beach in the heart of Sesimbra village, upscale hotel Sana Sesimbra brings the luxury of an acclaimed chain to a small town. Its central location and fabulous views enhance the hotel's cool retro look.

✪ Sesimbra Hotel & Spa

Rua Navegador Rodrigues Soromenho, tel. 212 289 800,
www.sesimbrahotelspa.com, €200-250 d

Built on a cliff overlooking Califórnia Beach and the Atlantic, modern Sesimbra Hotel & Spa has panoramic views from all rooms as well as from its infinity pool. Its plush interior and stylish seaside decor are relaxing and refreshing.

INFORMATION AND SERVICES

- **GNR police station:** Rua 4 de Maio, tel. 217 657 700, www.gnr.pt
- **Tourist office:** Rua da Fortaleza, tel. 212 288 500, daily 9am-9pm
- **Main post office:** Av. Padre António Pereira de Almeida 8

GETTING THERE

CAR

Sesimbra is 40 kilometers (25 miles) south of **Lisbon,** a 50-minute drive. By car, take the **A2** motorway over the **25 de Abril Bridge** and head southwest toward Setúbal. At the junction of the **N378** road, head directly south to Sesimbra. From **Setúbal,** Sesimbra is 30 kilometers (19 miles) west, a 45-minute drive along the **N10** road and **Avenida 25 de Abril.**

BUS

Public transport between Setúbal and Sesimbra is frustratingly sparse, with around a dozen departures a day on weekdays and just four or five on weekends, making a day trip difficult via public transport. The service, line 230, is operated by **Transportes Sul do Tejo** and costs €3.30. In Sesimbra, the bus stops on the main **Avenida da Liberdade**, 350 meters (0.2 miles) from the beach.

Transportes Sul do Tejo (tel. 707 508 509, www.tsuldotejo.pt) runs an inexpensive express-bus service (line 207 or 260) between Lisbon's Praça da Espanha and Sesimbra (1 hour, €4.35); tickets can be purchased from the driver.

Cabo Espichel

Wind-battered and rugged, Cabo Espichel is the Setúbal Peninsula's most southwesterly headland, a barren cape with massive cliffs and an eerie, desolate feel. Everything about Cabo Espichel is wild—the waves roar, the scenery is untamed, and there are few modern comforts.

SIGHTS

✪ CABO ESPICHEL PROMONTORY AND LIGHTHOUSE
(Promontório e Farol do Cabo Espichel)

EM 569 Cabo Espichel, open 24/7

Perched on the promontory, this hexagonal lighthouse guards the entire Setúbal Peninsula. The structure stands 32 meters (105 feet) tall but is still dwarfed by the sheer size of the cliffs. On a clear night, sailors can see the powerful beam from the lighthouse 40 kilometers (25 miles) out to sea. The lighthouse is open to the public Wednesday 2pm-5pm only. Entry is free, and visitors can climb to the top to see the lamp.

DINOSAUR FOOTPRINTS
(Pegadas dos Dinossauros)

open 24/7, free

Within walking distance of the lighthouse is a unique sight: dinosaur footprints. Likely made by sauropods, theropods, and ornithopods that inhabited the area millions of years ago, two sets of prints can be clearly seen in the cliffs. Directly above the prehistoric prints, the isolated 15th-century Chapel of Ermida de Memória perches perilously close to the cliff's edge. The chapel's interior is clad in traditional tile depicting "The Lady of the Cape"—the Virgin Mary is said to have appeared to an elderly couple in that spot in 1410.

OUR LADY OF THE CAPE SANCTUARY
(Santuário da Nossa Senhora do Cabo)

tel. 212 231 031, weekdays 9:30am-1:30pm and 2:30pm-5pm, weekends 9:30am-1:30pm and 2:30pm-6pm, free

Built in 1701, the Baroque Our Lady of the Cape Sanctuary was designed

Cabo Espichel Lighthouse

first as a place of defense, then to provide shelter. Two long arms stretching out from either side of the church include rooms that housed pilgrims. The church itself has a simple marble interior.

FOOD AND ACCOMMODATIONS

Most visitors to Cabo Espichel plan on meals and lodging in nearby Sesimbra or Setúbal, though there are a few eateries nearby.

A Fátima

Estrada do Cabo Espichel, tel. 212 685 164,
www.restauranteafatima.com,
Tues.-Sun. noon-3:30pm and 7pm-10pm, €10
A Fátima restaurant serves traditional homemade Portuguese fish and meat dishes at good prices.

Hotel dos Zimbros

Facho de Azóia, tel. 210 405 470,
www.hotelzimbros.com, €150-200 d
Incongruous with the wild landscape, the sleek 38-room Hotel dos Zimbros is on the main road into Cabo Espichel.

GETTING THERE

Taking public transport to Cabo Espichel is difficult, so most visitors drive. Cabo Espichel is 14 kilometers (8.7 miles) west from **Sesimbra** via the **N379 road** (20 minutes) and 40 kilometers (25 miles) west from **Setúbal** via the main **Avenida 25 de Abril** (50 minutes).

A public bus, **line 201,** operated by **Transportes Sul do Tejo** (tel. 707 508 509, www.tsuldotejo.pt), runs between **Sesimbra's main bus** station and Cabo Espichel about eight times on weekdays, less frequently on weekends. The journey takes around 30 minutes and tickets cost about €3 one way.

ÓBIDOS

Not to be missed, enchanting

Óbidos (AW-bee-doosh) is a pretty example of a fortified town and a quintessential Portuguese village, with whitewashed houses that exude undiluted charm huddled within the walls of the castle, now a hotel. It is one of Portugal's best-preserved medieval towns; the local parking lot is usually packed with tour buses from dawn till dark. Over the centuries Óbidos's natural beauty and perfection made it a favorite among royals. In the 13th century, King Dom Dinis gifted the village to his wife, Queen Isabel, starting a tradition;

HIGHLIGHTS

✪ **ÓBIDOS VILLAGE:** Explore one of the most unique and picturesque fortified towns in Portugal; like an open-air museum, it exudes old-world charm (page 164).

✪ **GINJA:** While in Óbidos make sure you try a local *ginja* cherry liqueur, in a chocolate cup, with or without the cherry. **Bar Ibn Errik Rex** is one of the oldest bars in town (page 169).

✪ **QUINTA DO GRADIL WINERY:** Lean more about the region's wine-producing tradition at Quinta do Gradil, a working wine farm that once belonged to one of Portugal's most important statesmen, the Marquis of Pombal (page 171).

ÓBIDOS

centuries later, in 1441, King Afonso V famously wed his cousin, Princess Isabella of Coimbra, here when they were age 9 and 10, respectively. The regal favoritism gave the village its nickname "Village of Queens," a legacy that makes the town treasured and well looked after by its residents.

Home to some of the country's biggest and best-known festivals that take over the entire town, including a Medieval Fair and the Chocolate Festival, Óbidos is always buzzing. Walk through the main archway, the ancient tile-clad Porta da Vila, to a maze of cobblestone streets lined with gorgeous whitewashed houses adorned with flowers, and cute crafts shops touting souvenirs, including *ginja*, the famous Óbidos cherry liqueur. For a special view of the town (if you can handle heights), circumnavigate the historic center on the elevated battlements.

ORIENTATION

Parking is limited in Óbidos, and most visitors will be required to leave their cars in one of the parking lots located on the village doorstep. Tour buses also stop just outside the town walls. Entry to Óbidos is made via the **Porta da Vila** gateway. Flights of steps are found regularly along the battlements, allowing visitors to climb the walls. Óbidos's main street, **Rua Direita,** stretches between the Porta da Vila and the historic **Pousada Castelo Óbidos** castle, now a hotel. It is along this street that most of the town's main attractions and little craft shops are found. Key sights, such as the **Santa Maria Church and Municipal Museum,** are off this main shopping street. But venture off the thoroughfare to see some of Óbidos's more picturesque backstreets and colorful little houses. At the top end of Rua Direita is Óbidos Castle and the area where its famous events, such as the **Medieval** and **Christmas Markets,** are set up. The **aqueduct** is located outside the town walls, opposite the main parking lot.

PLANNING YOUR TIME

Allocate a full day to visit Óbidos, its attractions, and surroundings, located just over an hour's drive (about 80 km/50 mi) north of Lisbon. Set aside a good few hours to really explore the

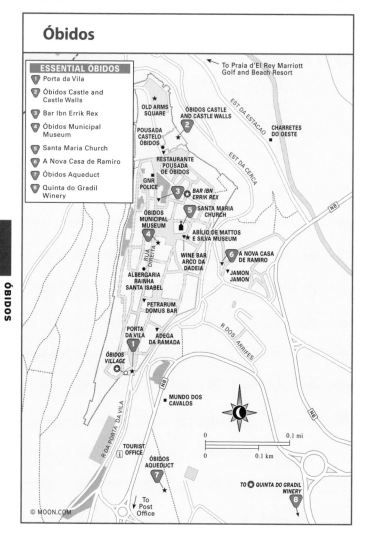

Óbidos

ESSENTIAL ÓBIDOS

1. Porta da Vila
2. Óbidos Castle and Castle Walls
3. Bar Ibn Errik Rex
4. Óbidos Municipal Museum
5. Santa Maria Church
6. A Nova Casa de Ramiro
7. Óbidos Aqueduct
8. Quinta do Gradil Winery

To Praia d'El Rey Marriott Golf and Beach Resort

OLD ARMS SQUARE

ÓBIDOS CASTLE AND CASTLE WALLS

EST DA ESTAÇÃO

CHARRETES DO OESTE

POUSADA CASTELO ÓBIDOS

2

EST DA CERCA

RESTAURANTE POUSADA DE ÓBIDOS

GNR POLICE

3 BAR IBN ERRIK REX

N8

5 SANTA MARIA CHURCH

ÓBIDOS MUNICIPAL MUSEUM

4

ABÍLIO DE MATTOS E SILVA MUSEUM

RUA DIREITA

WINE BAR ARCO DA DADEIA

6 A NOVA CASA DE RAMIRO

JAMON JAMON

ALBERGARIA RAINHA SANTA ISABEL

PETRARUM DOMUS BAR

R DOS ARRIFES

PORTA DA VILA

ADEGA DA RAMADA

1

ÓBIDOS VILLAGE

N8

MUNDO DOS CAVALOS

R DA PORTA DA VILA

0   0.1 mi

TOURIST OFFICE

0   0.1 km

ÓBIDOS AQUEDUCT

7

TO ⊙ QUINTA DO GRADIL WINERY

8

To Post Office

© MOON.COM

town's attractions, or spend a night here to enjoy the less-busy hours before 9am and after 8pm, when the tour buses leave. Due to its popularity and high volume of visiting tour buses, Óbidos can become very busy, especially during the holidays.

Start your visit with a full circle around the town along the **castle walls,** and then wander the maze of cobbled streets embraced by the battlements. If you still have time after your trip to Óbidos, nip over to the **Quinta do Gradil winery.**

Itinerary Idea

ESSENTIAL ÓBIDOS

To make the most of your trip to Óbidos, jump in the car (or on the tour bus) as early as possible.

1 Park in one of the nearby parking lots and admire the traditional tiling on the vaulted **Porta da Vila** on the way into the town.

2 Start your visit by walking the **castle embattlements:** take care, they can be uneven and there are no railings.

3 Stroll along the main Rua Direita, exploring the arts and crafts shops and trying a *ginja de Óbidos* at **Bar Ibn Errik Rex.**

4 Pop into the **Óbidos Municipal Museum.**

5 Make your way to the well-preserved castle, now a hotel, stopping at the Santa Maria Square en route to see the **Santa Maria Church** and town pillory.

6 On your way back from the castle, wander the backstreets and stop for lunch at **A Nova Casa De Ramiro,** well away from the crowds.

7 Admire the sprawling **aqueduct** before heading off.

8 If traveling independently, drive to **Quinta do Gradil** (30 minutes south) and wander amid the vineyards until dinner (book in advance) before heading back to Lisbon.

Sights

⭑ ÓBIDOS VILLAGE
(Vila de Óbidos)

Authentic and magical, Óbidos is the archetypal fortified Portuguese town, referred to locally as the "wedding gift town." Its classic beauty and layers of history make it a top destination for day trips from Lisbon, competing with Sintra and Cascais. Due to the high number of visitors, especially during popular annual events, its narrow streets can often be crowded.

The main entrance to Óbidos, the Porta da Vila (village gateway), is a sight in itself, cased in traditional blue-and-white *azulejo* tiles depicting the Passion of Christ. Absorb the historic ambience of the atmospheric town as you stroll the main shopping street, Rua Direita, from the Porta da Vila to the castle, with its plethora of traditional shops and delightful little houses with colorful flowers hanging from roofs and doorways. No trip is complete without trying a *ginja de Óbidos,* strong cherry liqueur served in shops throughout the town, usually in a chocolate cup. Plenty of shops along Rua Direita offer tastings. To flee the crowds, wander off the main street and explore Óbidos's cobbled labyrinth of side streets.

SANTA MARIA CHURCH
(Igreja de Santa Maria)

Praça de Santa Maria, tel. 262 959 633, daily 9:30am-12:30pm and 2:30pm-5pm Oct.-Mar., daily 9:30am-12:30pm and 2:30pm-7pm Apr.-Sept., free

In the middle of town, in a little square, the Praça de Santa Maria, along the main Rua Direita is the pretty 12th-century Santa Maria Church, with its striking white bell tower and fancy Renaissance portal. Inside, the walls are clad from the floor to the painted wooden ceiling in 18th-century *azulejo* tiles, and the church also houses the tomb of Dom João de Noronha, a 16th-century commander of Óbidos. In front of the church is the 15th-century town pillory, decorated with fishing net in homage to the fishermen who recovered the body of Afonso, the son of Queen Leonor and King João II, who died in a riding accident by the Tagus River.

Santa Maria Church

ÓBIDOS CASTLE AND CASTLE WALLS
(Castelo de Óbidos)

Walls open 24/7, free; for information on Pousada Castelo Óbidos hotel see www.pousadas.pt/en/hotel/pousada-obidos

Originating from the 12th century, Óbidos's excellently preserved medieval castle dominates the village. The main part, including the keep, is today an outstanding luxury *pousada* (hotel). The castle was gifted as a wedding present by King Dom Dinis to his

Óbidos Castle

new wife, Queen Santa Isabel, in 1282 when they were married here. From then until 1834, the village was owned by each queen of Portugal, earning its nicknames *Vila de Rainhas* (Village of Queens) and "wedding gift town." Over the centuries, the queens spent much time in Óbidos, and each left her influence on the village, including the local aqueduct.

The castle, now the Pousada Castelo Óbidos hotel, remains one of Óbidos's most impressive and romantic features, invoking a real sense of a bygone era, protectively guarding the village. The castle was extensively reinforced during the 14th century, so most of what can be seen today is from that era, with little surviving evidence of its earlier incarnation. A visually interesting structure, it blends four main architectural styles that characterize the centuries of its origins and expansion: Romanesque, Manueline, Baroque, and Gothic.

The hub of the town's main events is the grounds adjacent to the castle, the Old Arms Square. The sturdy castle walls, accessible via stony flights of stairs dotted around the village, were built in the 14th century when the castle's keep and battlements were reinforced; the walls encircle Óbidos and make for a unique stroll around the town. The circuit takes an hour and offers bird's-eye views over the village center. Note that walking the walls is not for everyone—the height, lack of railings, and unevenness underfoot require balance, agility, and a tolerance for heights.

ÓBIDOS MUNICIPAL MUSEUM
(Museu Municipal de Óbidos)

Rua Direita 97 - Solar da Praça de Santa Maria, tel. 262 955 500, www.obidos.pt, Tues.-Sun. 10am-1pm and 2pm-5pm, free

Pop into the small but well-formed Óbidos Municipal Museum to learn more about the town's devout religious history, conveyed in its permanent collection of artwork. Among the works displayed are 16th- and

165

Óbidos Aqueduct

17th-century paintings by André Reinoso, Portugal's first Baroque painter, and influential artist Josefa D'Obidos. Also has a little bookshop and clean bathrooms.

ABÍLIO DE MATTOS E SILVA MUSEUM
(Museu Abílio de Mattos e Silva)

Santa Maria Square, tel. 262 955 500,
Tues.-Sun. 10am-1pm and 2pm to 6pm, free

Located just off Rua Direita (the main street) to the rear of Santa Maria Square, this curious museum is worth a look. It showcases several old marionettes and artwork by Óbidos resident and renowned painter and set and costume designer Abílio de Mattos e Silva.

ÓBIDOS AQUEDUCT
(Aqueduto de Óbidos)

Across from the main parking lot and Porta da Vila

On the outskirts of town, across from the main parking lot and Porta da Vila entrance, is the long, spindly Óbidos Aqueduct, also known as the Aqueduct of Usseira. Remarkable in its slenderness and intactness, it was built at the order of Queen Dona Catarina of Austria, wife of Dom João III, in 1573 to bring water from the nearby Usseira spring to the village's fountains.

Festivals and Events

International Chocolate Festival (Festival Internacional de Chocolate)

www.festivalchocolate.cm-obidos.pt, €4, Feb., Mar., or Apr.

A 12-day event over a series of weekends in February, March, or April, the International Chocolate Festival is staged in the Old Arms Square, next to the castle, where small shacks emit the glorious sweet scent of warm chocolate. The festival showcases cocoa-based goodies from traditional Portuguese sweets to contemporary concoctions, and the obligatory hot chocolate or *ginja* liqueur served in a chocolate cup. Guests can also take cocoa-making classes for all ages.

ginja liqueur served in a chocolate cup

Medieval Fair (Feira Medieval)

www.mercadomedievalobidos.pt, €7, July-Aug.

Every year from a Thursday in mid-July to the Sunday in the first week of August, Óbidos's quaint streets are transformed into a medieval village for the Medieval Fair, complete with colorful bunting, fire-eaters, wizards, court jesters, jousting knights on horseback, falconry, and medieval gastronomy. The hub of activity is in the Old Arms Square, adjacent to the castle, where little shacks form a medieval marketplace selling food and handicrafts typical of the era. A costume shop rents outfits for just €5 if you want to get into the theatrical spirit of the fair. This is one of Portugal's most famous events and well worth a visit.

Christmas Village (Óbidos Vila Natal)

www.obidosvilanatal.pt, Dec.

Every year during December, Óbidos becomes a real-life snow globe, full of festive spirit and sparkly trimmings, when it hosts its famous annual Christmas Village. Hundreds of stalls sell gifts and hot chocolate, and fairground rides, shows, and entertainment fill the quaint streets. Dress warmly; this open-air event has an authentic winter chill.

Óbidos's Medieval Fair

Food

Jamon Jamon
Rua da Biquinha, tel. 916 208 162, Tues.-Sat.
noon-3pm and 7pm-10pm, Sun. noon-3pm,
€15

Traditional Portuguese cuisine is
served with a generous helping of
warm hospitality at this popular little tavern. Highly recommended are
the chef's duck rice special and pork
cheeks.

A Nova Casa de Ramiro
Rua Porta do Vale 12, tel. 967 265 945,
Mon. 7pm-11pm, Tues.-Thurs. noon-3pm and
7pm-11pm, Fri. 1pm-4pm and 7pm-11pm, €18

Located away from the throngs, just
outside the city walls, this theatrically
glamorous restaurant with its chandeliers and open fireplace is highly
regarded among locals and highly
rated by visitors. It serves luscious
Mediterranean cuisine; fresh fish and
seafood are menu staples.

Adega da Ramada
Travessa Nossa Sra. do Rosario 3, tel. 964
606 711, www.adegadoramada.com, Mon.
noon-10pm, Tues.-Sat. noon-4pm and
6:30pm-9:30pm, Sun. noon-4:30pm, €20

Tucked away on one of Óbidos's
quaint cobbled backstreets just off
the main drag, Adega da Ramada is a
simple tavernlike eatery with stepped
outdoor seating. It serves tasty grilled
meat and fish dishes on traditional

an outdoor café in Óbidos

clay crockery from its streetside
open grill; local specialties include a
black pig grilled skewer with hand-
cut chips. Good house wine to boot.

Restaurante Pousada de Óbidos
Pousada Castelo de Óbidos hotel, Paço Real
s/n, tel. 262 955 080, www.pousadas.pt/en/
hotel/pousada-obidos, daily 1pm-3pm and
7:30pm-10pm, €45

For fine dining with a difference,
head to the Pousada Castelo de
Óbidos castle hotel and enjoy a romantic meal in a historic setting.
The menu features traditional gourmet fare, inspired by regional ingredients and recipes.

⚙ GINJA: ÓBIDOS'S OWN CHERRY LIQUOR

Like many of Portugal's most famous sweet treats, history has it that this popular drink, an infusion of macerated morello cherries in *aguardente* alcohol, originates from the country's convents. Dating to the 17th century, its original recipe is to this day a closely guarded secret, known only to a privileged few. That recipe is thought to have been first brewed by a friar—possibly with medicinal purposes as *ginja* is a renowned digestive aid—and later local families would compete to see who could best replicate the recipe. Its popularity sky-rocketed hand-in-hand with Óbidos's tourism. Thanks to its specific microclimate, the Óbidos region produces some of the finest cherries in Europe.

Try *ginja* for yourself in Óbidos at **Bar Ibn Errik Rex** or **Petrarum Domus Bar,** or at any of the many other shops that sell it along **Rua Direita.**

ginja

Bars and Nightlife

⚙ Bar Ibn Errik Rex

Rua Direita 100, tel. 262 959 193, daily 11am-1am

Don't miss Bar Ibn Errik Rex, one of the oldest and best *ginja* bars in town, open since 1956. A medieval-style, family-run bar on the main street, it has more than 1,800 dusty miniature bottles hanging from the ceiling.

Petrarum Domus Bar

Rua Direita 38, tel. 262 959 620, www.petrarumdomus.com, Weds.-Mon. noon-10pm

A medieval-feeling bar and restaurant in a historic building with natural stone and wood features. Petrarum Domus showcases local wines and takes traditional tipple *ginja* and transforms it into delicious long drinks and cocktails.

Wine Bar Arco da Cadeia

Rua do Hospital, tel. 917 368 328, www.facebook.com/arcodacadeia, Tues.-Sun. 11am-2am, Mon. 11am-5pm

Hidden away on a backstreet under the old prison archway, this medieval wine bar serves fruity cocktails, refreshing sangria, and excellent wines. Snacks and tapas also available.

Accommodations

Albergaria Rainha Santa Isabel

Rua Direita 63, tel. 262 959 323, www.obidoshotel.com, €50-100 d

Inside the town walls on the main street, the charming and casual three-star Albergaria Rainha Santa Isabel is in a historic whitewashed building, with 20 simple old-fashioned rooms and a cozy guest lounge. Breakfast is included.

Pousada Vila Óbidos

Largo Dr. João Lourenço, tel. 210 407 635, www.pousadas.pt, €100-€200 d

Opened in 2018, the Pousada Convento de Óbidos is one of the most recent of the Pestana Group's fascinating conversions of local historic buildings, this time of Óbidos's old town hospital. Providing a "home-tel" experience, this lovely little building offers a tranquil and comfortable refuge with 17 rooms of modern and stylish décor and a pretty courtyard, conveniently located inside the walls of the bustling town.

✪ Praia d'El Rey Marriott Golf and Beach Resort

Av. D. Inês de Castro 1, Vale de Janelas, tel. 262 905 100, www.marriott.com, €200-300 d

The sprawling Praia d'El Rey Marriott Golf and Beach Resort is on the coast, 23 kilometers (14 miles) west of Óbidos and 57 kilometers (35 miles) south of Nazaré. This upscale place has 177 airy rooms and suites, a spa, and an 18-hole golf course.

ÓBIDOS
ACCOMMODATIONS

Pousada Castelo Óbidos

✪ QUINTA DO GRADIL WINERY

Quinta do Gradil Winery

Twenty-five kilometers (15.5 miles) south of Óbidos in the parish of Cadaval is the Quinta do Gradil Winery (Estrada Nacional 115, tel. 262 770 000, www.quintadogradil. wine), a unique 120-hectare (297-acre) estate between sea and hills that once belonged to the family of the Marquis of Pombal, an important 18th-century Portuguese statesman. It sits on the western foothills of the Montejunto mountain range in a region of varied geology, climate, and vegetation that create a distinctive terroir that produces fine wines. These include **Mula Velha,** the eponymous **Quinta do Gradil,** and **Castelo do Sulco.** The farm's endless rows of vines make an excellent stop to learn more about wine-making.

The elegant Quinta opens its doors to the public every **harvest** (Sept.-Oct.) for visitors to take part in the grape-picking process, and **year-round wine tastings** (Mon.-Sat. 11:30am and 3:30pm, Sun. 11:30am, from €9) are offered that can be combined with degustation menus (from €70). Dinner is also an option at the excellent on-site **Restaurant Quinta do Gradil** (tel. 917 791 974, Weds.-Mon. lunch 10am-6pm, Fri.-Sat. dinner 7pm-10pm, €25), converted from a former cereal storehouse. Large groups should reserve in advance.

GETTING THERE
From Óbidos, Quinta do Gradil is a 20-minute, 25-kilometer (15.5-mile) drive south on the **A8** motorway. The easiest way to get here by public transport is by **taxi,** which costs around €25 one way. Taxis are available just outside the Porta da Vila.

✪ Pousada Castelo Óbidos

Paço Real, tel. 210 407 630, www.pousadas. pt/en/hotel/pousada-obidos, €250-350 d

Spend a night in the heart of Óbidos town in the imposing 700-year-old Castelo Óbidos, which is today a luxury *pousada* (hotel). Each of the 11 rooms, 3 of which are in the castle keep, is individually decorated, while the adjacent 8-room Casa do Castelo cottage offers authentic yet comfortable medieval lodging.

Information and Services

- **National emergency number:** tel. 112
- **GNR police:** Rua Direita, tel. 262 955 000, www.gnr.pt
- **Tourist office:** Rua da Porta da Vila, ground floor, tel. 262 959 231, www.obidos.pt, Mon.-Fri. 9:30am-6pm, Sat.-Sun. 9:30am-12:30pm and 1:30pm-5:30pm
- **Post office:** Praça Santa Maria, tel. 262 955 041, www.ctt.pt, Mon.-Fri. 9am-12:30pm and 2:30pm-6pm

Getting There and Around

GETTING THERE

CAR

Óbidos is 80 kilometers (50 miles) north of Lisbon, a fast and easy drive on the A8 motorway (tolls apply) that takes just over one hour. Cars can be parked in a large parking lot (€2 for 1.5 hours) just outside the Porta da Vila gate, opposite the tourist information center. When it gets full, especially common in summer, there is a large overflow parking lot just across the road by the aqueduct.

BUS

An express-bus service named the Rápida Verde (1 hour, Mon.-Fri. hourly, less frequently Sat.-Sun. and holidays, €7.70), operated by bus company Rodoviária do Tejo (tel. 249 787 878, www.rodotejo.pt), runs between Lisbon's Campo Grande station, near Alvalade stadium, and Óbidos's parking lot, just outside the city walls near the Porta da Vila gate. The same service also runs to Alcobaça and Nazaré.

National bus service Rede Expressos (tel. 707 223 344, www.rede-expressos.pt) operates a similar service from its main Lisbon hub, Sete Rios.

GETTING AROUND

Óbidos is easily seen in one day and can be explored comfortably on foot. Cars are not allowed within the historic center and must park in the parking lot just outside the city walls, a two-minute walk south of the Porta da Vila gate.

CARRIAGE RIDES

Take a step back in time and rumble along the cobbled streets in an old-fashioned horse and carriage (30 minutes, 4 adults from €30 outside the walls, €65 inside the walls). Charretes do Oeste (tel. 262 835 562, www.charretesdooeste.com) and Mundo dos Cavalos (tel. 968 881 805 or 918 509 521, www.mundodoscavalos.pt) operate year-round, awaiting passengers in the main parking lot, but rides are subject to weather conditions.

NAZARÉ

Before becoming a monster-

wave surfing hot spot, Nazaré was a fishing town and popular traditional seaside resort. Today the town's charming main seafront avenue is flanked by dense construction. Famed for its excellent fresh seafood as much as for incredible surfing conditions, Nazaré can feel overrun, especially in peak season, and modern development has taken the shine off its fishing-town charm. Nonetheless, authentic traits and traditions persevere.

Watch the laden dragnets brought in to the shouts of local fisherwomen, who still wear the

HIGHLIGHTS

✪ **SUBERCO VIEWPOINT:** Take the vertiginous Nazaré funicular to Sítio headland and enjoy panoramic views of Nazaré town and beach from the Suberco viewpoint (page 178).

✪ **ALCOBAÇA MONASTERY:** Marvel at this Gothic masterpiece just 15 minutes' drive from Nazaré (page 179).

✪ **SURFING:** Time it right and you could see the world's bravest surfers tackle monster waves that dwarf the local lighthouse (page 181).

traditional seven skirts and headscarves. Along the beachfront, you'll see boards of butterflied fish left to cure in the open air, sold by the fisherwomen as a local delicacy. You can also enjoy the fresh catch at one of the many local beachfront seafood restaurants.

ORIENTATION

Nazaré's main landmarks are mostly located along its **beachfront** and up on the **Sítio headland** that towers over the town. Fantastic fresh fish restaurants line the vast crescent moon of golden sand that is Nazaré's famous beach. The **funicular** up to Sítio is located at the north end of the beachfront, along which there is a pleasant seafront promenade and main avenue, **Avenida da República.** An interesting part of Nazaré town is the **fishermen's quarters,** located between **Manuel de Arriaga square** and **Avenida Vieira Guimarães.** The **lighthouse,** Suberco viewpoint, and Memorial Hermitage are all located up on the Sítio headland, which is where the older part of Nazaré is situated. From up here in winter, visitors can watch surfers ride the monster waves.

PLANNING YOUR TIME

At a push, a half a day could suffice to see Nazaré's main attributes and enjoy a fresh fish lunch or dinner; you could pop up here for a quick look around after visiting **Óbidos,** for example. But the traditional little town warrants a full day, especially if you want to watch the surfing and tie in a trip to the nearby **Alcobaça Monastery.** Located 1.5 hours' drive north of **Lisbon** (121 km/75 mi), in summer Nazaré teems with holidaymakers young and old—it caters to both thanks to a remarkably vibrant nightlife—and **parking** can become a bit of an issue, as can beach space. But visit off season for a quieter experience and enjoy the bracing sea breeze and huge waves.

Itinerary Idea

BEACH DAY IN NAZARÉ

Set off from Lisbon after breakfast and head for **Alcobaça** on the A8 motorway (this route passes almost directly through Óbidos).

1 Spend an hour or two exploring the **Alcobaça Monastery** before making the 20-minute drive northwest to Nazaré.

2 Enjoy fresh fish or the local specialty of octopus with olive oil for lunch at **Pangeia Restaurante.**

3 Walk off lunch with a stroll along the promenade at **Nazaré Beach** and admire the colorful, typical wooden fishing boats and fisher-folk on the beach.

4 Head to the northern end of the beach to the **funicular** and ride up to the Sítio headland.

5 Enjoy the views from the **Suberco viewpoint.**

Nazaré Beach and promenade

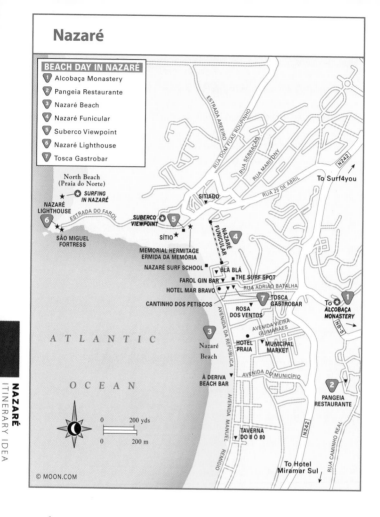

Nazaré

BEACH DAY IN NAZARÉ

1. Alcobaça Monastery
2. Pangeia Restaurante
3. Nazaré Beach
4. Nazaré Funicular
5. Suberco Viewpoint
6. Nazaré Lighthouse
7. Tosca Gastrobar

North Beach
(Praia do Norte)

★ ✿ SURFING
IN NAZARÉ

NAZARÉ
LIGHTHOUSE

ESTRADA DO FAROL

SÃO MIGUEL
FORTRESS

SITIADO ★

SUBERCO ✿ 5
VIEWPOINT

SÍTIO ★

To Surf4you

MEMORIAL HERMITAGE
ERMIDA DA MEMÓRIA

NAZARÉ SURF SCHOOL

FAROL GIN BAR ▼

HOTEL MAR BRAVÓ ●

CANTINHO DOS PETISCOS

BLÁ BLÁ

4 NAZARÉ FUNICULAR

THE SURF SPOT

RUA ADRIÃO BATALHA

7 TOSCA
GASTROBAR

ROSA
DOS VENTOS

To ✿
ALCOBAÇA
MONASTERY

A T L A N T I C

O C E A N

3

Nazaré
Beach

À DERIVA
BEACH BAR

HOTEL
PRAIA

MUNICIPAL
MARKET

AVENIDA VIEIRA
GUIMARÃES

AVENIDA DA REPÚBLICA

AVENIDA DO MUNICÍPIO

AVENIDA MANUEL REMÍGIO

2

PANGEIA
RESTAURANTE

N242

RUA CAMINHO REAL

0   200 yds
0   200 m

TAVERNA
DO 8 Ó 80 ▼

To Hotel
Miramar Sul

© MOON.COM

NAZARÉ
ITINERARY IDEA

6 Walk to the **lighthouse** to gaze at the hypnotic sea surrounding it.

7 Head back down to Nazaré town, where you can have a lighter dinner at **Tosca Gastrobar** before returning to Lisbon.

Sights

NAZARÉ FUNICULAR
(Ascensor da Nazaré)

Rua de São Lázaro, tel. 262 550 010, www.
cm-nazare.pt, daily 7:30am-8:30pm
Oct.-May, daily 7:30am-midnight
June-mid-July and late Sept., daily
7:30am-2am mid-July-mid-Sept., €1.20

The dizzying Nazaré Funicular takes passengers from the urban beachfront up to Sítio, an older extension of the town on a headland atop cliffs to the north.

The modern funicular cabs climb a historic track, ascending 318 meters (1,043 feet) in 15 minutes, between residential buildings at the bottom, through a tunnel, offering astounding views of Nazaré as they ascend to the top. This fun, easy, and cheap experience is a short trip and a good way to get to Sítio without a car—parking at the top can be hard to find, especially on weekends. The funicular runs every 15 minutes or so.

SÍTIO

Soar up the vertiginous rock face on Nazaré's famed funicular to the elevated part of town, on cliffs to the north of Nazaré main beach, known as Sítio, comprising a lovely large square flanked by stunning views, quaint shops and restaurants, a large sanctuary, and a chapel. In summer, Sítio can offer some respite from the throngs in the main part of town. From Sítio's main piazza, it is a short walk down to the lighthouse, where

view from the top of the Nazaré funicular

NAZARÉ
SIGHTS

177

THE FASCINATING FOLKTALES OF THE MEMORIAL HERMITAGE

Once upon a time, the Sítio promontory teemed with deer, and a bizarre contemporary **statue** of a surfer with a deer's head, which stands halfway down the road to the São Miguel Fortress, pays tribute to the locale's blended history.

According to local legend, in 1182 nobleman Dom Fuas Roupinho was hunting in dense fog and stopped just short of the edge of the cliff where his deer vanished. Just as he was about to fall to his death, he cried out to Our Lady of Nazaré, who appeared before him and stopped his horse. The rider ordered a chapel, the **Memorial Hermitage** (Ermida da Memória, Rua 25 de Abril, open 24/7, free), built in honor of this miracle; it can be visited just off Sítio's main square.

Memorial Hermitage

This enthralling piece of folklore is depicted in the traditional 17th-century *azulejos* that completely clad the interior of the small, square chapel, with its pyramidlike roof. A supposed **hoofprint** of the nobleman's horse is engraved in a stone found in a crypt beneath the chapel. Other folktales claim explorer Vasco da Gama prayed here before setting off on his voyages. The chapel was built above a cave in the cliffs where, during Moorish occupation, there stood a small statue of a black Madonna nursing the baby Jesus.

you can view the underwater canyon made famous by the photos of the huge monster waves.

✪ SUBERCO VIEWPOINT

Sítio promontory, just beyond the funicular exit

Make sure to stop at the Suberco viewpoint for breathtaking vistas of Nazaré and the beach.

SÃO MIGUEL ARCANJO FORTRESS

Estrada do Farol, tel. 938 013 587, https:// praiadonorte.com.pt/sobre/forte-s-miguel-arcanjo, daily 10am-6pm, €1

Built in 1577 by order of King Sebastian of Portugal and later expanded in 1644 by D. João VI, the fortress of São Miguel Arcanjo sits in a privileged position on a jagged promontory. Surrounded by the fearsome Atlantic, it has become one of Nazaré's top attractions and is the ultimate viewpoint for big-wave surfing competitions. Open year-round, the fortress also houses an interpretive center on the underwater Nazaré Canyon as well as surf-related exhibitions.

NAZARÉ LIGHTHOUSE

Estrada do Farol, tel. 265 561 967, http:// wlol.arlhs.com, daily 10am-6pm, €1

The best place to observe the fearsome spectacle of the monster waves is at the Nazaré Lighthouse, within the stone walls of the São Miguel Arcanjo Fortress on a promontory near **North Beach** (Praia do Norte), a short walk from the Sítio headland's main square. This outcrop was made famous in 2011 after photos of Garrett McNamara's big-wave victory traveled the globe, showing the tiny lighthouse dwarfed by the huge swells in the background. As well as spectacular views, the lighthouse also hosts an exhibition of paraphernalia relating to the local surfing scene.

OUTSIDE NAZARÉ
✪ ALCOBAÇA MONASTERY
(Mosteiro de Alcobaça)

Praça 25 de Abril, tel. 262 505 120, www.
mosteiroalcobaca.pt, daily 9am-6pm
Oct.-Mar., daily 9am-7pm Apr.-Sept., €6

Understated Alcobaça (al-koh-BAH-ssah) is on the tourist map for its staggering focal monument, the Alcobaça Monastery. A 15-minute drive inland from coastal Nazaré, it's worth passing through, even just to gaze at this feat of Gothic architecture.

Founded by the Order of Cistercians in 1153, Alcobaça Monastery, also known as the Royal Abbey of Santa Maria, is one of Portugal's foremost monuments, a masterpiece of Gothic architecture whose purity and finesse earned its classification by UNESCO as a World Heritage Site. It was Portugal's first truly Gothic building, constructed by Afonso Henrique I after victory over the Moors at Santarém in 1147. Construction began in 1178, with the main central church—the largest church in Portugal at the time—completed in the mid-13th century. Additions were made in the centuries that followed.

Hidden behind the monastery's lavish Baroque facade is the phenomenal Gothic **church** (free), whose narrow length and soaring ribbed ceiling in the nave let light flood in, illuminating the interior. It is the final resting place of 14th-century Pedro I and Inês de Castro, famous for their tragic love story. Their intricately carved tombs face each other.

Added to the monastery in the late 13th century, the **Cloister of Silence (Claustro do Silencio)** is one of the largest medieval Cistercian cloisters

Alcobaça Monastery

in Europe. Its sheer size and exquisitely carved Gothic architecture are remarkable, its name evocative of the silently moving monks who inhabited its walls. The cloister centers on a peaceful garden with a lovely Renaissance fountain in the middle.

More features worth seeing inside the monastery include the Kings Room (Sala dos Reis), where sculptures of Portuguese kings peer down on visitors and old *azulejos* clad the walls; the Chapter House (Sala do Capítulo), where monks gathered to discuss the daily running of the complex; a huge upstairs dormitory; a refectory (dining hall) with a pulpit embedded in the wall; and the impressive kitchen, with its gigantic tile-clad chimney.

A combined ticket to the Alcobaça Monastery, Batalha Monastery, and Tomar Convent of Christ (€15) is valid for seven days. Alcobaça is 122 kilometers (76 miles) north of Lisbon, a 1.5-hour drive via the A8 motorway and 16 kilometers (10 miles) east from coastal Nazaré, a 15-minute drive via the IC9 road.

The best way to get to Alcobaça by public transport is the direct bus service from Lisbon. Rodoviária do Tejo (tel. 249 787 878, www.rodotejo.pt) runs several express buses (2 hours, €9.85), leaving Lisbon's Campo Grande almost hourly on weekdays, less frequently on weekends and holidays. Rede Expressos (tel. 707 223 344, www.rede-expressos.pt) operates similar bus service from its main Lisbon hub, Sete Rios (2 hours, €10.90). Rodoviária do Tejo (tel. 249 787 878, www.rodotejo.pt) also operates over a dozen daily services between Nazaré and Alcobaça (20 minutes, €2.30). The bus station in Alcobaça is on Avenida Manuel da Silva Carolino, a 10-minute walk east of the monastery.

Sports and Recreation

BEACHES
Nazaré Beach
(Praia da Nazaré)

Nazaré beachfront, República Avenue, limited parking

A huge crescent-moon stretch of glimmering blond sand favored for fishing and surfing is Nazaré's calling card. Due to the offshore underwater formation that creates the famously huge waves, the water here can be choppy and cool, although calmer in summer when the beach is packed with holidaymakers. Nazaré's main beach is fringed by a long seafront avenue and the main avenue, Avenida da República, with its end-to-end shops, bars, and restaurants. Even though the sea here can be cold and rough, even in summer, and strong undercurrents are also something to watch out for, the main beach is sheltered by the Sítio headland and therefore calmer and less breezy than just around the corner, on Praia do Norte (North Beach).

North Beach
(Praia do Norte)

Rua Praia do Norte, parking available

While the main Praia da Nazaré beach is surfable, particularly in winter, the famous big-wave surfing is not on this beach; the hot spot for extreme surfing is a little further north, just after

Garret McNamara surfing in Nazaré

Since the 1960s, Nazaré has been a popular place among experienced surfers looking for a challenge—but recently it gained a whole new level of fame as one of the planet's top spots for extreme big-wave surfing. Once a year, typically in **November,** Nazaré's underwater canyon creates perfect conditions for enormous waves.

In November 2011, U.S. professional big-wave surfer Garrett McNamara conquered a monstrous 24-meter (79-foot) wave in Nazaré, setting a world record for the largest wave ever surfed. His name is now synonymous with Nazaré's surf scene, having almost single-handedly catapulted the once-sleepy coastal resort onto the must-surf map. (McNamara's record has since been smashed by Brazilian surfer Rodrigo Koxa, who surfed a 24.4-meter/80-foot wave in November 2017.)

THE MONSTER WAVE PHENOMENON
The monster waves are formed by a unique underwater canyon off Nazaré, a finger-shaped crevice pointing toward the town; the colossal waves create a year-round attraction, as visitors hope to witness Mother Nature's full fury unleashed—especially in winter. Outside November, the waves can still be big but nowhere near as spectacularly fearsome. There are plenty of surf schools and shops throughout Nazaré and along the beachfront where boards can be rented.

the Sítio headland, where the deep finger-shaped underwater canyon channels colossal swells. This beach is the wild and windy Praia do Norte (North Beach).

✪ SURFING

Nazaré, particularly **Praia do Norte,** is known as a surfing mecca, whether you want to try some of the legendary waves yourself or watch the pros.

Surf4you
Rua Fernando Ybarra 21, tel. 926 384 594, www.surf4-you.com

Local surf company Surf4you is popular for lessons and coaching.

Nazaré Surf School
Avenida da Republica, edificio S.Miguel s/n (basement), tel. 916 386 907, www. nazaresurfschool.pt
The beachfront Nazaré Surf School also offers lessons and board rentals.

The Surf Spot
Rua Mouzinho de Albuquerque 5, tel. 916 966 328, daily 10am-11pm
If it's clothing or equipment you want, head to specialist store The Surf Spot.

NAZARÉ
SPORTS AND RECREATION

LOCAL SPECIALTY: OCTOPUS WITH OLIVE OIL

Given the town's seafront location, Nazaré's local gastronomy is based on fresh seafood. A typical dish is *polvo á lagareiro* (octopus cooked in a pressure cooker and served with lashings of hot olive oil). The octopus should be soft, not chewy, and is usually served with small baked potatoes and lots of garlic.

WHERE TO TRY IT

Two top places to try this local delicacy are ✪ **Pangeia Restaurante** (Rua Abel da Silva 50, Nazaré, tel. 917 934 726, www.pangeiarestaurante.com, Thurs.-Tues. noon-3pm and 7pm-10pm, Weds. noon-3pm, €20) and tapas eatery **Cantinho dos Petiscos** (Rua Alexandre Herculano, Nazaré, tel. 915 064 325, Wed.-Mon. 10:30am-2am, €20).

polvo á lagareiro

Food

Municipal Market (Mercado Municipal)

Av. Vieira Guimarães, tel. 262 550 010, Tues.-Sun. 8am-1pm

Get up close and personal with the locals at the lively Nazaré Municipal Market. Sellers' benches are piled high with colorful fresh fruit and veggies, sweets, and local delicacies, as they noisily go about their business as they have for decades. This place is an authentic working Portuguese market with genuine local soul. A great place to sample local flavor and stock up with picnic supplies for a day at the beach.

Tosca Gastrobar

Rua Mouzinho de Albuquerque 4, tel. 262 562 261, Thurs.-Tues. noon-3pm and 7pm-10pm, €15

Local products meet international favorites at Tosca Gastrobar, a small, trendy gastropub where creative snack-size dishes take center stage. Baked camembert with walnuts and red fruit coulis, shrimp pasta, and spinach, apple, and cheese strudel are on the innovative menu. Reservations are recommended.

Sitiado

Rua Amadeu Guadêncio, tel. 262 087 512, Weds.-Mon. 11:30am-3pm and 7pm-10pm, €15

The quirky vintage decor at Sitiado, a colorful, petite restaurant (note the bicycle hanging on the wall), does little to convey the traditionally Portuguese essence of its menu. Simple salads, juicy grilled tuna steaks, beef steaks, and a range of tasty tapas (try the *casquinhas*, potato skins) make up the menu.

Rosa dos Ventos

Rua Gil Vicente 88, tel. 918 267 127, Fri.-Weds. noon-3:15pm and 7pm-9:30pm, €18

It might not be a beachfront place, but the seafood at Rosa dos Ventos is second to none. Set back from the beach on the main road through the top end of town, near the funicular, Rosa dos Ventos serves fresh fish and shellfish, simply boiled or grilled. Tasty fish stews and homemade desserts round out the offerings.

Bars and Nightlife

Taverna do 8 ó 80
Av. Manuel Remígio, tel. 262 560 490, www.tavernado8o80.pt, Weds.-Mon. noon-midnight, €20
Busy, sociable tavern-turned-wine-bar Taverna do 8 ó 80 is a beachfront restaurant that specializes in traditional favorites with a modern twist. The food is pricy because of the restaurant's location and reputation; specialties include sea bream ceviche, fried goat cheese, and mushrooms with *alheira* sausage.

Farol Gin Bar
Praça Sousa Oliveira 25, tel. 962 393 721, daily 10am-4am
For great gins (over 20 to choose from!) and refreshing cocktails the Farol Gin Bar is the place to go; it is one of the most popular and busiest little bars lining the Praça square.

À Deriva Beach Bar
Avenida Manuel Remígio 87, tel. 967 029 890, daily 10am-8pm
Enjoy a sundowner in style at this salt-tinged beach bar, toward the southern end of the main avenue. Watch the sun set with a cool beer in hand after a day at the beach.

Blá Blá
Rua do Guilhim 3, tel. 914 005 180, www.blabla.club, daily 10pm-dawn in summer, weekends only during winter
A late-night hangout, Blá Blá nightclub has long been a reference on Nazaré's club scene. It offers themed nights, such as reggae and afrobeat, and live DJ sets.

Accommodations

Hotel Miramar Sul
Cam. Real, tel. 262 590 000, www.miramarnazarehotels.com, €100-200 d
Part of the local Miramar Nazaré Hotels group, the Miramar Sul is located toward the southern end of Nazaré's beachfront, a laid-back, light and bright, affordable four-star hotel with two pools, sea views, and plenty of sun beds.

Hotel Mar Bravo
Praca Sousa Oliveira 71, tel. 262 569 160, www.marbravo.com, €100-200 d
A fantastic little 16-room hotel at the northern end of Nazaré's main beach. Hotel Mar Bravo's clean and contemporary décor enhances the summery vibes of the dazzling white sands and deep blue sea of its beachfront location.

Hotel Praia

Av. Vieira Guimarães 39, tel. 262 569 200,
www.hotelpraia.com, €100-200 d

Located in the center of Nazaré, just two minutes' walk from the beachfront, this hotel blends great location, comfort, and modern style. Family apartments are available, it has a pool, and parking costs an extra €5/day.

Getting There and Around

GETTING THERE

CAR

By car, Nazaré is 122 kilometers (76 miles) north of **Lisbon,** a 1.5-hour drive, following the **A8** motorway (tolls apply). From **Óbidos,** Nazaré is a 40-kilometer (25-mile), 30-minute drive north along the **A8.**

BUS

Rodoviária do Tejo (tel. 249 787 878, www.rodotejo.pt) operates the Rápida Verde express-bus service between Lisbon's **Campo Grande station** and Nazaré (1.75 hours, Mon.-Fri. hourly, less frequently Sat.-Sun. and holidays, €9.85). **Rede Expressos** (tel. 707 223 344, www.rede-expressos.pt) operates similar bus service from its main Lisbon hub, **Sete Rios** (1.75 hours, €10.90).

    Rodoviária do Oeste (tel. 262 767 676, www.rodoviariadooeste. pt) operates buses three times a day between **Óbidos** and Nazaré (1.25 hours, €4), and there is an evening Rápida Verde bus between the towns. The main **bus station** in Nazaré is on **Avenida do Município,** a few streets back from the beachfront, about a 10-minute walk.

GETTING AROUND

Most of Nazaré can be easily covered **on foot.** The main beachfront drag, **Avenida da República,** between the little **port** to the south and the **funicular** at the northern end of the main **Praia da Nazaré,** is about 1.5 km (1 mi), a 20-minute walk from one end to the other. The funicular is the best way to get from the main town to Sítio, although there are **stairs.** You could also drive, but **parking** is at a premium in Nazaré, especially up in Sítio and during holidays and on weekends.

TOMAR

A sense of history and grandeur

pervades the town of Tomar, which straddles the pretty Nabão River. Shrouded in mystery and packed with fascinating sights and ruins, the town was a key pillar in the formation of Portugal. During the 13th century, Tomar was a powerful town as the seat of the Knights Templar, a Catholic military order founded in 1119.

In addition to ruins with intriguing history, Tomar offers leisurely, picturesque walks along the Nabão River or a stroll through lovely Mouchão Park. Browse the many traditional

HIGHLIGHTS

✪ **CONVENT OF CHRIST:** A UNESCO World Heritage Site, the Convent of Christ is a fascinating complex of ancient buildings once inhabited by the enigmatic Knights Templar (page 189).

✪ **ALMOUROL CASTLE:** Atop an island of rocky boulders in the middle of the Tagus River, Almourol Castle is a sight to behold and requires a fun boat ride to get there (page 192).

✪ **QUEIJADAS:** Finger-licking sticky and sweet, the delectable local *queijada* cakes are made from the unusual combination of almond and squash. Try one at **Café Estrelas de Tomar** (page 194).

shops and cafés in the sleepy town center and indulge in one of Tomar's typical cakes, such as the almond and squash *queijadas* (sticky cakes) or the *fatias de Tomar* (Tomar slices) made with egg yolks, sugar, and water slowly cooked in a bain-marie in a special pan invented by a local tinsmith in the mid-20th century. As the locals say, the secret is in the pan.

ORIENTATION

The **Nabão River** flows tranquilly through the middle of Tomar; the town's main square, **Praça da República**, the **train station**, and other attractions such as the **Matchbox Museum** and the fascinating **Convent of Christ** are all on the western side of the river. The Convent complex is a 10-minute uphill hike from the main square, or a 15-minute walk from the train station, and the

vistas en route are fantastic. Or take one of the **tuk-tuks** that can be found zipping around.

PLANNING YOUR TIME

Located approximately 140 km (87 mi) north of Lisbon (1.5 hours), a full day should be allocated to Tomar. It is possible to do Tomar as a day trip, by **car** or by **train**, although a car is recommended if you want to visit the **Almourol Castle** too. The **Convent of Christ** alone warrants the journey. Spend a full morning or afternoon exploring the Convent of Christ, enjoy lunch in one of Tomar's many little local eateries, and use the rest of the day to wander around charming Tomar town or make the half-hour drive south to visit the Almourol Castle—a must-see when in this part of Portugal.

Itinerary Idea

ESSENTIAL TOMAR

Set off from Lisbon after an early breakfast and head for Tomar—aim to arrive mid-morning.

1 Head straight to the **Convent of Christ** and allow a good couple of hours to explore its nooks and crannies.

2 Make your way back down to the main town; enjoy lunch and a *queijada* at **Café Estrelas de Tomar.**

3 Walk off lunch with a stroll though Tomar's quaint streets, to the Nabão River and **Mouchão Park.**

4 Explore the quirky **Matchbox Museum** before heading back to your car.

5 Make the half-hour drive south to **Almourol Castle,** a dramatic castle arrived at by boat (make sure you allow enough time for the last boat back!).

Convent of Christ garden

Tomar

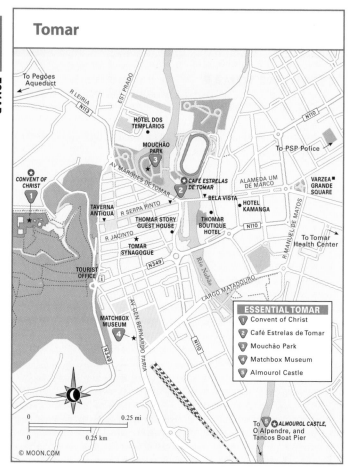

To Pegões Aqueduct

R LEIRIA N113

EST. PRADO

HOTEL DOS TEMPLÁRIOS

MOUCHÃO PARK

AV. MARQUES DE TOMAR

N110

To PSP Police

CONVENT OF CHRIST **1**

CAFÉ ESTRELAS DE TOMAR **2**

ALAMEDA UM DE MARCO

VARZEA GRANDE SQUARE

BELA VISTA

TAVERNA ANTIGUA

R SERPA PINTO

THOMAR STORY GUEST HOUSE

THOMAR BOUTIQUE HOTEL

HOTEL KAMANGA

N110

R. MANUEL DE MATOS

To Tomar Health Center

R JACINTO

TOMAR SYNAGOGUE

N349

Rio Nabão

TOURIST OFFICE

LARGO MATADOURO

MATCHBOX MUSEUM **4**

AV. GEN BERNARDO FARIA

N349

N110

ESSENTIAL TOMAR
1 Convent of Christ
2 Café Estrelas de Tomar
3 Mouchão Park
4 Matchbox Museum
5 Almourol Castle

0   0.25 mi

0   0.25 km

To **5** ALMOUROL CASTLE, O Alpendre, and Tancos Boat Pier

© MOON.COM

Sights

✪ CONVENT OF CHRIST
(Convento de Cristo)

Igreja do Castelo Templário, tel. 249 315 089 or 249 313 434, www.conventocristo. gov.pt, daily 9am-5:30pm Oct.-May, daily 9am-6:30pm June-Sept., €6

The 12th-century Convent of Christ is a great work of Renaissance architecture, blending Romanesque, Gothic, and Manueline features in its remodeling over the centuries. The compound is on a hill overlooking Tomar, its lofty location dominating the skyline and enhancing the feeling of power and secrecy that cloaked the Order of the Knights Templar.

The Templars settled in Portugal in the early 12th century and built what is today the Convent of Christ in 1160 under the leadership of Gualdim Pais, provincial master of the order in Portugal. In the early days the convent was a symbol of the Templars' privacy and their desire to recapture the kingdom, but later, having been occupied by Henry the Navigator in the 15th century, it became an emblem for Portugal opening to the world.

The sumptuous interior outweighs the striking exterior and should be seen. The Convent of Christ refers to a complex of buildings rather than just the convent used by the Templars (who later became the Order of Christ) for at least 130 years as their seat in Portugal, a mix of a classic 12th-century castle and eight cloisters added in the 15th

Convent of Christ

For at least 130 years Tomar's Convent of Christ was the hub of the Templars in Portugal as they fought to free the country from Moorish control. In 1190 a Moorish invasion crossed the Tagus River and attacked Tomar, capturing nearby castles, but the Templars withstood a six-day siege and eventually claimed victory. With this and similar conquests in the region, the Templars gradually started the reconquest of Portugal from the Moors.

The Knights Templar order came to an abrupt end in the early 14th century when Philip IV of France, allegedly jealous of their prowess and conquests, convinced the pope to extinguish the order. While most Templars had their wealth and land repossessed, in Portugal they were spared that fate by King Dinis. He protected the Templars by persuading the pope to agree to a new order, renaming them the Order of Christ and moving their hub to Castro Marim. A century later, Tomar was restored to its full glory as the headquarters of the Order of Christ by Prince Henry the Navigator, an exceptional figure who played a pivotal role in the Age of Discoveries.

and 16th centuries, plus vast gardens. The centerpiece is the castle's unusual **Charola,** the oratory of the Templars, an exuberantly decorated, light-filled church built by the first great master of the Templars and inspired by the architecture of the Holy Land. Outside, the church has a 16-sided polygonal structure, while inside it has a central octagonal structure, its lavish decor with floor-to-ceiling paintings indicative of the order's wealth and power.

It's possible to spend a few hours wandering this incredibly beautiful complex. Construction began in the 12th century on land donated by King Afonso Henriques to thank the Templars for their role in the *reconquistas*. It evolved into an impressive military complex. Henry the Navigator added a palace in the 15th century, when he was grand master of the order. He extended the monastic premises by adding two new cloisters and transformed the military house into a convent to be used by the clergy. The complex was completely remodeled in the 16th century by Manuel I, who also became master of the order, and was embellished throughout with elaborate sacred art, mural paintings, and decorative plasterwork. Classified

a UNESCO World Heritage Site in 1983, it has intricate details and surprises around every corner, such as the many masons' inscriptions that linger from its days as the seat of the Templars.

Audio guides are available. A combined ticket to the Convent of Christ, Alcobaça Monastery, and Batalha Monastery (€15) is valid for seven days. Note that there are narrow, uneven passages, cobbled floors, and lots of worn stairs; accessibility could be problematic for people with limited mobility.

TOMAR SYNAGOGUE
(Sinagoga de Tomar)

Rua Dr. Joaquim Jacinto 73, tel. 249 329 823, www.cm-tomar.pt, Tues.-Sun. 10am-1pm and 2pm-6pm Oct.-Apr., Tues.-Sun. 10am-1pm and 3pm-7pm May-Sept., free

Built in the 15th century in Tomar's historic center, the Tomar Synagogue is a rare example of a medieval Jewish temple in Portugal and is the best preserved. Tomar's Jewish community thrived until 1496-1497, when the Jews were forced to convert to Roman Catholicism or be expelled by Manuel I. Subsequently, the synagogue served as a prison, a Christian chapel, a hay

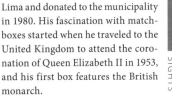

Lima and donated to the municipality in 1980. His fascination with matchboxes started when he traveled to the United Kingdom to attend the coronation of Queen Elizabeth II in 1953, and his first box features the British monarch.

Mouchão Park

storehouse, and a grocery warehouse. From the outside, it blends in with the simple whitewashed houses on the street, distinguished by the blue Star of David above the door. Inside, Gothic vaulted ceilings connecting to the floor with spindly stone columns are an impressive sight. The synagogue's present-day north-facing entrance is not an original feature; the pointy Gothic east-facing arch was the main entrance in the Middle Ages. In 1921 the building was classified a National Monument, and it also houses a small Jewish museum, which hosts several medieval tomb slabs from across Portugal.

MATCHBOX MUSEUM
(Museu dos Fosforos)

Av. Gen. Bernardo Faria, tel. 249 329 814,
Tues.-Sun. 10am-1pm and 3pm-6pm, free
The quirky, colorful Matchbox Museum, located in the São Francisco convent, houses an extraordinary collection of 43,000 matchboxes, collected over 27 years from 127 countries and dating back to 1827, filling cabinets and creating a striking visual effect. The collection was started by local man Aquiles da Mota

MOUCHÃO PARK
(Parque do Mouchão)

Rua do Parque, tel. 249 313 326, 24/7, free
Straddling the heart of Tomar town and a sliver of land called Mouchão Island in the Nabão River, Mouchão Park is a public park with many trees for shady tranquility on hot days. Stroll the lovely gardens and hear the river running nearby. An old wooden waterwheel stands guard near one of the park's entrances, and a campsite is located nearby. The park is divided into two areas, with a playground, a sports field, and pavilion on one side and the verdant island on the other, connected by a bridge.

PEGÕES AQUEDUCT
(Aqueduto de Pegões)

Looming above the Ribeira dos Pegões valley, on the northwestern outskirts of Tomar, the 16th-century Pegões Aqueduct was originally built to supply the Convent of Christ with water. Like a caterpillar on long legs, the colossal water channel with its succession of lofty double-tiered arches winds around the hills for over 6 kilometers (3.7 mi). Its highest point is 30 meters (98 feet). Construction started in 1593 by Italian architect and engineer Filipe Terzi and was completed in 1641 by Portuguese architect Pedro Fernandes Torres.

✪ ALMOUROL CASTLE

Almourol Castle

Set on a solitary islet that juts out into the Tagus River, in a parish known as Praia do Ribatejo (Ribatejo Beach), the **Almourol Castle** (Castelo de Almourol, Ilhota do Rio Tejo, Praia do Ribatejo, Vila Nova da Barquinha, tel. 249 720 358, www.igespar.pt, daily 10am-1pm and 2:30pm-5pm Nov.-Feb., daily 10am-1pm and 2:30pm-7pm Mar.-Oct., €2.50 includes boat trip) rises from a rocky outcrop. The castle dates to the 12th century, and its origins are shrouded in mystery. It is believed to have been built on the site of an ancient Lusitanian *castro* (a pre-Roman fortification) that was conquered by the Romans in the 1st century BC and later held by invading Visigoths and Moors. It remains unclear when the structure was founded, although an inscription on the main entrance suggests it was circa 1171.

Enigmatic and powerful, Almourol is symbolic of the Christian reconquest, distinguished from other monuments by its riverside location on land that once fell under the protection of the Knights Templar. Almourol Castle forms part of a protective belt that was a frontline of defense along the Tagus River in the Middle Ages, along with the castles of Tomar, Zêzere, and Cardiga. It was abandoned with the extinction of the Knights Templar in Portugal, but from the 19th century it was rediscovered, and in the 20th century the castle was used by the government to host many important meetings.

GETTING THERE

Reach the castle from the nearby **Tancos boat pier,** in the parish of Vila Nova da Barquinha, sailing across the Tagus on a little boat to the islet. Boats depart hourly and allow visitors 40 minutes to wander the castle before the return trip. The castle is a magnificent fairy-tale sight as the boat approaches. The views from the castle are phenomenal.

Vila Nova da Barquinha and Almourol Castle is a 25-minute, 22-kilometer (13.6-mile) drive northeast from Tomar on the **N110** and **A13** roads.

CP (tel. 707 210 220, www.cp.pt) trains run six times daily from **Tomar** to Tancos train station (1-2 hours, €3.15); the journey may require a transfer at Entroncamento. Tancos train station is a 10-minute walk east of the boat pier.

Festivals and Events

Tray Festival
(Festa dos Tabuleiros)

June or July

One of Tomar's most ancient local traditions, the Tray Festival is a spectacle like no other. Staged every four years in June or July (there was one in 2019), it takes its name from the festival's high point: a procession of local girls wearing headdresses made from bread piled staggeringly high, parading through the streets with male partners as attendants. The headdresses, called *tabuleiros,* are decorated with colorful flowers and topped off with a white dove, symbolizing Christianity's Holy Spirit. The festival also features other traditional ceremonies and celebrations. The day after the procession, the *pêza* takes place, when bread and meat are shared among the local people. The festival is believed to have originated in rituals dating to the 13th century. Almost the entire local population— thousands of men, women, and children—takes part in this event.

Knights Templar Festival
(Festival dos Templários)

tel. 249 310 040,

www.templarknights.eu, July

The annual Knights Templar Festival is a series of celebrations dedicated to

Knights Templar Festival

the Templars, held over four days at the beginning of July. These include a torchlit Knights Parade, medieval banquets, and a reenactment of the 1190 Moorish siege of Tomar. The festival dates to 2013, when Tomar was chosen to be world headquarters of the International Order of the Knights Templar (OSMTH)—the oldest Knights Templar organization in the world. The entire town dresses in its best medieval finery to recreate the mysticism and magic of the bygone era, with costumes, arts and crafts, and food and drink galore.

Food

✪ Café Estrelas de Tomar
R. Serpa Pinto 12, tel. 249 313 275, www. estrelasdetomar.pt, daily 8am-8pm, €5

Established in 1960, this riverfront café and bakery is one of the oldest and most celebrated in Tomar, producing fresh local sweets and "conventual" confectionary (traditional recipes that allegedly seeped down from the country's guarded convents), including Tomar's famous *queijadas* and *fatias,* every day. Located on the west bank, near the Rua Marquês de Pombal Bridge.

Taverna Antiqua
Praça da República 23-25, tel. 249 311 236, www.tavernaantiqua.com, Tues.-Sun. noon-11pm, €15

Fitting for a town so closely linked to knights, this medieval-themed restaurant, on the main Praça da República square, offers a unique dining experience with food, crockery, and entertainment of the era. Think banquet vibes, heavy wood tables, rock walls, and candlelight.

O Alpendre
Rua Principal 13, tel. 919 562 990, Mon.-Thurs. noon-2:30pm, Fri. noon-2:30pm and 7:30pm-10pm, Sat. 7:30pm-10pm, €15

Portuguese food doesn't get any better than at O Alpendre, a homey, inexpensive eatery on the Nabão's east bank, with rich regional favorites including excellent beef dishes and homemade desserts.

Bela Vista
Rua Marquês de Pombal No. 68, tel. 249 312 870, http://abelavista.pt, Weds.-Sun. noon-3pm and 7pm-9:30pm, Mon. noon-3pm, €15

Sitting pretty on the Nabão riverbank, Bela Vista serves authentic regional meat and fish dishes like octopus rice and roast kid. Founded in 1922, it boasts stunning views over the river, Mouchão Park, and the convent hill.

Accommodations

Hotel Kamanga
Rua Major Ferreira do Amaral 16, tel. 249 311 555, www.hotelkamanga.com, €55 d

In a good location on the east side of the Nabão River, within walking distance of Tomar's attractions and an 11-minute walk to the train station, Hotel Kamanga is budget lodging at its best. Rooms are clean, with simple wood furnishings and colorful, crafty quilts; some offer views of the convent.

Thomar Story Guest House
Rua João Carlos Everard 53, tel. 925 936 273, www.thomarstory.pt, €60 d

In the heart of historic Tomar, modern little Thomar Story Guest House occupies a late-19th-century building that oozes character and charm. Each of the 12 tastefully decorated rooms is designed to reflect the town's history.

Thomar Boutique Hotel

Rua Santa Iria 14, tel. 249 323 210,
www.thomarboutiquehotel.com,
€63 d

This chic and contemporary urban boutique hotel is within walking distance of Tomar's main sights. Located on the Nabão riverside, it has a nice rooftop with great views over the historic town center.

⭐ **Hotel dos Templários**

Largo Candido dos Reis 1, tel. 249 310 100,
www.hoteldostemplarios.com, €92 d

Overlooking the Nabão River, at the foot of the Convent of Christ hill, the central, four-star Hotel dos Templários has spacious rooms and sizable indoor and outdoor pools. Its great location makes a good base for exploring the region.

Information and Services

- **National emergency number:** tel. 112
- **PSP police:** Rua Dom Lopo Dias de Sousa 8D, tel. 249 328 040, www. psp.pt
- **Tourist office:** Av. Dr. Cândido Madureira 531, tel. 249 329 800, www.cm-tomar.pt, daily 8am-6pm
- **Tomar Health Center:** Rua Nabância 14, tel. 249 329 710, Mon.-Fri. 9am-12:30pm and 2pm-5:30pm

Getting There and Around

GETTING THERE

CAR

Tomar is a 1.5-hour, 140-kilometer (87-mile) drive north from **Lisbon** on the **A1** motorway.

BUS

Rede Expressos (tel. 707 223 344, www.rede-expressos.pt) runs four daily buses between Lisbon's **Sete Rios** hub and Tomar (1.75 hours, €9.50). **Rodoviária do Tejo** (tel. 249 810 700, www.rodotejo.pt) has seasonal buses (May-Sept.) that connect Santarém's main destinations, including **Nazaré,** stopping at the monasteries of Batalha and Alcobaça) along the **IC9** road. Tomar's **bus station** (Avenida Combatentes da Grande Guerra, tel. 249 787 878) is located on the west side of the Nabão river, a 15-minute walk south of the Convent of Christ.

TRAIN

CP (tel. 707 210 220, www.cp.pt) trains run from Lisbon's **Santa Apolónia** and **Oriente** stations to Tomar (2 hours, €10.10) roughly every couple of hours. Tomar's **railway station** is adjacent to the bus station on Avenida Combatentes da Grande Guerra, a short walk from the historic city center.

GETTING AROUND

Tomar is easy to navigate, with most of the main sights and transport terminals being packed into the town of the west side of the river. The town is easily (and best) covered **on foot.**

There is plenty of **parking** in Tomar, such as the free parking lot in the **Varzea Grande square** in front of **Tomar Station** and an **underground parking garage** on the opposite side of the river. However, seeing as the Covent is somewhat of an uphill hike (albeit a relatively short one), driving up or even getting a local *tuk-tuk* is also an option (Tuk Lovers, Praça da República main square, tel. 918 541 229 or 918 350 329, www.tuklovers.com, prices from €10).

ÉVORA

In the heart of the Alentejo, Évora

(EH-voh-rah) is the region's biggest city, built on a small hill amid the surrounding plains 133 kilometers (82 miles), or a 1.5-hour drive, from Lisbon. Wonderfully preserved, Évora is home to unusual historic monuments and leading wine producers, and it is a university city that blends the old with the demands of modern youth.

Often called the megalithic capital of Iberia, Évora, a UNESCO World Heritage Site, has sites that date from prehistory. The most famous is Almendres Cromlech, on the city's outskirts, with

HIGHLIGHTS

✪ **CHAPEL OF BONES:** The chilling Chapel of Bones is a gruesome but unmissable highlight of Évora (page 201).

✪ **MEGALITHS AT ALMENDRES CROMLECH:** This Neolithic-era site comprises mysterious *menhirs* that predate England's Stonehenge (page 203).

✪ **CARTUXA ESTATE:** Learn about the essence of the Alentejo's famous wines at the iconic Cartuxa vineyards (page 204).

menhirs (standing stones) that predate England's Stonehenge. Évora's city center is well preserved. First inhabited by Celts, the city was conquered by the Romans in the 1st century BC, and relics of their occupancy, such as the Roman Temple, remain along with surviving architectural influences from the subsequent Moorish occupancy. In the 15th century, Évora was home to Portugal's kings, which brought great wealth, and more prestige came in the 16th century when Évora was elevated to an ecclesiastical city.

ORIENTATION

Évora is not that big, and its main sights can be covered **on foot** in one day. Central **Giraldo Square (Praça do Giraldo)** is the city's main meeting point. Flanked by historic monuments and buildings and lined with elegant cafés and restaurants, it has a grand feel, with the **Bank of Portugal** at its southern end and a charming church and marble fountain at the northern end. The **Roman Temple of Évora, Évora Cathedral,** and **Évora University** are all northeast from the square; the **Chapel of Bones** is in the opposite direction, southwest of the square. Évora's historic center is encircled by strapping 14th-century **walls,** and the city itself is encircled by the busy IP2 main ring road. The **aqueduct** is outside the city, on the other side of the IP2, north of Évora, and the **Cartuxa wine estate** is just a little further in the same direction.

PLANNING YOUR TIME

Plan to spend at least one day in Évora exploring the **monuments,** mazelike **cobbled streets,** and the many excellent **cafés** and **restaurants.** Allow another day or two to venture outside the city center and discover a host of acclaimed **vineyards** and quaint **villages.** As Évora is a 1.5-hour drive east of Lisbon (about 140 kilometers/87 miles), an overnight stay is ideal. The city can be eye-wateringly hot in summer, so if visiting in summer, plan activities outside the times of most intense heat, between midday and 4pm. Be aware that Évora's **historic center** (inside the walls) can be very busy with traffic; parking is limited and mostly paid. There are free **parking lots** outside the city walls.

Itinerary Ideas

ESSENTIAL ÉVORA

Leave Lisbon nice and early to make the 1.5-hour drive to Évora.

DAY 1

1 Start your exploration of Évora in its heart, enjoying a coffee in the bustling **Giraldo Square.**

2 Head southwest to the creepy **Chapel of Bones.**

3 Afterward, follow the walls northeast to see the **Aldeia da Terra** miniature sculptures, a lighthearted take on Portuguese village life.

4 Enjoy lunch at **Chão das Covas Café,** one of Évora's many excellent restaurants.

5 Walk off lunch by following the walls to the **Roman Temple.**

6 Nearby you can also see **Évora Cathedral.**

7 Wrap up Day 1 with a romantic dinner at **Taberna Típica Quarta Feira.**

DAY 2

1 On Day 2, make the short trip north outside the city to see the **Água da Prata** aqueduct.

2 Then, keeping in the same direction, head to the **Cartuxa Estate** for a tour of the vineyards.

3 After your tour of Cartuxa, start heading south back to Lisbon, stopping at the **Almendres Cromlech** en route.

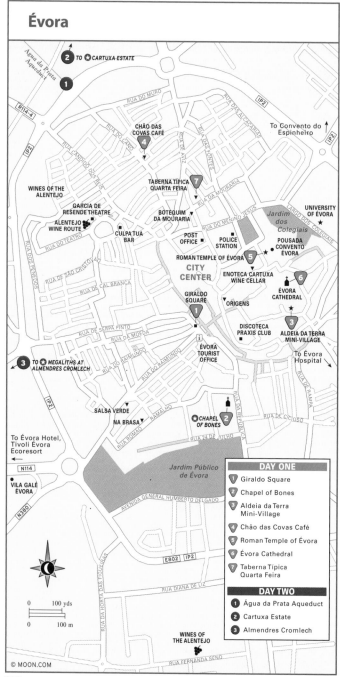

Évora

Água da Prata Aqueduct

R114-4

2 TO ✪ CARTUXA ESTATE

1

RUA DO MURO

IP2

RUA DE AVIZ

RUA DAS ALCAÇARIAS

To Convento do Espinheiro

IP2

RUA CÂNDIDO DOS REIS

IP2

RUA DO CANO

CHÃO DAS COVAS CAFÉ **4**

RUA DAS FONTES

RUA DA MOURARIA

TABERNA TÍPICA QUARTA FEIRA **7**

WINES OF THE ALENTEJO

GARCIA DE RESENDE THEATRE

BOTEQUIM DA MOURARIA

RUA DO MENINO JESUS

UNIVERSITY OF ÉVORA

Jardim dos Colegiais

LARGO DOS COLEGIAIS

ALENTEJO WINE ROUTE

CULPA TUA BAR

POST OFFICE

POLICE STATION

POUSADA CONVENTO ÉVORA

RUA DO TEATRO

RUA DE SÃO CRISTÓVÃO

ROMAN TEMPLE OF ÉVORA **5**

CITY CENTER

ENOTECA CARTUXA WINE CELLAR

ÉVORA CATHEDRAL **6**

RUA DE CAL BRANCA

GIRALDO SQUARE **1**

ORIGENS

RUA DOS PENEDOS

RUA DE SERPA PINTO

RUA DA MOEDA

DISCOTECA PRAXIS CLUB

ALDEIA DA TERRA MINI-VILLAGE **3**

To Évora Hospital

3 TO ✪ MEGALITHS AT ALMENDRES CROMLECH

RUA DO RAIMUNDO

ℹ️ **ÉVORA TOURIST OFFICE**

RUA DO RAIMUNDO

IP2

RUA DE RAMPA

RUA DA REPÚBLICA

SALSA VERDE

NA BRASA

RAMALHO

✪ CHAPEL OF BONES **2**

RUA DE CICIOSO

To Évora Hotel, Tivoli Évora Ecoresort

RUA ROMÃO

RUA 24 DE JULHO

N114

VILA GALÉ ÉVORA

N380

Jardim Público de Évora

AVENIDA GENERAL HUMBERTO DELGADO

E802 IP2

RUA DIANA DE LIZ

```
0        100 yds
0        100 m
```

WINES OF THE ALENTEJO

RUA DA HORTA DAS FIGUEIRAS

RUA FERNANDA SENO

© MOON.COM

Sights

☼ CHAPEL OF BONES
(Capela dos Ossos)

Praça 1 de Maio 4, tel. 266 704 521, www.igrejadesaofrancisco.pt, daily 9am-5pm winter, daily 9am-6:30pm summer, €4

The odd and chilling Chapel of Bones is next to the entrance of the Church of Saint Francis (Igreja de São Francisco) in the heart of the city. The inner walls and pillars of this 16th-century chapel are clad with the tightly packed human bones and skulls of 5,000 local residents who were exhumed from the overcrowded cemeteries that once sprawled on the city's fringes. Local monks decided to put their remains on display as a warning about the superficiality of materialism and the certainty of death. This is explained in a message above the chapel door: *"Nós ossos que aqui estamos, pelos vossos esperamos,"* or "We bones that are here are awaiting yours."

Chapel of Bones

ROMAN TEMPLE OF ÉVORA
(Templo Romano de Évora)

Largo do Conde de Vila Flor, tel. 266 769 450, www.cultura-alentejo.pt, 24/7

A sacred site dating from the 1st century AD, the Roman Temple of Évora

Roman Temple of Évora

is one of the best-preserved Roman temples on the Iberian Peninsula. Also referred to incorrectly as the Temple of Diana, it is one of Portugal's most recognizable landmarks. The temple is believed to honor Emperor Augustus, who was worshipped as a god. Its remains are a series of Corinthian stone columns on a solid base, but the Roman architecture is still evident. In the historical center, near the cathedral, the temple is on the highest point in the city in front of the manicured public Garden of Diana (Jardim de Diana), pleasant for a shady stroll and with a café with glorious views over Évora.

ÉVORA CATHEDRAL
(Catedral de Évora)

Largo do Marquês de Marialva 809, tel. 266 759 330, www.evoracathedral.com, daily 9am-5pm, cathedral €2, cloister, roof, and museum €4.50

The grand Évora Cathedral, or Sé, is the largest medieval cathedral in Portugal. Similar to Lisbon's monumental cathedral, Évora Cathedral has two massive towers, Gothic cloisters, a

Manueline chapel, and a magnificent Baroque chapel. Also of note, among many other unique features, are the striking six-turret lantern-tower and the main portal, whose huge marble columns have impressive carvings of the apostles.

Built on the highest ground in the city, near the Roman Temple, the Gothic structure also bears Romanesque, Manueline, and Baroque architectural touches in its add-ons over the centuries. Construction ran from 1280 to 1350 to mark the victory of the Christian Crusaders over the Moors. The cathedral has the look of a fortress, evident in features such as the battlement-encircled terrace. Its main facade is made of rose granite. Inside are ornamental cloisters and beautiful rose windows that give an ethereal feel, a contrast to the simple exterior.

Évora Cathedral cloisters

Évora Cathedral also houses a **museum** packed with religious art and has the only Gothic statue of the pregnant Virgin Mary in Portugal, over a gilded altar inside the church. An added bonus is the view from the rooftop; the climb up is via a narrow 135-step spiral staircase through the bell tower, suitable only for the agile.

UNIVERSITY OF ÉVORA
(Universidade de Évora)

Largo dos Colegiais 2, tel. 266 740 800, www.uevora.pt, Mon.-Sat. 9am-8pm, €3, children under 12 free

The University of Évora is monumental but overshadowed by the city's more famous attractions. Founded in the 16th century, the university comprises several restored historical structures around the city, identified with a dove sculpted into a marble circle above the main entrance. The university's main building is the spectacular square Espírito Santo College, a magnificent edifice with an imposing facade of successive grand arches on marble columns, encasing a courtyard and central fountain. Construction took place 1550-1559. Visitors can explore on their own the lecture halls and hidden works of art, which include ancient tile plaques and an old bookshop with a mural.

ALDEIA DA TERRA MINI-VILLAGE

Rua de São Manços 15-19, tel. 266 746 049, www.aldeiadaterra.pt, daily 10am-6pm, €3

The quirky Aldeia da Terra Mini-Village is a tongue-in-cheek portrayal of Portuguese village life. Translating as "Village of the Land," it is a colorful collection of pint-size clay sculptures by artist Tiago Cabeça. Opened in 2010, this open-air attraction comprises 2,000 clay figurines that were relocated in 2017 from the nearby town of Arraiolos to Évora.

ÁGUA DA PRATA AQUEDUCT
(Aqueduto da Água de Prata)

Supplying drinking water over a length of 9 kilometers (5.6 miles), this 16th-century stone aqueduct, literally "Silver Water Aqueduct," was a complex and challenging construction

✪ ALMENDRES CROMLECH

As well as its plethora of incredible monuments, Évora is home to another intriguing attraction, the **Megalithic Route,** a trail through the megalithic sites throughout the region. The finest and largest of these is the famous Almendres Cromlech, a Neolithic complex located in the deep Alentejo.

This circular twin set of prehistoric standing stones (or *menhirs*) is said to predate the world's most famous megaliths, Stonehenge in England, reportedly erected over several periods. It is the largest site of such structures on the Iberian Peninsula, which, along with Évora's other smaller

Almendres Cromlech

sites throughout the region, gives it its nickname "the megalithic capital of Iberia." Comprising 95 standing stones arranged facing downhill in two oval rings, many of which have enigmatic engravings whose meanings remain unknown, the mysterious Almendres site's construction is said to date back to the 6th millennium BC. While its purpose is not certain, it is believed to be a ceremonial site for celestial worship or a form of astronomical observatory.

GETTING THERE
The Almendres Cromlech is located near the village of Nossa Senhora de Guadalupe on the outskirts of Évora (30 minutes, 18 km/11 mi west from Évora). It is situated off the national roadway (N114) from Évora to Montemor-o-Novo, just after the village of Guadalupe, in the Herdade dos Almendres (Almendres Estate), a scenic hillside location swaddled by olive and cork trees.

Public transport to the site is sparse, but it is open 24/7 and there is no entry fee. Visitors are free to wander and touch the stones at leisure.

project for its era. Massive arches, at points 25 meters (82 feet) high, rise from the ground. The main arches are located outside the city walls, north of Évora near the ring road. In the city's core it blends in seamlessly, fused to houses and shops. Originally the aqueduct ran to a marble fountain in the main Giraldo Square, with a series of public fountains along the way.

It is possible to follow the route of the aqueduct by foot or bicycle through the city on the **Água de Prata Route** (Percurso da Água de Prata), which leads to the outskirts of the city, through farms and cork oaks. A shorter route is from **Porta da Lagoa,** where the aqueduct crosses the R114-4 road from Évora to Arraiolos, into the city center; follow the aqueduct and enjoy the sights along the way. Charming little shops have been built beneath some of the arches, and there is a Renaissance-style water box with a dozen Tuscan columns on Rua Nova. Other streets where you can see the aqueduct are Rua do Cano, Rua do Salvador, and Travessa das Nunes.

Wine Routes and Tours

Alentejo Wine Route
Wine Tasting Center
(Rota dos Vinhos do Alentejo)

Horta das Figueiras, Rua Fernanda Seno 12, Apartado 498, tel. 266 748 870, www.vinhosdoalentejo.pt, Mon.-Fri. 11am-7pm, Sat. 10am-1pm

Wine lovers are spoiled for choice, and the Alentejo Wine Route (Rota dos Vinhos do Alentejo) takes visitors through the region's various wine-growing areas, listing dozens of wineries. It aims to promote regional wine-making as well as other aspects of regional culture. The headquarters are just outside the historic city center, between the hospital and the train station. Staff can help organize a trip and winery visits.

Wines of the Alentejo
(Vinhos do Alentejo)

Praça Joaquim António de Aguiar 20, tel. 266 746 498, Mon.-Sat. 11am-7pm

Alternately, head to the central Wines of the Alentejo (Vinhos do Alentejo) tasting and information center, which harnesses the essence of the region's wines. As well as showcasing two different wines to taste from three different producers, the beautiful center, with vaulted ceilings, stone walls, and windows on a beautiful square, also provides information on what to see in the Alentejo.

✪ Cartuxa Estate

Quinta de Valbom, tel. 266 748 383, www.cartuxa.pt, daily 10am-7pm

One of Évora's most iconic vineyards is the Cartuxa Estate, 1.7 kilometers (1.1 miles) from the town center, a half-hour walk, a five-minute drive, or €5 by taxi. Producing iconic EA, Foral de Évora, and Pêra-Manca wines, the century-old 15-hectare (37-acre) organic vineyard offers guided tours (1 hour, in English, by appointment only), as well as wine and olive oil tasting (€10). Just next door is the Cartuxa Convent, built between 1587 and 1598, which houses monks.

Sports and Recreation

Skydive Portugal

Évora Municipal Airdrome, tel. 910 999 991, www.skydiveportugal.pt, from €115

Contact SkyDive Portugal to jump out of a plane over the stunning Alentejo plains.

Balonissimo

tel. 935 646 124, www.balonissimo.com, from €140

Enjoy the beauty of the Alentejo from the serenity of a hot-air balloon. Watch the sunrise as you glide over Évora, the aqueduct, and the rolling plains and vineyards with a glass of champagne in hand. Balonissimo offers free pickup from anywhere in Évora. Flights last about an hour, with the full excursion taking 3-4 hours.

Arts and Entertainment

Garcia de Resende Theatre (Teatro Garcia de Resende)

Rua do Teatro 10, tel. 266 777 000, www.cendrev.com

This magnificent century-old building is worth a look if only to admire the simple granite exterior, behind which hides an opulent Italian-style theater. Shaped like a horseshoe, the main concert hall has three tiers of balconies; their deep red lining, gold-trimmed rims, and incredible painted ceiling give the main room a regal, Baroque feel. Inaugurated in June 1892, the theatre is named after Évora-born poet, designer, and architect Garcia de Resende, who was an esteemed figure on Portugal's Renaissance scene. The playhouse has a busy year-round program of national and international plays and performances.

Food

Évora's food scene spans rustic restaurants to fine dining, centered on hearty, meaty regional dishes, although international cuisine and vegetarian restaurants can be found. The Alentejo is famous for its *porco preto* (black pig) and excellent wines, and most restaurants in Évora will serve both. Many of the city's best-known restaurants are in the Moorish Quarter *(centro histórico)*.

Chão das Covas Café

Largo Chão das Covas Évora, tel. 266 706 294, Tues.-Sun. 11am-11pm, €10

Don't be misled by the "café" in the name of Chão das Covas Café; this cute little eatery might be small, but its home-cooked Alentejano dishes and tapas are huge in flavor.

Salsa Verde

Rua do Raimundo 93A, tel. 266 743 210, www.salsa-verde.org, Mon.-Fri. 11am-3:30pm and 6pm-9:30pm, Sat. 11am-3:30pm, €10

Vegetarian restaurant Salsa Verde is an airy, colorful setup in a former convent, a true haven for veggie fans in a land of meat lovers. Meat-free twists on traditional Portuguese dishes use fresh local produce and herbs. There are no fixed menus; every day the offerings are fresh and different.

Na Brasa

Rua Romão Ramalho 82, tel. 266 771 609, Mon.-Thurs. 11am-4pm and 6:30pm-midnight, Fri.-Sat. 11am-4pm and 6:30pm-1am, Sun. 6:30pm-midnight, €15

Lofty barnlike steakhouse Na Brasa serves fabulous meat straight from the grill as well as seafood dishes.

Botequim da Mouraria

Rua da Mouraria 16A, tel. 266 746 775, Mon.-Fri. 12:30pm-3pm and 6:30pm-9:45pm, €15

One of Évora's most popular restaurants, Botequim da Mouraria is small, rustic, and tavernlike, run by a husband-and-wife team who

an outdoor café in Évora

prepare simple, unfussy, traditional Portuguese food. Be sure to try the *presunto* cured ham.

Origens

Rua de Burgos 10, tel. 964 220 790, www.origensrestaurante.com, Tues.-Sat. 12:30pm-3pm and 7:15pm-11pm, €18

Offering contemporary Portuguese fare, Origens is modern and gleaming, with a sleek menu to match. Don't miss the chilled fresh tomato cream soup with cottage cheese, dried fruit, and honey.

✪ Taberna Típica Quarta Feira

Rua do Inverno 18, tel. 266 707 530, Mon. 7:30pm-10pm, Tues.-Sat. 12:30pm-3pm and 7:30pm-10pm, €20

Unpretentious and atmospheric, the family-run Taberna Típica Quarta Feira serves tasty local and regional specialties such as Alentejo-style pork meat and grilled black pork chops.

✪ Enoteca Cartuxa Wine Cellar

Rua de Vasco da Gama 15, tel. 266 748 348, www.cartuxa.pt, Mon.-Sat. 10am-10pm, Sun. noon-3pm, €20

Cosmopolitan Enoteca Cartuxa Wine Cellar is a polished restaurant by the producers of the famous Cartuxa vineyard wines. The estate's wines are paired with Portuguese regional dishes such as cow tongue, pork cheek, sheep and goat cheese, smoked sausages, and cured meats.

LOCAL SPECIALTIES

Two local delicacies are *porco preto* (black pig) and the sweet treat *queijada d'Évora*.
Black pig, also known as Alentejano pig, is a darker-skinned animal than its relatives. Its origins can be traced to wild boars. The black pig is traditionally free-range and feeds on acorns, so the meat is moister, more succulent, and more fragrant, with a nutty taste.

   Queijada d'Évora is a small, sweet tartlet with a thin, crispy pastry crust and a creamy filling made from egg yolks and fresh sheep-milk cheese. It is a form of *doçaria conventual,* traditional Portuguese sweets whose closely guarded recipes come from convents.

Bars and Nightlife

Évora has a vibrant alfresco social scene. In summer especially, locals socialize in the cooler temperatures after dark, giving the city a bustling café-culture feel, topped with the energetic vibe of the university students.

Discoteca Praxis Club

Rua Valdevinos 21, tel. 963 937 388, www.praxisevora.wixsite.com, Tues.-Sat. 11pm-6am

Many of the city center hotels have upscale wine and cocktail bars, while the other bars around the historic center buzz with students and younger people, particularly on Wednesday night.

Discoteca Praxis Club has four bars and two dance floors popular with the younger crowd. Its packed calendar features resident and guest DJs, live bands, and themed evenings.

Culpa Tua Bar

Praça Joaquim António de Aguiar 6, tel. 969 533 692, Mon.-Sat. 5pm-3am, Sun. 5pm-midnight

The rustic Culpa Tua Bar is a busy little bar showcasing great local liquor, wine, and fruity cocktails. The bar is in a characterful old building with a vaulted ceiling, brick arches, and a cobbled floor.

Accommodations

Évora Hotel

Av. Túlio Espanca, tel. 266 748 800, www.evorahotel.pt, from €100-200 d

Sprawling, modern, upscale Évora Hotel, a five-minute drive from the city center, captures the essence of the Alentejo. Surrounded by quintessential countryside and decorated with tones and textures of the region, it has two outdoor pools and an indoor pool.

Vila Galé Évora

Av. Túlio Espanca, tel. 266 758 100, www.vilagale.com, €100-200 d

Sleek, modern, four-star Vila Galé Évora is a short walk from the city center, just outside the city walls. It has high-quality rooms, indoor and outdoor pools, a spa, and an on-site restaurant.

Tivoli Évora Ecoresort

Quinta da Deserta e Malina, tel. 266 738 500, www.ecorkhotel.com, from €100-200
Built using natural materials, refined countryside Tivoli Évora Ecoresort has an ecofriendly ethos with 56 private suites a 10-minute drive from the city center in the rolling Alentejo plains.

✪ Convento do Espinheiro

5.2 km (3.2 mi) north of Évora city center, tel. 266 788 200, www.conventodoespinheiro.com, from €150-250 d
Luxury boutique hotel Convento do Espinheiro, converted from a 15th-century convent, is one of Portugal's most famous and emblematic hotels. Surrounded by gardens, it offers 92 rooms (including 5 suites), divided between sumptuous conventual rooms and a modern wing with midcentury-inspired decor.

Pousada Convento Évora

Largo do Conde de Vila Flor, tel. 266 730 070, www.pousadas.pt/en/hotel/pousada-evora, €200-300 d
The serene 36-room Pousada Convento Évora, with a swimming pool, is in Évora's historic center, converted from a low-rise, whitewashed monastery dating to 1487. The luxurious rooms are former monks' cells.

Information and Services

- **PSP police station:** Rua Francisco Soares Lusitano, tel. 266 760 450, www.psp.pt
- **Main post office:** Rua Olivença, tel. 266 745 480
- **Évora Hospital:** Largo Senhor da Pobreza, tel. 266 740 100
- **Évora Tourist Office:** Praça do Giraldo 73, tel. 266 777 071, Mon.-Fri. 9am-6pm, Sat.-Sun. 10am-2pm and 3pm-6pm Nov.-Mar., daily 9am-7pm Apr.-Oct.

Getting There and Around

GETTING THERE

CAR

Évora is 1.5 hours' drive east of **Lisbon**, about 140 kilometers (87 miles), following the **A6** motorway.

BUS

Évora's main **bus station** (Av. Tulio Espanca, tel. 266 738 120) is a 10-minute walk west of the walled city center.

Rede Expressos (tel. 707 223 344, www.rede-expressos.pt) runs air-conditioned buses almost every half hour from Lisbon's **Sete Rios bus** station (1.5 hours, from €10.60). Tickets can be bought at the station's ticket office or booked online.

TRAIN

CP (tel. 707 210 220, www.cp.pt) trains run four times daily from

Lisbon's **Oriente, Sete Rios,** and **Entrecampos** stations (1.5 hours, 2nd class €12.40, 1st class €16.50).

The train station in Évora, **Largo da Estação,** is outside the city walls, 1 kilometer (0.6 mile) south, a 15-minute walk. The station is simple, but look for the old *azulejo* tile murals depicting local life.

GETTING AROUND

Most of Évora's sights can be covered **on foot,** but the old cobbled streets can be slippery and uneven. **Horse-drawn carriages** (around €30) can be found outside the cathedral for sightseeing trips.

CAR

Rent a car to explore the surrounding wine farms, villages, and Almendres Cromlech. Hotels work with local car rental companies; ask at reception. South of the walled city, between the IP2 road and the Circular de Évora ring road, are a number of car rental offices, including **Europcar Évora** (Estrada de Viana, Lote 10, tel. 266 742 627, www.europcar.pt), **Hertz** (Rua da Revendedora, Lote 7, Bairro da Torregela, Horta das Figueiras, tel. 219 426 300, www.hertz.pt), and **Sadorent** (Rua Manuel Correia Lopes 118, tel. 266 734 526, www.sadorent. pt), all open weekdays 9am-6pm.

Finding **parking** within the city walls can be difficult and must be paid for weekdays 8:30am-7:30pm and Saturday 9am-2pm. There are spacious parking lots outside the walls, such as at Portas de Lagoa, near the aqueduct, north of the city center. It is within walking distance of the center, with no steep hills or stairs. Parking outside the city walls is usually free.

TAXI

There are plenty of **taxis** near places of interest and the train and bus stations. Local company **Associação de Rádio Táxis de Évora** (Rua dos Altos, tel. 266 735 735) provides service anytime.

BUS

Local bus service **TREVO** (www.trevo. com.pt, €1 for 24 hours) serves Évora and its immediate fringes. **Lines 51** and **52** on the Blue Route cover the old city continuously weekdays 8am-8pm and Saturday 8am-2pm.

ESSENTIALS

Transportation

GETTING THERE

Traveling to Portugal from anywhere in Europe is quick and easy, with regular direct flights from many European cities as well as from Asia, the Middle East, North and South America, and Africa. Even better, flights can be pretty cheap within Europe, thanks to the growing number of low-cost airlines.

Lisbon Airport is the country's biggest and busiest. Most flights from outside Europe are to Lisbon, with direct flights from the United States, Canada, Brazil, Morocco, Tunisia, Turkey, Russia, Dubai in the United Arab Emirates, Angola, Mozambique, and China. Porto also has regular direct flights from Newark in the United States, Luanda in Angola, and Rio de Janeiro and São Paulo in Brazil, although far fewer than Lisbon. Faro has almost exclusively European flights, the vast majority from the United Kingdom, Germany, and France.

It is easy to travel to Portugal within Europe, with bus and train services connecting Portugal with Spain, France, Belgium, the Netherlands, and the United Kingdom. Driving to Portugal is also possible thanks to a good international road network and the EU (European Union) open-borders policy.

FROM NORTH AMERICA

Some transatlantic cruises include Lisbon, generally just for a short day trip, but the easiest, quickest, cheapest, and most convenient way to travel between the United States and Portugal is without doubt by air. Flights take seven hours eastbound from the Northeast, and nine hours westbound.

Portugal's national carrier, **TAP Air Portugal** (www.flytap.pt), has regular direct flights between mainland Portugal and New York (JFK and Newark), Boston, Miami, and Philadelphia. U.S. airline **United** (www.united.com) also has direct flights to Portugal.

TAP has invested heavily in the U.S. market, increasing the number of destinations it serves, and has also created the **Portugal Stopover** (www.portugalstopover.flytap.com)

program, where U.S. travelers on TAP to other destinations can spend a few days in Portugal before continuing onward. Portugal's national flag carrier also operates onward connecting flights from Lisbon to Porto, Faro, and the islands.

Regional Azores airline **SATA Azores Airlines** (www.azoresairlines. pt) and **Air Canada** (www.aircanada. com) operate direct flights between Portugal and Canada, including a stop in the Azores archipelago.

FROM EUROPE
Air

The vast majority of European flights to Portugal are from the United Kingdom, France, Germany, the Netherlands, and Belgium, all 2.5-3 hours away. Direct flights also operate from Finland as well as Eastern European countries such as Poland, the Czech Republic, and Hungary. Flights from neighboring Spain are only to Lisbon and Porto.

The ever-expanding availability of European flights includes a number of low-cost airlines such as Ryanair (Ireland), easyJet (UK), Vueling (Spain), Eurowings (Germany), and Transavia (France), meaning travel between two European destinations can cost less than €100 round-trip. Prices within Europe are heavily influenced by school holidays at Easter, summer, and Christmas-New Year's as well as peak tourist seasons in Portugal, especially July-August; pricing can vary widely.

Train

Getting to Portugal from other European countries by train isn't as straightforward as by air and can sometimes be more expensive. The train is slightly quicker than traveling by bus.

Getting to Portugal by train from most of Europe requires passing through an international terminal such as Paris or Madrid. Getting to Portugal from the United Kingdom takes around 24 hours and involves catching the Eurostar (www.eurostar.com) from London to Paris, then a TGV high-speed train from Paris to Hendaye-Irun at the border of southern France and Spain, and from there the overnight Sud Expresso train to Lisbon. There are two overnight sleeper trains from Spain: the Lusitania Hotel Train (www.cp.pt), linking Madrid's Chamartin Station to Lisbon in about 10 hours, and the Sud Expresso (www.cp.pt), which connects Lisbon to San Sebastian in Spain and Hendaye in southern France in about 11 hours.

The easiest way to get around Portugal—and the rest of Europe—by train is with a Eurail Pass (www.eurail.com). This EU-wide rail travel pass for non-EU citizens covers train travel in first or second class. The Eurail pass comes in three options: the Global Pass, covering 5 or more of up to 28 European countries; the Select Pass—covering 2, 3, or 4 bordering countries; or a single-country pass. Prices for Portugal range from €82 for a single-country pass to €307 for a basic Global Pass, although prices vary.

An identical pass is available to EU citizens and official residents: the Interrail Pass (www.interrail.eu) ranges from €80 for a single-country pass to €208 for a basic Global Pass, although prices vary.

Bus

The main bus lines offering intercity travel within Europe to Portugal are Eurolines (Lisbon tel. 218 957 398, Porto tel. 225 189 303, Bragança tel. 273 327 122, www.eurolines.com) and National Express (www.nationalexpress.com). These generally travel to Lisbon from many European countries. The most popular routes are from the United Kingdom, France, Spain, and the Netherlands. Transfers may be required; from London to Lisbon, for example, a change may be required in Paris. There are at least five buses a week between Paris and Lisbon. Bus prices from Amsterdam to Lisbon start from €110 one way and take around 36 hours; London to Lisbon is around €115 and 45 hours, and Paris to Lisbon €85 and 29 hours.

The main bus companies operating between Portugal and neighboring Spain are Avanza (tel. +34 912 722 832, www.avanzabus.com) and Alsa (tel. 902 422 242, www.alsa.com). A one-way trip from Madrid to Lisbon costs around €23, Seville to Lisbon €25, and Corunna to Lisbon €38.

Car

Europe is connected by a well-maintained motorway network, meaning international travel is straightforward between EU capital cities. Most of Europe exercises an open-borders policy, with no compulsory inspections at borders. Timewise, for example, driving nonstop from Paris to Lisbon takes around 16 hours; Madrid to Lisbon is 6 hours; and Berlin to Lisbon is 26 hours. Each country has different speed limits, driver alcohol tolerances, and other traffic laws.

Driving from the United Kingdom to Portugal is slightly more complicated, as it requires a ferry between the UK and mainland Europe. There are no direct ferries between the UK and Portugal, so the more common driving routes are from the UK by ferry to France or Spain. Ferries from the UK to France are quicker and cheaper than those to Spain, but also make the journey longer due to added driving time. Ferry trips between the UK and France often take just a few hours, while a ferry to Spain can take more than a day. There are many ferry routes between the UK and France, and the website **Direct Ferries** (www. directferries.co.uk) provides a comprehensive map of routes and prices.

Ferry crossings between the United Kingdom and Spain tend to change often, but the main crossings are between Plymouth and Santander, generally once a week, and Portsmouth to Bilbao or Portsmouth to Santander, three times a week. Other good ferry comparison sites are www.aferry.co.uk and www.ferries.co.uk. There are also direct ferries between Ireland and France.

The alternative to the ferry between the United Kingdom and mainland Europe is to take the Channel Tunnel, also known as the **Eurotunnel** (www. eurotunnel.com). Taking just 35 minutes to cross under the channel, the tunnel is cheaper and quicker than a ferry but is not for the claustrophobic. It connects Folkestone in the south of England to Calais in northern France via a 50-kilometer (31-mile) rail tunnel. At its lowest point, it is 75 meters (246 feet) below the seabed and 115 meters (377 feet) below sea level. Costs start from £30 per car (including up to nine passengers).

It is without doubt cheaper and quicker to fly to Portugal from anywhere in Europe than to drive, and tolls and the cost of gasoline can vary noticeably from country to country. But a road trip is always an adventure, as long as you do your research

and mapping in advance, and there's no reason why driving to Portugal can't be an enjoyable—if perhaps costly—experience.

FROM AUSTRALIA AND NEW ZEALAND

There are no direct flights between Portugal and Australia or New Zealand. Connecting flights are generally via Dubai in the United Arab Emirates, with a daily direct flight between Lisbon and Dubai on **Emirates** (www.emirates.com), or via Asia. There is also a direct nonstop flight between Australia and London, from where there are many onward flights to Portugal. Most major European air carriers operate code-share flights to major Asian hubs. Singapore, for example, can be reached with just one connection, from Lisbon to Istanbul on Turkish Airlines, or Dubai on Emirates, or via the United Kingdom or Germany with Singapore Airlines.

FROM SOUTH AFRICA

There are no direct flights from South Africa to Portugal. TAP flies direct to Maputo in Mozambique and Luanda in Angola, also served by Angolan airline TAAG, and connecting flights can be arranged from there. Major European carriers such as British Airways, Germany's Lufthansa, Swissair, Spain's Iberia, and Air France fly direct to South Africa with connecting flights to Lisbon.

GETTING AROUND LISBON

Lisbon is a large European city with an efficient system of buses, trams, and Metro trains, along with ferries across the Tagus River. In addition, it's a wonderful city to explore on foot (despite the many hills), and public transportation is supplemented by taxi, ride share, *tuk-tuks* and hop-on, hop-off buses geared toward tourists.

BUS

The capital's bus service, **Carris** (www.carris.pt), also manages the city's tram system. It provides good coverage of the city, as well as service to neighboring towns and suburbs, and is inexpensive, with most trips under €2. Most buses run 6am-9pm daily, with the busiest lines running until midnight.

TRAM

Carris (www.carris.pt) operates a network of historic trams and funiculars, a unique way to get into the city's backstreets. Five tram routes carry 60 trams, most of which are vintage vehicles. Trams and funiculars generally operate 6am-11pm daily.

METRO

Inaugurated in 1959, Lisbon's **Metro** (www.metrolisboa.pt) has consistently grown, including a stop beneath the airport, making travel fast and easy. The Metro has four main lines—Green, Yellow, Red, and Blue—and is simple to navigate, covering the city's important points. Trains run regularly and reliably.

CAR

Getting around Lisbon without a car is easy and convenient thanks to the comprehensive public transport network. A car is only necessary to visit outlying areas.

EXPLORING OUTSIDE LISBON

TRAIN

Portugal's train service **Comboios de Portugal (CP)** (www.cp.pt/passageiros/en) is efficient and cheap

but complex. It operates on several tiers, from the painfully slow Urbano train service, which stops in every town and village; the modern Intercity service between main cities; and the high-speed Alfa-Pendular, which connects Porto to Lisbon and the Algarve with a few stops between.

Despite being comprehensive, the national rail network isn't as direct as bus services, and, oddly, some major cities have no train station, while many cities and towns have their train stations on the outskirts, requiring a taxi ride to the center. On the plus side, Portugal's trains tend to be spacious and well-kept on the inside, and offer cheaper second-class tickets and more privacy and comfort in first class, sometimes in private compartments.

BUS

There are many different bus companies in Portugal, including three major intercity long-distance bus companies, Algarve line **Eva Transportes** (www.eva-bus.com), national **Rede Expressos** (www.rede-expressos.pt), and northern **Rodonorte** (www.rodonorte.pt). Local and regional buses link towns, villages, and parishes within municipalities. In Lisbon, the local public transport company is **Carris,** which operates buses, trams, and funiculars. Bus travel in Portugal is cheap but not always the most comfortable, although long-distance express buses are mostly equipped with air-conditioning, TVs, toilets, and even onboard drinks and snacks. Pop into a local ticket office to check for updated timetables. Small discounts are given on round-trip tickets.

CAR

Driving in Portugal can, in certain places, require nerves of steel and patience. Lisbon has fast and furious traffic, where delaying at a traffic light will inevitably earn a blast of the horn from behind. There can also be a seeming lack of civility on Portugal's roads, with poor usage of turn signals, and passing seems to be a national sport. For the most part, navigating Portugal's roads is straightforward, and major road surfaces are of a decent standard.

Car Rental

The country's airports host many car rental companies, or ask at your hotel. Vehicles can be dropped off at most holiday lodgings. Use price comparison sites like **Auto Europe** (www.autoeurope.pt) or **Portugal Auto Rentals** (www.portugal-auto-rentals.com) to find the best deals. Booking well in advance will mean better prices. Beware of unexpected surprises by double-checking the opening and closing times of the car rental desk at the airport, fuel fees and excess insurance, and electronic toll payments.

Even though the minimum legal age to drive is 18, most rental companies require drivers to be age 21 or to have held a license for at least five years. Costs can vary greatly, from as little as €10 per day in low season but rising exponentially in high season. If you're just visiting one or two areas, a small car is useful as most town centers, including historic hamlets and large cities, have areas that are a tangle of narrow cobbled streets.

Road System

Portugal's road system is decent and major routes are kept in good condition, although the same cannot be said about smaller regional or municipal roads. Some are in urgent need of repair, particularly in rural areas, and on certain stretches signage could use updating.

Motorways are generally in good condition, although major motorways (*autoestradas*) have tolls, signaled with a large white V on a green background. Secondary and rural roads can be poorer quality, with potholes and sharp bends. In high-elevation areas, such as the Serra da Estrela, snowfall can close roads for hours or even days.

Roads are categorized as follows:

Motorways (*autoestradas*) start with an **A** (A1, A22) and are major highways between cities or regions. Most A roads have tolls, paid at booths or electronically. Some motorways, such as the A22, are exclusively electronic and have barriers. Electronic toll payment uses the **Via Verde** (www.viaverde.pt) transponder system. More information on tolls and motorways is available at www.portugaltolls.com. Motorways have service areas with cafés, gas stations, and toilet facilities at regular intervals. Emergency telephones are also found at regular intervals.

Main highways (*itinerário principal*) start with an **IP** (IP1, IP2). These are major roads that are alternatives to the motorways, although the road conditions are inferior, and generally link main cities.

Secondary highways (*itinerário complementar*) start with an **IC** (IC1, IC2). These roads complement the IPs by connecting them to big towns and cities.

National roads (*estrada nacional*) start with an **N** or **EN** (N125, also known as EN125) and are the main roads between towns and cities.

Local municipal roads (*estrada municipal*) start with an **M** or **EM** and are smaller roads within localities.

Portugal is also connected to the rest of Europe by an **international E-road system,** a numbering system for pan-Europe roads. The main European routes crossing Portugal are the E01, E80, E82, E90, E801, E802, E805, and E806.

General Road Rules

In Portugal traffic runs on the right side of the road. Drivers must be over age 18, and seat belts are compulsory for all occupants.

National speed limits are easy to remember, although many drivers seem to struggle to abide by them: 50 km/h (31 mph) in residential areas, 90 km/h (56 mph) on rural roads, and 120 km/h (74 mph) on motorways. Cars towing trailers are restricted to 80 km/h (50 mph).

The rule on roundabouts (rotaries, or traffic circles) is that the outer lane should be used only if turning off immediately. In practice, this rarely happens. Make allowances for it.

You must park facing the same direction as the traffic flow. It's also illegal to use a mobile phone while driving (although at times you might wonder), and that applies to talking and texting.

Punishment for drunk driving is harsh, ranging from hefty fines to driving bans. The legal limit is 0.5 gram (0.02 ounce) of alcohol per liter (34 ounces) of blood, or 0.2 gram (0.007 ounce) per liter for commercial drivers.

Driver's Licenses

EU citizens require a valid driver's license with a photo on it, issued by the bearer's home country, to drive in Portugal. Drivers from outside the EU require a license and an International Driving Permit, which must be shown both to rental agencies for renting a car and to the authorities if asked. When you are driving on Portugal's roads, the vehicle's documents must be in the vehicle at all times, and drivers need a valid ID, such as a passport. It is compulsory to have certain items in a vehicle. These are a reflective danger jacket, a reflective warning triangle, spare bulbs, a spare tire, and approved child seats for children under age 12 or 150 centimeters (5 feet). Check that you have these before driving off, as failure to produce them could result in a fine.

Refueling

Diesel *(gasóleo)* is cheaper than unleaded gasoline *(gasolina sem chumbo)* in Portugal, and gas stations can be found in abundance (although this is less the case in rural areas). Most large supermarkets and shopping centers have gas stations that offer low-cost fuel options, and there is almost always a gas station near an airport. The main gas stations in Portugal belong to BP, Galp, and Repsol. Most gas stations are open 7am-10pm daily, but stations at service areas on motorways or on main roads should be open 24 hours daily. Unleaded gasoline has a 95 or 98 octane rating, although both can be used in gasoline vehicles; the 98 is more expensive. All gas stations accept debit and credit cards as well as cash.

Parking

Parking can be hard to find in town centers given the narrow cobbled streets and tourist demand. Big towns and cities have designated parking lots and parking areas, which charge fees, especially in popular places like Faro, Lisbon, and Porto. The closer to the city center, the more expensive the parking will be.

Automobile Associations

A contact number for breakdowns should be provided by the vehicle's insurer. When collecting a rental car, always clarify what to do or who to call in the event of a breakdown or emergency. The **Auto Club Portugal (ACP)** (tel. 808 222 222, www.acp.pt) is the Portuguese equivalent of the American Automobile Association.

Visas and Officialdom

To enter Portugal, all travelers are required to have a valid ID. Most European citizens need only a valid ID or a passport and can circulate freely within the EU by land, air, or sea. People from other countries must have a passport and may require a visa. Always check with the relevant authorities before traveling or with your travel provider. Here are some basic guidelines.

PASSPORTS AND TOURIST VISAS
EU/SCHENGEN

EU nationals traveling within EU or Schengen states do not require a visa for entering Portugal for any length of stay. They do require a valid passport or official ID card (national citizen's card, driver's license, or residency permit, for example).

European citizens traveling between Schengen countries are not required to present an identity document or passport at border crossings, as an open-borders policy is in effect. However, it is recommended that travelers have ID documents with them at all times, as they may be requested at any time by the authorities. In Portugal the law requires everyone to carry a personal ID at all times.

Citizens of the United Kingdom and Ireland must produce a passport to enter Portugal, valid for the duration of the proposed stay, and can stay for up to three months. After that, they must register with the local authorities. The UK and Ireland are currently EU member states but are not part of the Schengen area, the 26 countries that abolished passport and other border controls at their shared borders. It is not yet known how the UK's departure from the EU, commonly referred to as Brexit, will affect travel policies.

UNITED STATES, CANADA, AUSTRALIA AND NEW ZEALAND

People from non-EU countries always require a passport, valid for at least six months, and some may require a visa. Australian, Canadian, New Zealand, and U.S. travelers require a valid passport but do not need a visa for stays of up to 90 days in any six-month period. While it is not obligatory to have an onward or return ticket, it is advisable to have one.

SOUTH AFRICA

South African nationals need to apply for a Portugal-Schengen visa. This should be done three months before travel. Applicants must have a South African passport valid for six months beyond the date of return with at least three blank pages. They also need a recent passport photo (specify to photographer that it has to meet the Schengen visa requirements), a completed original application form, round-trip tickets from South Africa to Portugal, and proof of prepaid lodging or a letter of invitation if staying with friends or family in Portugal, among other requisites.

CUSTOMS

Customs is mandatory for all travelers arriving in or leaving Portugal carrying goods or money, although certain limits apply to what can be brought in or taken out. Aeroportos de Portugal (ANA) states that all passengers traveling without baggage or transporting cash or monetary assets under the equivalent of €10,000 or carrying personal items not intended for commercial purposes and not prohibited should pass through the "Nothing to Declare" channel. Passengers carrying over €10,000 or whose baggage contains tradable goods in quantities greater than those permitted by law and that are not exempt from value-added tax (VAT) or excise duty must pass through the "Goods to Declare" channel.

Passengers age 17 or older can bring in the following:

From EU member states: 800 cigarettes, 400 cigarillos, 200 cigars, 1 kilogram (2.2 pounds) of smoking tobacco, 10 liters (11 quarts) of alcoholic spirits, 20 liters (21 quarts) of beverages with alcoholic content under 22 percent, 90 liters (95 quarts) of wine, 110 liters (116 quarts) of beer, medications in quantities corresponding to need and accompanied by a prescription.

For travelers from outside the EU: 200 cigarettes, 100 cigarillos, 50 cigars, 250 grams (0.6 pound) of smoking tobacco, 1 liter (1 quart) of alcoholic spirits, 2 liters (2 quarts) of beverages with alcoholic content under 22 percent, 4 liters (4 quarts) of wine, 16 liters (17 quarts) of beer, medications in quantities corresponding to need and accompanied by a prescription.

Quantities exceeding these must be declared, and passengers under age 17 don't get an exemption for alcohol or tobacco.

EMBASSIES AND CONSULATES

Australian Embassy: Av. da Liberdade 200, Lisbon, http://portugal.embassy.gov.au, tel. 213 101 500, Mon.-Fri. 10am-4pm

British Embassy: Rua de São Bernardo 33, Lisbon, tel. 213 924 000, emergency tel. 213 924 000, www.gov.uk/world/organisations/british-embassy-lisbon, Mon., Weds., and Fri. 9:30am-2pm

British Vice Consulate: Edificio A Fábrica, Av. Guanaré, Portimão (Algarve), tel. 213 924 000, Mon., Weds., and Fri. 9:30am-2pm

Canadian Embassy: Av. da Liberdade 196, Lisbon, tel. 213 164 600, www.canadainternational.gc.ca/portugal, Mon.-Fri. 9am-noon

French Embassy: Rua Santos-O-Velho 5, Lisbon, tel. 213 939 292, https://pt.ambafrance.org, Mon.-Fri. 8:30am-noon

Irish Embassy: Av. da Liberdade 200, Lisbon, tel. 213 308 200, www.dfa.ie/irish-embassy/portugal, Mon.-Fri. 9:30am-12:30pm

New Zealand Consulate: Rua da Sociedade Farmacêutica 68, 1st Right, Lisbon, tel. 213 140 780, consulado.nz.pt@gmail.com, www.mfat.govt.nz, office hours by appointment only

South African Embassy: Av. Luís Bívar 10, Lisbon, tel. 213 192 200, lisbon.consular@dirco.gov.

za, Mon.-Thurs. 8am-12:30pm and 1:15pm-5pm, Fri. 8am-1pm. The Consular Section (Annex) is open Monday-Friday 8:30am-noon.

Spanish Embassy: Praça de Espanha 1, Lisbon, tel. 213 472 381, www.exteriores.gob.es, Mon.-Fri. 9am-2pm

U.S. Embassy: Av. das Forças Armadas 133C, Lisbon, tel. 217 273 300, https://pt.usembassy.gov/embassy-consulate/lisbon, Mon.-Fri. 8am-5pm

U.S. Consulate: Príncipe de Mónaco 6-2F, Ponta Delgada (Azores), tel. 296 308 330, conspontadelgada@state.gov, Mon.-Fri. 8:30am-12:30pm and 1:30pm-5:30pm

Food

It's not hard to wax lyrical about Portugal's cuisine: fresh, flavorful, comforting, and generous, it is the soul of an unassuming seafaring nation. Largely Mediterranean, the staples are fresh fish, meat, fruit, and vegetables prepared with olive oil and washed down with excellent national wines. Dishes vary from light and fresh along the coast, with grilled fish and seafood, to hearty meaty stews and roasts in rural inland areas, and colorful cosmopolitan fusions in larger towns and cities.

Each region touts its own take on national staples such as the *cozido á Portuguesa* (Portuguese stew) and *caldeirada* (fish stew), as well as typical local sweets—all with a story attached to them. Another staple on most menus and one of Portugal's emblematic gastronomic ingredients is salted codfish, or *bacalhau,* for which the Portuguese are said to have a different recipe for every day of the year. The most famous cod dishes are *bacalhau à Brás* (cod mashed with egg, potato, and onion, topped with crunchy matchstick fries), *bacalhau à Gomes de Sá* (flaked cod layered with sliced potato and egg and baked in the oven), *bacalhau espiritual* (like *bacalhau á Bras* but with grated carrot), and *pastéis de bacalhau* (cod fritters), usually a snack with cold beer.

PORTUGUESE CUISINE
FISH
It is perhaps unsurprising that Portugal, an audacious seafaring nation, is renowned for its bounty of seafood. Coastal areas generally serve shellfish as an appetizer. One-pot dishes such as *caldeiradas* and *arroz de tamboril* (monkfish rice) are not to be missed. Salted codfish is a staple throughout Portugal, and grilled sardines are enjoyed voraciously during summer (sardine fishing is limited in winter to allow stocks to replenish); these, along with *dourada* (golden bream), *robalo* (sea bass), and *cavalas* (mackerel), are among the most common fish on menus. Prawns boiled or fried in olive oil and garlic are enjoyed as a snack or appetizer, while more unusual seafood includes razor clams and sea urchins.

MEATS
Most restaurants have grilled meat on the menu, most commonly *febras*

PORTUGAL: A TIMELINE

5000 BC	First agricultural societies in the region begin to form
700-300 BC	Celts invade Portugal region in waves, bringing materials such as iron and other cultural influences
300 BC-AD 500	Roman occupation of Portugal, starting in the south
500	Iberian Peninsula invaded and conquered by the Visigoths
711	Moors from present-day Morocco and Northern Africa claim and settle the Iberian Peninsula
800-1100	Pockets of Christian armies gradually drive back and reclaim territory from the Moors during an era known as the *reconquistas;* Moors completely driven out by 12th century
1139	Alfonso Henriques, one of the main leaders of the Christian armies, declares himself the first king of Portugal
1249	Alfonso III conquers the southern city of Faro; signs the Treaty of Windsor with the United Kingdom to protect Portugal from Spanish incursions
1415	Prince Henry the Navigator captures the Muslim outpost of Ceuta
1488	Portuguese navigators round the Cape of Good Hope under the leadership of Bartolomeu Dias
1498	Vasco da Gama reaches India
1500	Pedro Álvares Cabral claims Brazil

(pork steaks), *costeletas de porco* (pork chops), *entrecosto* (pork ribs), *entremeada* (pork belly), and the ubiquitous *frango piripiri* (chicken grilled and served with spicy chili sauce). Note that the word *grelhado* (grilled) usually means on charcoal.

Cured and smoked meats, especially the smoky, spicy *chouriço* sausage, *presunto* (cured ham), and *morcela* (black blood sausage), also represent a huge chunk of Portuguese gastronomy. They are often eaten simply as an appetizer, accompanied by fresh rustic bread, olives, and cheese, or added to stews and soups to enhance the flavor.

SOUPS

Almost all cafés and restaurants have a homemade vegetable soup on the menu. *Caldo verde,* potato and kale soup with hunks of smoky *chouriço* sausage, is a typical soup served at family tables and traditional festivities.

BREAD

It is customary in Portugal, especially in restaurants, for a basket of fresh bread to be brought out before a meal, along with olives and butter and fishy pâtés. Don't be misled: these items are not complimentary, and if you eat them, they will be added to the bill. If

1571	Established naval and colonial outposts connect Portugal to the coasts of Africa, the Middle East, India, and South Asia
1578	King Dom Sebastião I is killed in the Battle of Alcácer Quibir; Portuguese throne is claimed by Spanish King Phillip II
1668	After 28 years of the Portuguese Restoration War, Spain officially recognizes Portuguese independence
1755	Portugal is brought to its knees by the massive Lisbon earthquake
1890	Portuguese comply with United Kingdom ultimatum to withdraw all troops from African colonies
1910	Coup d'etat organized by the Portuguese Republican Party deposes the constitutional monarchy and proclaims a republican regime, the Estado Novo (First Republic)
1926	Another coup d'état paves the way for the military to seize power under the Diatdura Nacional (National Dictatorship)
1970	Longtime dictator António de Oliveira Salazar dies after almost half a century of oppressive rule; power is handed to slightly less radical Marcelo Caetano
1974	Marcelo Caetano overthrown in the Carnation Revolution, eradicating dictatorial power
1986	Portugal joins the European Union
1999	Macau, Portugal's last colonial possession, handed over to China

you don't want them, ask for them to be taken away. Portugal has amazing bread, almost always freshly made. From rustic hobs to seeded baguettes and pumpkin or carob bread, it's hard not to be sucked in by the amazing carbohydrates on offer, especially to soak up those delicious sauces and juices.

SWEETS AND PASTRIES

Portugal is renowned for its range of traditional sweets and pastries. Display cabinets in cafés and *pastelarias* (cake shops) throughout the country are piled every morning with freshly baked treats. Portugal is home to the unique *doces conventuais* (convent sweets), generally based on egg yolk and sugar and made to ancient recipes said to originate in the 15th century from the country's convents.

Arroz doce (rice pudding with a sprinkling of cinnamon), *bolo de bolacha* (cookie cake), *pudim flan* (custardy pudding with caramel on top), and *tarte de natas* (creamy chilled pie made from condensed milk with a ground cookie topping) are typical desserts, but the ever-present *pastel de nata* (custard tart) is Portugal's iconic sweet.

DRINKS

Perhaps not as eminent as France, Italy, or Spain, modest Portugal nonetheless boasts a gamut of acclaimed wines, including rosés and unique fresh and fizzy green wines. Even ordinary table wine tends to be palatable, and a small jug of house wine in a low-key restaurant costs as little as €3. Besides wine, Portugal produces beer, the most famous being Sagres, Cristal, and Super Bock. A growing number of craft beers are also on the market.

Traditional Portuguese tipples include *ginja* (a sweet cherry liqueur, also called *ginjinha*), *licor beirão* (a medicinal-tasting liqueur said to aid digestion, made from a long-guarded secret blend of herbs), *aguardente* (brain-blowing firewater), and *amarguinha* (a marzipan-tasting, toothachingly-sweet almond liqueur, often chilled). Besides port and madeira liquor-wines, make sure you try the local *poncha* in Madeira, a mix of alcohol distilled from sugarcane, honey, orange or lemon juice, or other fruit juices.

The legal age to drink and buy alcohol in Portugal is 18. Nondrinkers won't be disappointed with canned iced teas and Sumol sparkling fruit juices, the traditional flavors being pineapple and orange. The Algarve, especially the city of Silves, is renowned for incredibly sweet oranges, and fresh orange juice served here with plenty of ice is a real treat.

The Portuguese are big coffee drinkers, and the standard is a small, strong, black espresso. To get milk in it, ask for *café com leite* or *meia-de-leite* (in a cup and saucer), or *galão* (served in a tall glass), differing only in presentation. "Having a coffee" is synonymous with "catching up," and cafés are the social glue of neighborhoods.

DINING OUT

Restaurants in Portugal are incredibly varied, from down-to-earth, no-frills spots to high-end Michelin-starred eateries. Touristy areas have a wider range of well-known chains and international cuisines. Vegetarian and vegan restaurants are on the rise, while traditional Portuguese eateries can be found in spades.

For real local flavor, try to find a *casa de pasto,* literally a "grazing house," basic, cheap, and cheerful little diners found off the beaten track that cater to local laborers with good home-cooked food. These characterful places tout three-course "dish of the day" menus for as little as €7.50, including a bread basket with butter, pâtés, and olives, a fish or meat entrée, a coffee, dessert, and drinks. If your budget allows, head to a high-end eatery where the menu will be a contemporary take on fresh local products and time-honored recipes. If you have a sweet tooth, find a *pastelaria* (there seems to be one on almost every street) to enjoy a coffee and freshly made traditional cake or a toasted sandwich for just a few euros.

TIPPING

Restaurants tend to be the only places in Portugal where tipping is exercised, and a tip reflects how much patrons have enjoyed the food and service. As a general rule, 10-15 percent of the overall bill is the standard, but in less formal eateries it's okay just to leave any loose change you have, but at least €1. Gratuities are not included on bills. Waitstaff in Portugal appreciate tips, but they are not compulsory.

PICNIC SUPPLIES AND GROCERIES

A great way to save money is to buy your own food, and Portugal is a veritable buffet of fresh produce. Larger supermarkets have counters for fresh fish, cold meats, cooked meats, and deli, with the likes of olives and slaws, as well as a fresh bread section, baked in-house or supplied by local bakers.

Most towns have a farmers market at least once or twice a month, generally on Saturday morning, piled high with locally grown fruit and vegetables as well as treats like dried nuts, dried fruits, sweets, and eggs. Municipal markets, usually open mornings Monday-Saturday, are also great for fish, meats, vegetables, and fruit. Some municipal markets have ready-to-go food counters and sell jams, liqueurs, cured meats, and preserves.

MEALS AND MEALTIMES

Portugal has three main meals: a good breakfast in the continental style, with cereals, bread, cold meats and cheese, and jam, generally eaten before work or school; lunch at 1pm-3pm; and dinner starting from 7:30pm-8pm. Main meals tend to be hearty, and lunch and dinner are often preceded by a bowl of soup. The Portuguese also enjoy *lanche,* a light midafternoon snack, as well as a coffee and a pastry midmorning.

Accommodations

Accommodations range from run-of-the-mill hotels and tourist complexes to friendly family-run inns, campsites, budget-friendly hostels, and exclusive luxury retreats. Lisbon currently exercises a **tourist tax** *(taxa turística),* a surcharge of €1 per night per guest up to a maximum of seven nights. This is charged directly at reception on check-in.

ACCOMMODATIONS RATINGS

Portugal's rating system is governed by national law and implemented by the national tourism board, **Turismo de Portugal** (www.turismodeportugal. pt). Ratings are based on fulfilled minimum requisites stipulated for each category. Star ratings are generally indicative of the level of comfort and facilities an establishment provides and not necessarily subjective factors such as view or atmosphere. Hotels are classified one to five stars; a one-star property is a basic budget lodging, while a five-star hotel offers a luxurious

experience. *Estalagens* (inns) rate four to five stars, *pensões* (guesthouses) one to four stars, and apart-hotels rate two to five stars. Campsites are graded one to four stars.

MAKING RESERVATIONS

Most people nowadays make bookings online via price comparison websites or directly with hotels. It's always wise to follow it up with a phone call to ensure everything is confirmed and any special requests are clear. If planning to travel to Portugal in summer, book well ahead, as hotels sell out fast in peak season. Prices can also be much higher in peak season than in low season.

TYPES OF ACCOMMODATIONS
HOTEL

All of Portugal's main towns and cities offer hotels spanning three to five stars. The more popular the destination, the greater the choice. Lisbon is awash with smart hotels, most with their own pools. Prices vary greatly by season and the popularity of the resort.

Among the compulsory criteria, minimum requirements for four- and five-star hotels include air-conditioning, TV, and direct phone lines in all rooms; one- to three-star hotels don't necessarily have to have those features. Three- to five-star hotels must also provide room service, laundry service, and air-conditioning in public areas, whereas one- and two-star hotels don't. All categories except one-star hotels must have an on-site bar, a full bath, 24-hour reception, copy and fax service, and safes in the rooms.

ESTALAGEM (INN)

Portugal's inns (estalagens) are hotel-type lodgings in traditional buildings that, due to their architectural characteristics, style of fixtures and furnishings, and services provided, reflect the region and its natural environs. Inns are classified four or five stars. As a whole, inns must comply with criteria similar to corresponding hotels (24-hour reception, room service, restaurant, bar, air-con in public areas, etc.); the main differences are found in the actual rooms, which tend to be smaller. Generally speaking, inns are more modest than hotels and often rustic and family-run.

PENSÃO RESIDENCIAL

Smaller towns and villages will usually have a pensão residencial, or just residencial, private family-run boardinghouses in shared residential buildings. These provide affordable lodgings in central locations. Pensões usually have a restaurant. The word residencial is added when

the unit provides breakfast only. Residenciais are simple bed-and-breakfast lodgings.

APART-HOTEL

Apart-hotels are self-contained apartments with the full facilities of hotels. There is no room service.

POUSADA

Pousadas are state-owned monuments such as castles, palaces, monasteries, and convents converted into sumptuous accommodations reflecting the region and era of the monument. **Pousadas de Portugal** (www.pousadas.pt) is a brand that has iconic monument-hotels in exceptional locations, including Pousada Serra da Estrela, a former sanatorium in the snowy Serra da Estrela mountains; Pousada Convento Beja, an ancient convent; and Pousada Castelo Óbidos, a castle-hotel in the heart of the famous medieval town.

HOSTEL

Portugal is renowned for excellent hostels, regularly earning European awards. That doesn't mean all of the country's hostels are above par. It pays to do some research and read reviews before booking. For outstanding hostels in Portugal, see www.hostelworld.com.

ALDEAMENTO TURÍSTICO (TOURIST RESORT)

Tourist resorts, also known as tourist villages or complexes, are developments comprising different types of independent lodging, such as bungalows, apartments, or villas, in communal spaces. These resorts must also have an on-site four- or five-star hotel, entertainment facilities, and room service.

CAMPING

Portugal has over 100 campgrounds. Camping sites are classified by stars, from the most luxurious four stars to the minimum basic one star. Privately owned camping sites are classified in the same way, preceded by the letter *P*. Campsites tend to stay open year-round, as Portugal has a growing number of winter motorhome visitors, but prices can double from low to peak season. High-season prices may apply to holidays such as New Year's. Most campsites have on-site toilets and showers as well as facilities such as swimming pools and markets, bungalows, and chalets, which are reflected in the star rating. Some have sanitary facilities for RVs. Not all accept pets. For more on camping in Portugal, see www.campingportugal.org.

Festivals and Events

Most of the country's major events, such as the traditional Popular Saints festivities and local festivals, are held in summer.

SPRING

CARNIVAL
mid-Feb.-early Mar.

Carnival (or Carnaval) festivities take place throughout the country, but Lisbon's is especially spectacular, with colorful floats and concerts, music, masquerade balls, and other street events.

ÓBIDOS CHOCOLATE FESTIVAL
late Apr.-early May

This series of weekends in Óbidos showcases chocolate, from traditional Portuguese sweets to contemporary concoctions.

SUMMER

SANTO ANTÓNIO FESTIVAL
Jun.

Lisbon's patron saint, Saint Anthony, is celebrated throughout the city the entire month of June, peaking on June 12 with parades and processions lasting through the night.

TOMAR TRAY FESTIVAL
Jun.-Jul.

This ancient festival takes place every four years features a procession of local girls wearing *tabuleiros* traditional headdresses made from bread, along with other traditional celebrations and ceremonies.

ÓBIDOS MEDIEVAL FAIR
Mid-Jul.-early Aug.

This medieval fair in Óbidos features fire-eaters, wizards, court jesters, and jousting knights, along with food and handicrafts typical of the era.

WINTER

ÓBIDOS CHRISTMAS FAIR
late Nov.-early Jan.

With hundreds of stalls selling gifts and hot chocolate and myriad shows and entertainment filling the streets, Óbidos' Christmas Village is a festive though crowded time to visit the town.

Conduct and Customs

The Portuguese are characteristically warm and welcoming and proud to show off their heritage, although they are also modest and conservative. Striking up a conversation about food or soccer, two of Portugal's best-loved pastimes, is a surefire way of opening communication. Conscious that tourism is a main source of income, the Portuguese are generally friendly and helpful toward visitors, although in rural pockets of the country foreigners are still eyed with curiosity. Staunchly traditional and understated, Portugal is a country where recent acquaintances may be greeted like long-lost friends, but raucous behavior, such as drunken rowdiness, is eschewed. Decorum is much appreciated, which is not to say you can't let your hair down and let loose in the appropriate places. As long as you show courtesy and respect to the locals, you can expect the same back.

GENERAL ETIQUETTE

Typically friendly and humble, the Portuguese love to show off their language skills and impress visitors, and few are the people who don't know at least a few key phrases in English. Likewise, the Portuguese very much appreciate efforts by visitors in learning even just a few words of the national language. Modest and somewhat reserved, the Portuguese tend to be quite formal in greetings among those less well acquainted. Men usually shake hands while women give air kisses on each cheek; women hardly ever shake hands in Portugal. Children are greeted in the same way as adults. Family is the foundation of

Portuguese households and takes precedence over most other social and professional affairs.

COMMUNICATION STYLES

The Portuguese appreciate polite directness. Eye contact, a smile, and a firm handshake are the cornerstones of communication. Saying *"Bom dia"* (Good day or Hello), *"Por favor"* (Please), and *"Obrigado/a"* (Thank you) go a long way. Overtly exuberant or loud behavior is not appreciated. The Portuguese tend to socialize on the weekends rather than after work during the week.

BODY LANGUAGE

A big no-no in Portugal is pointing—especially pointing at someone. While conversations can sound heated and loud, the Portuguese are not overly demonstrative with hand gestures or body language. Finger-snapping to get someone's attention is also frowned upon.

TERMS OF ADDRESS

An overtone of formality is required when addressing people, especially strangers. Men should be addressed as *senhor* (abbreviation *Sr.*) and women *senhora (Sra.)* at all times. A young girl would be *menina* (miss), and a boy, *menino*.

TABLE MANNERS

Table manners are relaxed but courteous. Sharing from a bowl while talking animatedly is a mainstay around a family table, although politeness, such as wishing everyone *"Bom apetite"*

(Bon appétit) before a meal and saying "Thank you" afterward, is expected. Domestic dining begins at the say-so of the head of the table or the cook, and feel free to raise a glass to toast (saúde) everyone. Dining out depends on the type of establishment; laid-back eateries are a family-style affair, while upmarket venues require upmarket manners and dress. Arriving late to a meal with friends is acceptable; arriving late to a dinner reservation is not.

If invited to dine at someone's home, take a small gift, such as a bottle of wine or flowers.

PHOTO ETIQUETTE

Places where photos are banned will be signed. Taking photos inside churches during mass is considered disrespectful. If you want to take a picture of a local, Portuguese people are generally happy to collaborate, but always politely seek permission beforehand.

Health and Safety

Overall, travel and health risks in Portugal are relatively low, with food- and water-borne illnesses like traveler's diarrhea, typhoid, and giardia not a concern in Western Europe. Insect-transmitted diseases, such as Lyme disease and tick fever, however, are found in Portugal. A number of precautionary steps can reduce the risk: prevent insect bites with repellents, apply sunscreen, drink plenty of water, avoid overindulging in alcohol, don't approach wild or stray animals, wash your hands regularly, carry hand sanitizer, and avoid sharing bodily fluids.

Basic medications such as ibuprofen and antidiarrheal medication can be bought over-the-counter at any pharmacy in Portugal. For emergency medical assistance, call 112 and ask for an ambulance. If you are taken to a hospital, contact your insurance provider immediately. Portugal also has a 24-hour free health help line (tel. 808 242 424) in Portuguese only. For detailed advice before traveling, consult your country's travel health website: www.fitfortravel. nhs.uk (United Kingdom), https://wwwnc.cdc.gov/travel (United States), www.travel.gc.ca (Canada), or www.smarttraveller.gov.au (Australia).

VACCINATIONS

There are no compulsory immunization requirements to enter Portugal. The World Health Organization (WHO) recommends all travelers, regardless of destination, are covered for diphtheria, tetanus, measles, mumps, rubella, and polio. See your doctor at least six weeks before departure to ensure your routine vaccinations are up-to-date.

HEPATITIS A

Recommended for all travelers over age one and not previously vaccinated against hepatitis A. In 2017 a number of European countries, Portugal included, recorded an outbreak of hepatitis A. It is transmitted through contaminated food and water, as well direct contact with infected individuals via the fecal-oral route.

HEPATITIS B

The hepatitis B vaccination is suggested for all nonimmune travelers who may be at risk of acquiring the disease, which is transmitted via infected blood or bodily fluids, such as by sharing needles or unprotected sex.

HEALTH CONSIDERATIONS

SUNSTROKE AND DEHYDRATION

The sun and heat in Portugal can be fierce, especially June-September and particularly July-August. Apply a strong sunblock and use a hat and sunglasses. Avoid physical exertion when the heat is at its peak (noon-3pm) and keep well hydrated by drinking plenty of water or electrolyte-replenishing fluids. Avoid excessive alcohol during the hottest hours or being out in the sun with a hangover.

UNDERTOW

Some beaches, especially along the western coast, which is fully exposed to the Atlantic, can experience strong undercurrents when the sea is roughest, particularly in winter and spring. During summer, generally May-September, the sea is calmer and beaches are staffed by lifeguards; off-season they are not. Always obey flags.

TAP WATER

Tap water is consumable throughout Portugal and is safe to brush teeth, wash fruit, or make ice, although many people drink bottled water, as opposed to tap water, even at home.

STRAY ANIMALS

Portugal still battles errant and abandoned animals. In some places it's not unusual to see stray dogs and cats, even in packs and colonies. A huge amount of work has been done by private and public entities to sterilize and rehome animals, and things have greatly improved since the 1980s, but more work remains. Travelers are advised to not approach, pet, or feed strays. If you are bitten by a stray animal, wash and disinfect the wound, and seek medical advice promptly.

SEXUALLY TRANSMITTED DISEASES

Travelers are at high risk of acquiring sexually transmitted diseases (STDs) if they engage in unprotected sex. According to research, Portugal has one of the poorest control rates of sexually transmitted infections; gonorrhea and syphilis are common.

HEALTH CARE

MEDICAL SERVICES

Portugal's state-funded public health service (SNS, Serviço Nacional de Saúde) provides quality care, particularly in emergency situations and those involving tourists. There are also private hospitals operating throughout Portugal, such as the **Hospital Particular do Algarve** (tel. 707 282 828, www.grupohpa.com) group in the Algarve and the **CUF Hospitals and Health Units** (tel. 210 025 200, www.saudecuf.pt) in Lisbon and the north. For minor illnesses and injuries, head to a pharmacy: most pharmacists speak good English and can suggest treatment. If the problem persists or worsens, seek a doctor. Portugal has two types of pharmacies: traditional pharmacies *(farmácia),* identified with a big flashing green cross outside, and parapharmacies *(parafarmácia),* selling only nonprescription medicines.

INSURANCE

EU citizens have access to free emergency medical treatment through the European Health Insurance Card (EHIC), which replaces the defunct E111 certificate. Non-EU citizens for whom there is no reciprocal agreement for free medical care between Portugal and the traveler's home country should consider fully comprehensive health insurance for serious illness, accident, or emergency. Opt for a policy that covers the worst-case event, like medical evacuation or repatriation. Find out in advance if your insurance will make payments to providers directly or reimburse you later for overseas health expenditures. Travelers to the Azores and Madeira are advised to acquire wide-ranging travel insurance that provides for medical evacuation in the event of serious illness or injury; serious or complicated problems sometimes require medical evacuation to the mainland.

PRESCRIPTIONS

A prescription issued by a doctor in one EU country is valid in all EU countries. However, a medicine prescribed in one country may not be authorized for sale or available in another country, or it might be sold under a different name. EU doctors can issue cross-border prescriptions valid in all EU countries. Opt for paper copies of prescriptions as opposed to electronic copies.

If you're traveling from outside the EU, have enough of your prescription medication to cover the trip. Talk to your doctor beforehand and travel with a doctor's note, a copy of any prescriptions, or a printout for the medication. Medications should be carried in labeled original bottles or packaging, although this is not compulsory. Some prescription medicines may require a medical certificate; always check with your doctor. Ask for an extra written prescription with the generic name of the drug in the event of loss or if your stay is extended. Portuguese pharmacies will accept prescriptions from countries outside the EU, but drugs have to be paid for in full. Even without the state subsidies, drugs are generally cheaper in Portugal than many other EU countries and the United States. Alternatively, visit a Portuguese doctor and obtain a prescription in Portugal.

Many types of medication—including heart medication, antibiotics, asthma and diabetes medicines, codeine, injectable medicines, and cortisone creams—can be acquired in Portugal only with a prescription.

It is illegal to ship medication to Portugal. When traveling, always transport medicines in carry-on luggage.

BIRTH CONTROL

Birth control is widely available throughout Portugal. Female contraceptive pills, patches, and rings can be bought over the counter in pharmacies, as can the morning-after pill, without a prescription. Condoms are also widely available in pharmacies, supermarkets, gas stations, and some nightlife venues.

SAFETY
POLICE

Portugal has three police forces: the **PSP (Public Safety Police—Polícia de Segurança Pública)** (tel. 218 111 000, www.psp.pt), in cities and larger towns; the road traffic police **GNR (National Republican Guard— Guarda Nacional Republicana)** (tel. 213 217 000, www.gnr.pt), also responsible for policing smaller towns and villages and investigating crimes against animals or nature; and the **PJ (Judiciary Police—Polícia Judiciária)** (tel. 211 967 000, www.pj.pt), the criminal investigation bureau, responsible for investigating serious crimes.

The common European emergency number is tel. **112,** which redirects calls to the appropriate services.

CRIME

Portugal has a relatively low serious crime rate, but opportunistic crime is recurrent, particularly in busy places popular among tourists, such as Lisbon and the Algarve. Popular beaches are hot spots for car theft, so keep valuables on your person or at least hidden from view. Don't leave anything of value, such as passports or computers, in vehicles. Pickpocketing is also common, particularly on the busy trams in Lisbon and Porto. Use a concealed crossbody pouch to carry cash and your ID, and keep money and documents separate. Take the same precautions you would at home—keep valuables safe and avoid walking alone at night or on backstreets.

HARASSMENT

Harassment is not something visitors to Portugal will usually have to deal with. Opportunistic petty drug pushers in busy nightspots and overenthusiastic restaurant or bar staff trying to attract clientele are about the extent of the pestering. Saying a polite but firm "No, thanks" and walking away are generally enough to deter unwanted attention.

DRUGS

Since 2001, Portugal has a decriminalized drug system, and being caught with a small amount of some recreational drugs, such as marijuana, is no longer a crime but a medical health issue, addressed with rehabilitative action like therapy as opposed to jail. This health-focused legal shift saw drug-related deaths drop dramatically, but that's not to say it's okay to do drugs in Portugal; drug use is prohibited. The law does not differentiate between citizens and visitors, and tourists caught with drugs will be subject to the same process, which could include fines or being brought before a dissuasive committee or a doctor. Producing or dealing drugs in Portugal is a serious criminal offense punishable with lengthy jail terms. The use of recreational drugs is common in the nightlife areas of places such as Lisbon and Albufeira. Beware being approached by people selling drugs.

Practical Details

MONEY

CURRENCY

Since 1999 Portugal's currency has been the euro; before that it was the escudo. There are 100 cents in 1 euro (€1).

CHANGING MONEY

The ability to exchange currency varies greatly by location. In tourist-dense Lisbon, Porto, and the Algarve, foreign currency can be exchanged at almost every hotel, currency exchanges, and even some shops. Airports have exchange bureaus, although their commission rates, along with those in hotels, are more expensive. Keep an eye on exchange rates in the months before you travel to see how they fluctuate, and change some cash beforehand when the rates are favorable. In Portugal, hunt around, do some groundwork, and compare rates to choose the best option. It is almost always more favorable for UK travelers with British pounds to change their cash for euros in the United Kingdom; in Portugal the Scottish pound can sometimes be refused. For up-to-date exchange rates, see www.xe.com.

BANKS

Banks in Portugal are generally open Monday-Friday 8:30am-4pm. In larger towns and cities, they will stay open during lunch, but in smaller locales, banks close 1pm-2pm. Portugal's banks close Saturday-Sunday and national holidays. Banks rarely offer foreign currency exchange services.

ATMS

ATM cash withdrawal machines (*multibanco*) can be found widely in most towns and cities. Smaller villages may have just one or two, normally at bank branches, in supermarkets, on main streets and squares, and at major bus and train stations and airports. Charges apply to foreign transactions. There is an option for instructions in English. Maximum withdrawals are €200 a time, but this can be withdrawn several times a day.

CREDIT CARDS

Credit cards are widely accepted in bigger towns and cities, but not so much in smaller locales. Visa, Mastercard, and American Express cards are widely accepted in hotels, shops, and restaurants. Gas stations usually take only debit cards and cash.

SALES TAX

The standard sales tax rate in Portugal is 23 percent. On wine it is 13 percent, and on medications, books, and optical lenses 6 percent. In Madeira the tax is 22 percent, and in the Azores 18 percent. Many stores throughout Portugal have adopted the Europe Tax Free (ETS) system, which allows non-EU shoppers to recover VAT or sales tax as a refund. Stores adhering to the ETS system have an ETS sign at the entrance. For more information, see www.globalblue.com/tax-free-shopping/portugal.

BARGAINING

Haggling is increasingly a thing of the past in Portugal, as standardized retail prices are enforced in municipal markets and farmers markets. However, haggling at a flea market is still part of the experience.

SPECIAL DISCOUNTS

Students, seniors (65 and over), and children generally benefit from discounts on state-run services such as monuments, museums, municipal swimming pools, and public transport.

BUDGETING

As one of Europe's most affordable countries, Portugal still offers value for money. Far cheaper than London, Paris, or Barcelona, Lisbon doesn't have to be expensive. As with all the sunshine destinations in Southern Europe and the Mediterranean, hotel rates peak in summer and drop in winter, meaning spring and autumn can offer the best value in terms of lodging and weather. Car rental rates fluctuate with the tourist seasons, and airfares are influenced by EU school holidays. Portugal has a range of inns, vacation rentals, and some of the best hostels in Europe, so how much you spend depends on you.

A British study found Portugal's Algarve was Europe's third-cheapest holiday destination for sun-loving Britons in 2018, mainly driven by a strengthening pound. Including everyday items such as coffee, beer, meals, wine, public transport, and sunblock, it is still much cheaper than other European destinations.

OPENING HOURS

In the past most shops and services in Portugal would close 1pm-3pm for lunch. This is still in practice in many establishments, although a growing number of state and private entities such as banks, post offices, and pharmacies now remain open during lunch.

Major national monuments like castles, churches, and palaces are open every day of the week, and those that aren't tend to close on Monday.

Attractions stay open longer in summer, opening an hour or so earlier than in winter and closing an hour or so later. Theme parks, especially water parks, and even some hotels and restaurants close for a month or two in winter. Smaller museums and monuments also close for lunch.

PUBLIC HOLIDAYS

Almost all close on bank holidays, such as Christmas Day, New Year's Eve, and New Year's Day. Major holidays such as Carnival (late February or early March) and Lisbon's Santo António festivities (June) may result in closures of banks or other state entities, though bars and restaurants are often open and at their busiest.

- **New Year's Day (Anno Novo):** January 1
- **Good Friday (Sexta-feira Santa):** Friday before Easter Sunday
- **Easter Sunday (Domingo de Páscoa)**
- **Freedom Day (Dia da Liberdade):** April 25
- **Labor Day (Dia do Trabalhador):** May 1
- **Portugal Day (Dia de Portugal):** June 10
- **Corpus Christi (Corpo de Deus):** 60 days after Easter Sunday
- **Assumption Day (Assunção de Nossa Senhora):** August 15
- **Republic Day (Implantação da República):** October 5
- **All Saints' Day (Dia de Todos-os-Santos):** November 1
- **Restoration of Independence (Restauração da Independência):** December 1
- **Immaculate Conception Day (Imaculada Conceição):** December 8
- **Christmas Day (Natal):** December 25

COMMUNICATIONS

PHONES AND CELL PHONES

Making Calls

Portugal's country code is +351 (00351). To call a phone number in Portugal from abroad, first dial the country code. Within Portugal, there are regional prefixes, and all start with 2. Lisbon, for example, is 21, Faro is 289, and Porto is 22. These are incorporated into phone numbers, which are always nine digits. There is no need to dial 0 or 1 before the number. Mobile phone numbers start with 9. Toll-free numbers start with 8. Portugal's main landline provider is **Portugal Telecom** (www.telecom.pt).

Mobile Phones

The main mobile providers are **Nós** (www.nos.pt), **Meo** (www.meo.pt), and **Vodafone** (www.vodafone.pt). Mobile phone coverage is decent throughout the country, particularly in major cities and populous areas along the coast, although it can be patchy in rural or high-elevation areas. Foreign handsets that are GSM compatible can be used in Portugal. Using a prepaid SIM card in Portugal is recommended, particularly for non-EU visitors. They are widely available from the stores of the main mobile phone providers, which can be found on retail streets and shopping centers. You will need a copy of your passport or ID to buy one.

In 2017 the EU abolished roaming surcharges for travelers, meaning that people traveling within the EU can call, text, and use data on mobile devices at the same rates they pay at home, but this applies only to EU countries. Surcharges may apply if your consumption exceeds your home usage limits.

INTERNET ACCESS

Portugal has an up-to-date communications network, with good phone lines and high-speed internet. Wi-Fi is widely available, and most hotels will either have free Wi-Fi throughout or in designated Wi-Fi areas. Elsewhere, major cities offer Wi-Fi hotspots, as do some public buildings, restaurants, and cafés. Internet cafés can be found throughout Portugal.

SHIPPING AND POSTAL SERVICE

Portugal's national postal service is **Correios de Portugal** (tel. 707 262 626, www.ctt.pt), with post offices in all population centers. Postal services range from regular *correio normal* to express *correio azul*. Shipping costs for a 2-kilogram (4.4-pound) package range from €4.50 sent domestically to €15 sent abroad. Postcards and letters up to 20 grams (0.7 ounce) cost €0.86 within Europe, €0.91 to other countries. Express mail letters cost €2.90.

Other shipping services operate in Portugal, including **FedEx** (tel. 229 436 030, www.fedex.com) and **DHL** (tel. 707 505 606, www.dhl.pt).

WEIGHTS AND MEASURES

CUSTOMARY UNITS

Portugal was the second country after France to adopt the metric system, in 1814. Length is in centimeters, meters, and kilometers, and weight is in grams and kilograms. Temperatures are in degrees Celsius.

In addition, shoes and clothing sizes differ from the British and U.S. systems. For example:

- shoe sizes: U.S. men's 7.5, women's 9 = U.K. men's 7, women's 6.5 = Portugal 40

- women's dresses and suits: U.S. 6, 8, 10 = U.K. 8, 10, 12 = Portugal 36, 38, 40
- men's suits and overcoats: U.S. and U.K. 36, 38, 40 = Portugal 46, 48, 50

TIME ZONE

Mainland Portugal is in the Western European time zone (WET), the same as the United Kingdom and Ireland. Complying with European daylight saving time (DST), clocks advance one hour on the last Sunday in March and lose one hour on the last Sunday in October. The Azores archipelago is always one hour earlier than mainland Portugal. Madeira is in the same time zone as the mainland. In relation to the United States, Portugal is seven or eight hours later than Los Angeles, four or five hours ahead of Miami and New York, five or six hours ahead of Chicago, and ten or eleven hours ahead of Hawaii.

ELECTRICITY

Portugal has 230-volt, 50-hertz electricity and type C or F sockets. Type C plugs have two round pins; type F have two round pins with two grounding clips on the side. Travelers from the United Kingdom, Australia, and most of Asia and Africa will require only an adapter to make the plugs fit. Visitors from the United States, Canada, and most South American countries require an adapter and for some devices a voltage converter. These are available in airports, luggage shops, and most electrical shops. Universal adapters are a great investment as they can be used anywhere.

WHAT TO PACK

Key items to pack include mosquito repellent and sunblock (sunblock is expensive in Portugal) plus a hat for May-October, a windbreaker for all seasons (Portugal can be breezy year-round), and warm sweaters, a jacket, and a light raincoat for winter. Comfortable shoes for walking are advised if your trip is more than a beach holiday, and don't forget an electrical adapter for chargers. Pack a concealable pouch to carry documents and cash while out and about exploring, and never carry cash and documents together.

TOURIST INFORMATION

Portugal is a tourism-oriented destination with widely available visitor information. Each region—Porto and the North, Central Portugal, Lisbon, the Alentejo, the Algarve, Azores and Madeira—has its own tourism board to promote the area, while the national **Turismo de Portugal** (www.turismodeportugal.pt) promotes the country as a whole. Each main town has at least one tourist office, as do popular villages. Most hotels provide good information on what to do and see locally. Portugal's official tourism website, www.visitportugal.com, provides a wealth of information on history, culture, and heritage as well as useful contacts.

TOURIST OFFICES

Tourist offices can be found in every city, town, and village that has a tourist attraction or monument. Major cities and destinations like Lisbon, Porto, and the Algarve have numerous tourist offices where visitors can drop in with questions and get maps, public transport timetables, and excursion information. Tourist office staffers speak good English.

Download maps of Portugal and its various regions free from www. visitportugal.com. Most hotel reception desks have maps of the vicinity, or ask at tourist offices.

Traveler Advice

ACCESS FOR TRAVELERS WITH DISABILITIES

Portugal prides itself on being an accessible destination for travelers with disabilities, and massive efforts have been made to become inclusive for all. The main airports have services and facilities for wheelchair users, and infrastructure is gradually being modernized to facilitate mobility. There are a number of wheelchair-friendly accessible beaches along the coast, with equipment and facilities for all to enjoy the beach safely and comfortably. Some monuments, however, are not wheelchair friendly, and people with mobility issues might struggle with everyday infrastructures (such as cobbled streets and high sidewalks).

In 2018 the national tourism board launched an interactive app, **TUR4all Portugal,** that contains a wealth of information about facilities and services for those with special needs visiting Portugal. It can be downloaded for free from www.accessibleportugal. com.

TRAVELING WITH CHILDREN

Youngsters in family-friendly Portugal are fawned over and welcomed practically everywhere. It's not unusual to see children dozing on their parents' laps in a café late on a summer night. Restaurants are very accommodating of younger diners, although kids' menus can be limited to the staple chicken nuggets or fish fingers.

Activities for children range from Lisbon's award-winning Oceanarium and riverfront cable cars, to spotting wildlife in the Mafra Royal Hunting Grounds, surfing on some of Portugal's best beaches, riding the beach train in Costa da Caparica, and playgrounds in almost every public park. Kids also benefit from discounts on public transport, at museums, and at most main attractions.

When the weather is warm, tourist trains and ice cream are found throughout towns and villages, while most resorts and hotels have kids' clubs or at least activities and facilities for children. For some grown-up-time, ask your hotel to arrange a babysitter.

To enter and leave Portugal, all minors must have their own passport and be with both parents. If children are not traveling with both parents, legal documentation with formalized permission from the other parent is required. Portugal's border and immigration officials will ask for such papers.

Breastfeeding is applauded in Portugal, although it's rarely done in public, and if it is, it's done discreetly.

WOMEN TRAVELING ALONE

Portugal is a great destination for women traveling alone, given that it is one of Europe's safest and most peaceful countries, and people as a whole are respectful and obliging. If you want to share lodging or to meet new people, Portugal has clean and cheap, well-regulated and well-run hostels, a great way to mingle with fellow travelers. Most people speak decent English and are happy to assist. Besides petty crime in major towns and cities, the serious crime rate is low, and lone women travelers should have no problems. As with any place, common sense should prevail, and taking dark backstreets or walking along deserted streets at night should be avoided.

SENIOR TRAVELERS

With a year-round pleasant climate and placid, laid-back lifestyle, Portugal is a magnet for senior travelers and a top destination for Northern European retirees who make it their second home. Compact, peaceful, and well equipped, with medical facilities (providing you have the right insurance coverage), it meets the needs of travelers of all ages. Geographically, Lisbon and Porto are hilly and a challenge on foot; sticking to the flatter downtown and riverside areas and using the plethora of public transport can help travelers avoid issues with aches and pains.

Portugal has discounts for senior travelers (65 and over) with ID on public transport and in museums, and plenty of attractions, like wine-tasting and spa visits, to appeal to the mature tourist.

LGBTQ+ TRAVELERS

LGBTQ travelers will find Portugal mostly welcoming; it legalized same-sex marriage in 2010, the eighth country in Europe to do so. Portugal is currently a popular destination for same-sex weddings. Most Portuguese have a laid-back attitude toward LGBTQ visitors, although attitudes toward same-sex couples can vary by region. Despite being progressive, Portugal is traditionally a Roman Catholic society, and inhabitants of remote and small towns might raise an eyebrow or scowl at same-sex displays of affection, but rarely will verbal or physical hostility be directed at you.

While the LGBTQ scene is still underground in much of Portugal, Lisbon and Porto, and to a lesser extent the Algarve, have a vibrant and inclusive LGBTQ scene. Lisbon and Porto host colorful pride marches and have numerous gay bars, nightclubs, and LGBTQ-friendly accommodations, although tourists being denied a room or a table based on their sexual orientation or gender identity is not unheard of. The International Gay & Lesbian Travel Association (IGLTA, www.iglta.org) provides a wealth of information on LGBTQ travel in Portugal, including organized trips, tours, tips, and travel advice.

TRAVELERS OF COLOR

Portugal is widely regarded as one of Europe's safest, most peaceful, and most tolerant countries, and allegations of color-motivated discrimination and attacks are rare. However, in recent times there have been sporadic reports of incidents involving racial bias, specifically at the doors of popular nightspots in Lisbon. Management of these venues strongly deny that bouncers discriminate against clubgoers' entry based on their race, but allegations to that effect have made the rounds on social media. That said, Portugal is home to large communities of Africans from the former colonies, and while racially motivated incidents do happen, they are extremely rare. For the most part, travelers and immigrants of all colors are welcomed and accepted in Portugal, which has one of the most integrated immigrant communities in Europe.

Portuguese Phrasebook

PRONUNCIATION

VOWELS

The pronunciation of **nonnasal vowels** is fairly straightforward:

a pronounced "a" as in "apple," "ah" as in "father," or "uh" as in "addition."

e pronounced "eh" as in "pet." At the end of a word, it is often silent or barely pronounced.

i pronounced "ee" as in "tree."

o pronounced "aw" as in "got." At the end of a word or when it stands alone, it is generally pronounced "oo" as in "zoo."

u pronounced "oo" as in "zoo."

The **nasal vowels** are much more complicated. Nasal vowels are signaled by a tilde accent (~) as in *não* (no), or by the presence of the letters **m** or **n** following the vowel, such as *sim* (yes) or *fonte* (fountain). When pronouncing them, it helps to exaggerate the sound, focus on your nose and not your mouth, and pretend there is a hidden "n" (or even "ng") on the end. Note that the **ão** combination is pronounced like "own" as in "town."

CONSONANTS

Portuguese consonant sounds are easy compared with the nasal vowels. There are, however, a few exceptions to be aware of.

c pronounced "k" as in "kayak." However, when followed by the vowels **e** or **i**, it is pronounced "s" as in "set." When sporting a cedilla accent (**ç**),

it is pronounced with a longer "ss" sound as in "passing."

ch pronounced "sh" as in "ship."

g pronounced "g" as in "go." However, when followed by the vowels **e** or **i**, it is pronounced "zh" like the "s" in "measure."

h always silent.

j pronounced "zh" like the "s" in "measure."

l usually pronounced as in English. The exception is when it is followed by **h**, when it acquires a "li" sound similar to "billion."

n usually pronounced as in English. The exception is when it is followed by **h**, when it acquires a "ni" sound similar to "minion."

r pronounced with a trill. When doubled (**rr**), it should be pronounced with a longer roll.

s pronounced "s" as in "set" when found at the beginning of a word. Between vowels, it's pronounced like "z" as in "zap." At the end of a word, it's pronounced like "sh" as in "ship."

x pronounced "sh" as in "ship" when found at the beginning of a word. Between vowels, the pronunciation varies between "sh" as in "ship," "s" as in "set," "z" as in "zap," and "ks" as in "taxi."

z pronounced "z" in "zap" when found at the beginning of a word. In the middle or at the end of a word, it is pronounced "zh" like the "s" in "measure."

STRESS

Most Portuguese words carry stress on the second-to-last syllable. There are, however, some exceptions. The stress falls on the last syllable with words that end in **r** as well as words ending in nasal vowels. Vowels with accents over them (~, ´, `, ˆ) generally indicate that the stress falls on the syllable containing the vowel.

PLURAL NOUNS AND ADJECTIVES

In Portuguese, the general rule for making a noun or adjective plural is to simply add an **s.** But there are various exceptions. For instance, words that end in nasal consonants such as **m** or **l** change to **ns** and **is**, respectively. The plural of *estalagem* (inn) is *estalagens,* while the plural of *pastel* (pastry) is *pastéis.* Words that end in nasal vowels also undergo changes: **ão** becomes **ãos, ães,** or **ões,** as in the case of *irmão* (brother), which becomes *irmãos,* and *pão* (bread), which becomes *pães.*

GENDER

Like French and Spanish, all Portuguese words have masculine and feminine forms of nouns and adjectives. In general, nouns ending in **o** or consonants are masculine, while those ending in **a** are feminine. Many words have both masculine and feminine versions determined by their **o** or **a** ending, such as *menino* (boy) and *menina* (girl). Nouns are always preceded by articles—*o* and *a* (definite) and *um* and *uma* (indefinite)—that announce their gender. For example, *o menino* means "the boy" while *a menina* means "the girl." *Um menino* is "a boy" while *uma menina* is "a girl."

BASIC EXPRESSIONS

Hello *Olá*
Good morning *Bom dia*
Good afternoon *Boa tarde*

Good evening/night *Boa noite*
Goodbye *Tchau, Adeus*
How are you? *Como está?*
Fine, and you? *Tudo bem, e você?*
Nice to meet you. *Um prazer.*
Yes *Sim*
No *Não*
I don't know. *Não sei.*
and *e*
or *ou*
Please *Por favor*
Thank you *Obrigado* (if you're male), *Obrigada* (if you're female)
You're welcome. *De nada.*
Excuse me (to pass) *Com licença*
Sorry/Excuse me (to get attention) *Desculpe* (if you're male), *Desculpa* (if you're female)
Can you help me? *Pode me ajudar?*
Where is the bathroom? *Onde é o banheiro?*
What's your name? *Como se chama?*
My name is . . . *Meu nome é …*
Where are you from? *De onde é que vem?*
I'm from . . . *Sou de …*
Do you speak English? *Fala inglês?*
I don't speak Portuguese. *Não falo português.*
I only speak a little Portuguese. *Só falo um pouquinho português.*
I don't understand. *Não entendo.*
Can you please repeat that? *Pode repetir, por favor?*

TERMS OF ADDRESS

I *eu*
you *você* (formal), *tu* (informal)
he *ele*
she *ela*
we *nós*
you (plural) *vocês*
they *eles* (male or mixed gender), *elas* (female)
Mr./Sir *Senhor*
Mrs./Madam *Senhora*
boy/girl *menino/menina*

child *criança*
brother/sister *irmão/irmã*
father/mother *pai/mãe*
son/daughter *filho/filha*
husband/wife *marido/mulher*
uncle/aunt *tio/tia*
friend *amigo* (male), *amiga* (female)
boyfriend/girlfriend *namorado/ namorada*
single *solteiro* (male), *solteira* (female)
divorced *divorciado* (male), *divorciada* (female)

TRANSPORTATION

north *norte*
south *sul*
east *este*
west *oeste*
left/right *esquerda/direita*
Where is . . . ? *Onde é . . . ?*
How far away is . . . ? *Qual é a distância até . . . ?*
far/close *longe/perto*
car *carro*
bus *autocarro, camioneta*
bus terminal *terminal das camionetas*
subway *metro*
subway station *estação do metro*
train *comboio*
train station *estação de comboio*
plane *avião*
airport *aeroporto*
boat *barco*
ship *navio*
ferryboat *ferry, balsa*
port *porto*
first *primeiro*
last *último*
next *próximo*
arrival *chegada*
departure *partida*
How much does a ticket cost? *Quanto custa uma passagem?*
one-way *uma ida*
round-trip *ida e volta*
I'd like a round-trip ticket. *Quero uma passagem ida e volta.*

gas station *bomba de gasolina*
parking lot *estacionamento*
toll *portagem*
at the corner *na esquina*
one-way street *sentido único*
Where can I get a taxi? *Onde posso apanhar um táxi?*
Can you take me to this address? *Pode me levar para este endereço?*
Can you stop here, please? *Pode parar aqui, por favor?*

ACCOMMODATIONS

Are there any rooms available? *Tem quartos disponivéis?*
I want to make a reservation. *Quero fazer uma reserva.*
single room *quarto de solteiro*
double room *quarto duplo*
Is there a view? *Tem vista?*
How much does it cost? *Quanto custa?*
Can you give me a discount? *É possível ter um desconto?*
It's too expensive. *É muito caro.*
Is there something cheaper? *Tem algo mais barato?*
for just one night *para uma noite só*
for three days *para três dias*
Can I see it first? *Posso ver primeiro?*
comfortable *confortável*
change the sheets/towels *trocar os lençóis/as toalhas*
private bathroom *banheiro privado*
shower *chuveiro*
soap *sabão*
toilet paper *papel higiênico*
key *chave*

FOOD

to eat *comer*
to drink *beber*
breakfast *pequeno almoço*
lunch *almoço*
dinner *jantar*
snack *petisco*

dessert *sobremesa*
menu *ementa*
plate *prato*
glass *copo*
cup *chávena*
utensils *talheres*
fork *garfo*
knife *faca*
spoon *colher*
napkin *guardanapo*
hot *quente*
cold *frio*
sweet *doce*
salty *salgado*
sour *azedo, amargo*
spicy *picante*
I'm a vegetarian. *Sou vegetariano* (if you're male), *Sou vegetariana* (if you're female).
I'm ready to order. *Estou pronto para pedir* (if you're male), *Estou pronta para pedir* (if you're female).
Can you bring the bill please? *Pode trazer a conta, por favor?*

MEAT

meat *carne*
beef *carne, bife*
chicken *frango, galinha*
pork *porco, leitão*
ham *fiambre*
cured ham *presunto*
sausage *salsicha*

FISH AND SEAFOOD

fish *peixe*
seafood *frutas do mar, mariscos*
shellfish *marisco*
codfish *bacalhau*
sardines *sardinhas*
tuna *atum*
shrimp *camarão*
crab *caranguejo*
squid *lula*
octopus *polvo*
lobster *lagosta*

EGGS AND DAIRY

eggs *ovos*
hard-boiled egg *ovo cozido*
scrambled eggs *ovos mexidos*
whole milk *leite gordo*
skim milk *leite desnatado*
cream *creme de leite*
butter *manteiga*
cheese *queijo*
yogurt *iogurte*
ice cream *gelado*
sorbet *sorvete*

VEGETABLES AND LEGUMES

vegetables *verduras, legumes*
salad *salada*
lettuce *alface*
spinach *espinafre*
carrot *cenoura*
tomato *tomate*
potato *batata*
cucumber *pepino*
zucchini *courgette*
eggplant *berinjela*
mushrooms *cogumelos*
olives *azeitonas*
onions *cebolas*
beans *feijões*

FRUITS

fruit *fruta*
apple *maçã*
pear *pêra*
grape *uva*
fig *figo*
orange *laranja*
lemon *limão*
pineapple *ananás*
banana *banana*
apricot *damasco, abricó*
cherry *cereja*
peach *pêssego*
raspberry *framboesa*
strawberry *morango*
melon *melão*

SEASONING AND CONDIMENTS

salt *sal*
black pepper *pimenta*
hot pepper *pimenta picante*
garlic *alho*
oil *óleo*
olive oil *azeite*
mustard *mostarda*
mayonnaise *maionese*
vinegar *vinagre*

BAKED GOODS AND GRAINS

bread *pão*
pastry *pastel*
cookies *biscoitos*
cake *bolo, torta*
rice *arroz*

COOKING

roasted, baked *assado*
boiled *cozido*
steamed *cozido no vapor*
grilled *grelhado*
fried *frito*
well done *bem passado*
medium *médio*
rare *mal passado*

DRINKS

beverage *bebida*
water *água*
sparkling water *água com gás*
still water *água sem gás*
soda *refrigerante*
juice *sumo*
milk *leite*
coffee *café*
tea *chá*
with/without sugar *com/sem açúcar*
ice *gelo*
beer *cerveja*
wine *vinho*
Do you have wine? *Tem vinho?*
Red or white? *Tinto ou branco?*
Another, please. *Mais uma, por favor.*

MONEY AND SHOPPING

money *dinheiro*
ATM *multibanco*
credit card *cartão de crédito*
Do you accept credit cards? *Aceita cartões de crédito?*
Can I exchange money? *Posso trocar dinheiro?*
money exchange *câmbio, troca de dinheiro*
It's too expensive. *É muito caro.*
Is there something cheaper? *Tem algo mais barato?*
more *mais*
less *menos*
a good price *Um preço bom.*

HEALTH AND SAFETY

I'm sick. *Estou doente.*
I have nausea. *Tenho nausea.*
I have a headache. *Tenho uma dor de cabeça.*
I have a stomachache. *Tenho uma dor de estômago.*
Call a doctor! *Chame um doutor!, Chame um médico!*
Call the police! *Chame a polícia!*
Help! *Socorro!*
pain *dor*
fever *febre*
infection *infecção*
cut *corte*
burn *queimadura*
vomit *vômito*
pill *comprimido*
medicine *remédio, medicamento*
antibiotic *antibiótico*
cotton *algodão*
condom *preservativo*
contraceptive pill *pílula*
toothpaste *pasta de dentes*
toothbrush *escova de dentes*

NUMBERS

0 zero
1 *um* (male), *uma* (female)
2 *dois* (male), *duas* (female)
3 *três*
4 *quatro*
5 *cinco*
6 *seis*
7 *sete*
8 *oito*
9 *nove*
10 *dez*
11 *onze*
12 *doze*
13 *treze*
14 catorze, *quatorze*
15 *quinze*
16 *dezesseis*
17 *dezessete*
18 *dezoito*
19 *dezenove*
20 *vinte*
21 *vinte e um*
30 *trinta*
40 *quarenta*
50 *cinquenta*
60 *sessenta*
70 *setenta*
80 *oitenta*
90 *noventa*
100 *cem*
101 *cento e um*
200 *duzentos*
500 *quinhentos*
1,000 *mil*
2,000 *dois mil*
first *primeiro*
second *segundo*
third *terceiro*
once *uma vez*
twice *duas vezes*
half *metcde*

TIME

What time is it? *Que horas são?*
It's 3 o'clock in the afternoon. *São três horas da tarde.*
It's 3:15. *São três e quinze.*
It's 3:30. *São três e meia.*
It's 3:45. *São três e quarenta-cinco.*
In half an hour. *Daqui a meia hora.*
In an hour. *Daqui a uma hora.*
In two hours. *Daqui a duas horas.*
noon *meio-dia*
midnight *meia-noite*
early *cedo*
late *tarde*
before *antes*
after *depois*

DAYS AND MONTHS

day *dia*
morning *manhã*
afternoon *tarde*
night *noite*
today *hoje*
yesterday *ontem*
tomorrow *amanhã*
tomorrow morning *amanhã de manhã*
week *semana*
month *mês*
year *ano*
Monday *segunda-feira*
Tuesday *terça-feira*
Wednesday *quarta-feira*
Thursday *quinta-feira*
Friday *sexta-feira*
Saturday *sábado*
Sunday *domingo*
January *janeiro*
February *fevereiro*
March *março*
April *abril*
May *maio*
June *junho*
July *julho*

August *agosto*
September *setembro*
October *outubro*
November *novembro*
December *dezembro*

SEASONS AND WEATHER

season *estação*
spring *primavera*

summer *verão*
autumn *outuno*
winter *inverno*
weather *o tempo*
sun *sol*
rain *chuva*
cloudy *nublado*
windy *vento*
hot *quente*
cold *frio*

Index

List of Maps

Photo Credits

Liked this book? Travel deeper with more & Beyonds from Moon:

Barcelona
Budapest
Copenhagen
Florence
Lisbon
Marrakesh
Milan
Prague
Venice

OR TAKE THINGS ONE STEP AT A TIME

AMSTERDAM WALKS — *See the City Like a Local*

LONDON WALKS — *See the City Like a Local*

NEW YORK CITY WALKS — *See the City Like a Local*

PARIS WALKS — *See the City Like a Local*

ROME WALKS — *See the City Like a Local*

TOKYO WALKS — *See the City Like a Local*

Moon's pocket-sized city walks with fold-out maps are the perfect companion!

Sights Around the World

MOON
BALI & LOMBOK
CHANTAE REDEN

MOON
CANADIAN ROCKIES
WITH BANFF & JASPER NATIONAL PARKS
HIKE·CAMP
SEE WILDLIFE
ANDREW HEMPSTEAD

MOON
ECUADOR
& THE GALÁPAGOS ISLANDS
BETHANY PITTS

MOON
FIJI

MOON
ICELAND
JENNA GOTTLIEB

MOON
JAPAN
JONATHAN DEHART
PLAN YOUR TRIP, AVOID THE CROWDS,
AND EXPERIENCE THE REAL JAPAN

MOON
MOROCCO

MOON
PRAGUE, VIENNA
& BUDAPEST
AURA WALKER
DAVID JOHN CALON

MOON
YOSEMITE
SEQUOIA &
KINGS CANYON
ANN MARIE BROWN

Outdoor Adventure

MOON
Drive & Hike
APPALACHIAN
TRAIL
THE BEST TRAIL TOWNS, DAY HIKES,
AND ROAD TRIPS IN BETWEEN
TIMOTHY MALCOLM

MOON
Drive & Hike
PACIFIC CREST
TRAIL
THE BEST TRAIL TOWNS, DAY HIKES,
AND ROAD TRIPS IN BETWEEN
CAROLINE HINCHLIFF

MOON
YELLOWSTONE TO
GLACIER NATIONAL PARK
Road Trip
JACKSON HOLE, CODY, THE GRAND TETONS
& THE ROCKY MOUNTAIN FRONT
CARTER G. WALKER

MAP SYMBOLS

═══	Expressway	┄┄┄	Unpaved Road	▬▬▬	Railroad
═══	Primary Road	-----------	Trail	▭▭▭	Pedestrian Walkway
═══	Secondary Road	············	Ferry	▨▨▨	Stairs

○	City/Town	ⓘ	Information Center	▲	Park
◉	State Capital	Ⓟ	Parking Area	⚲	Golf Course
✪	National Capital	⛪	Church	✚	Unique Feature
✪	Highlight	🍇	Winery/Vineyard	🖎	Waterfall
★	Point of Interest	TH	Trailhead	Λ	Camping
•	Accommodation	🚉	Train Station	▲	Mountain
▼	Restaurant/Bar	✈	Airport	🎿	Ski Area
▪	Other Location	✕	Airfield	🗺	Glacier

CONVERSION TABLES

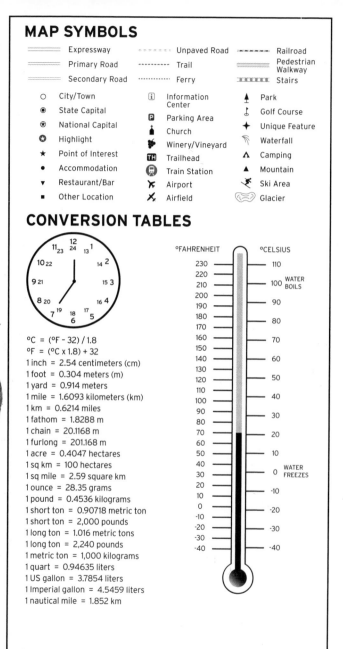

°C = (°F − 32) / 1.8
°F = (°C x 1.8) + 32
1 inch = 2.54 centimeters (cm)
1 foot = 0.304 meters (m)
1 yard = 0.914 meters
1 mile = 1.6093 kilometers (km)
1 km = 0.6214 miles
1 fathom = 1.8288 m
1 chain = 20.1168 m
1 furlong = 201.168 m
1 acre = 0.4047 hectares
1 sq km = 100 hectares
1 sq mile = 2.59 square km
1 ounce = 28.35 grams
1 pound = 0.4536 kilograms
1 short ton = 0.90718 metric ton
1 short ton = 2,000 pounds
1 long ton = 1.016 metric tons
1 long ton = 2,240 pounds
1 metric ton = 1,000 kilograms
1 quart = 0.94635 liters
1 US gallon = 3.7854 liters
1 Imperial gallon = 4.5459 liters
1 nautical mile = 1.852 km

MOON LISBON & BEYOND
Avalon Travel
Hachette Book Group
1700 Fourth Street
Berkeley, CA 94710, USA
www.moon.com

Editor: Megan Anderluh
Managing Editor: Hannah Brezack
Copy Editor: Matt Hoover
Graphics Coordinator: Rue Flaherty
Production Coordinator: Rue Flaherty
Cover Design: Faceout Studio, Charles Brock
Interior Design: Megan Jones Design
Moon Logo: Tim McGrath
Map Editor: Kat Bennett
Cartographers: Erin Greb, Alison Ollivierre, Kat Bennett
Proofreader: Lori Hobkirk
Indexer: François Trahan

ISBN-13: 978-1-64049-339-1

Printing History
1st Edition — May 2020
5 4 3 2 1

Front cover photo: restaurant in Lisbon © Rainer Martini / LOOK-foto / Getty Images
Back cover photo: Monserrate Palace © Stefano Valeri | Dreamstime.com

Printed in China by RR Donnelley